# Bang-up and Smash
## Women's Prisons, Bail Hostels and Probation

### ASBO

London, September 2017

Bang-up and Smash: Women's Prisons, Bail Hostels and Probation, ASBO

First printing: September 2017, Active Distribution

Cover © Enki Bilal, Sacha

Printed in Croatia by Što čitaš?
www. stocitas.org/english-sto-citas.htm

Copyleft: download, distribute, discuss, dismiss

For more information contact the author: asbo.hmp@riseup.net

If you are reading this in prison please ask someone outside to email your
postal details.

ISBN 9781909798489

# Contents

## ACKNOWLEDGEMENTS

To everyone who has supported me this last while. You know who you are.

Thank you to PM Press and Active Distribution for help with publishing, and to Lee Jackson and Just Seeds for some of the images.

This book is dedicated to all those resisting and rejecting authority, inside and out. The money from this project is for you.

"There is violence
in the slow wilt of these stems;
in the warp and seethe of the skyline and in the ragged gait of wire-thin animals
that meet your eyes in the city at night."
Kelly Rose Pflug-Back, *Stone*


## CONTENT WARNING

This publication contains content that may be distressing or triggering. There are references throughout to physical violence, sexual assault, sexual abuse (including paedophilia), and drug/alcohol use. It also includes several examples of discriminatory language, suicide and self-harm.

All attempts have been made to make legal references as accurate as possible.

# AIMS

If these sound grandiose, I do not apologise. If they sound unrealistic, it is only because our dreams have been so downtrodden by those who seek to control us, both inside and outside our cages.

In no particular order...

- To provide people facing a custodial sentence (and those supporting them) with ideas for dealing with everyday prison life in women's prisons in the UK, by combining anarchist literature, practical examples and case studies from jail, and prison-related support organisations.
- To highlight gender issues in relation to the range of texts that already exist about the UK prison system, and to critically analyse feminist arguments around women's prisons.
- To show the many ways in which the prison industrial complex (PIC) is both dependent on, and perpetuates, discrimination and multiple forms of oppression.
- To give an overview of the concept of social exclusion, whilst critiquing organisations which promote 'inclusion' as an antidote to the PIC.
- To discredit concepts such as reform and rehabilitation, and to expose them for the dangerous façades that they are.
- To use anecdotal evidence and first-hand examples of the violence of the prison regime and 'criminal justice system' (CJS).
- To problematise the idea of prison abolition and highlight it's limitations from an anarchist perspective.
To show how the frameworks, institutions and technologies used for discipline and control extend far beyond prison walls and create the 'prison society'.

# INTRODUCTION

"She lives in a mansion of aching hearts,
she's one of a restless throng." *Roddie Doyle[1]*

Prison is designed to control, to oppress, to separate and alienate. However, even in "a mansion of aching hearts" there are ways to keep your head held high. It's easy to fixate on the moment you will leave jail and walk through the gate, but there are many possibilities for rebellion and solidarity along the way. As Albert Libertad said: "Those that envision the goal from the first steps, those that want the certitude of reaching it before walking, never arrive"[2].

"We do not want the pardon of the state, we only desire its destruction" *Monica Caballero* and *Francisco Solar[3]*

This is a practical guide, though for obvious security reasons some things are best left unsaid. You can find them out inside. Prison is messy. Relentless. Just like critique and analysis, it is ongoing and painful. But it is not omnipotent.

"What would you have us do with criminals then?" I asked
"Give them medals" Sorros said "For daring to be anti-social
in the face of an anti-social order...They put humans in a cage
and they call it justice." *Margaret Killjoy[4]*

One of my mates inside called me ASBO and I hope I will always be anti-

---

1 Doyle, *A Star Called Henry 1999*
2 Libertad, (1875-1908) *We Go On*
3 Letter from Prison of Villabona, Spain 2015
4 Killjoy, *A Country of Ghosts, 2014*

social. The title of this publication comes from two features of prison life: 'Bang-up' (being locked in your cell) and 'Smash' (or rather, the budget prison issue version of it, reconstituted potato). I hope it will provide some 'food for thought' when the monotony of enforced solitude and cheap carbs threatens to suffocate you in jail!

## Anonymity?

> "Run from what's comfortable. Forget safety. Live where you fear to live. Destroy your reputation. Be notorious."
> *Jalal al-Din Rumi*[5]

> "When you do something out of conviction, my dear, it should be because you believe it's the right thing to do. If you look for approval from everyone, you'll never be able to act."
> *Leslie Feinberg*[6]

One of the first things I want to highlight is how uncomfortable I feel writing with a lot of imperatives and telling people what to do. I *much* prefer writing in the third person, and obviously all the random bits of information and advice outlined here are just *suggestions*. Everyone rides their sentence in their own way, and every sentence is different. All prisoners have coping strategies: spice, self-harm, sex, socialising, subutex, smoking, scandal, stories, schemes, sessions in the gym, whatever your poison, whatever gets you through (as long as it ain't snitching!). As Jean Weir has outlined: "Simply staying alive, holding onto one's individuality and keeping ones spirits and head high is in itself a form of rebellion in the context of an institution that is deliberately built to put people down and humiliate them."[7]

Writing this text is one of the hardest things I have ever done. I am *not* saying this for sympathy. Nor am I saying this because I do not stand by my ideas and actions. I am saying this in order to acknowledge the complexity of feelings I have had towards this project. Every day I mourn my loss of anonymity, and even though I am using an alias, it is probably easy for the reader to ascertain who has assembled these words.

> "When you start doing what could drive people to your side instead of what you think is right, you do politics. From the

5 1207-1273
6 Feinberg, *Stone Butch Blues, 1993*
7 Weir, *Tame Words from a Wild Heart, 2016*

moment you impose limitations on yourself out of fear of not being understood, you are, *de facto* already a political entity, and therefore you become part of the problem, one of the many cancers that infect our existence. One should never measure his own words and actions just to become acceptable to people, to the crowd, otherwise there is great risk of being transformed by the very 'intermediate' objective he wants to achieve." *Alfredo Cospito*[8]

## The Prison Industrial Complex (PIC)

"The prison industrial complex (PIC) is a term we use to describe the overlapping interests of government and industry that use surveillance, policing, and imprisonment as solutions to economic, social and political problems. Through its reach and impact, the PIC helps and maintains the authority of people who get their power through racial, economic and other privileges." *Critical Resistance website*

In England and Wales in 2008, it cost £56,000 to incarcerate someone in a women's prison for a year. The cost now is undoubtedly much higher. England and Wales have the highest imprisonment rate in Western Europe, locking up 147 people per 100,000. The prison population in England and Wales has gone over 85,000 after an increase of more than 1,000 people from the beginning of September 2016. The number of people in prison now stands at 85,108.[9] At the time of publication the total 'useable operational capacity' of the UK prison estate was 86,146, meaning there are just over 1,000 places available before it is unable to take any more people[10].

According to monthly prison newspaper *Inside Time* (IT), in June 2016 some prisons were operating at 160% of their certified capacity (HMP Leeds was operating at 176%). There were 3,876 people in women's prisons (and 81,691 in men's prisons). The situation has got so bad that for the first time since their records began, the Prison Service no longer publishes monthly statistics on overcrowding. Figures are now be published annually because apparently "statistics for the number of prisoners held over a prison's capacity does not indicate the number of prisoners held in crowd-

8 CCF Imprisoned Members Cell, *A Few Words on Freedom: Interview with Alfredo Cospito, 2017*
9 Statistics published by the MoJ in 2016, cited by the PRT, prisonreformtrust.org.uk/PressPolicy/News/ItemId/375/vw/1
10 PRT, 2016

ed conditions."[11]

The Prison Reform Trust (PRT) has described "chronic levels of over-crowding" and how it is connected to "sentence inflation". This inflation is attributed to the dramatic increase in the length of sentences and tariffs (the minimum term an indeterminate prisoner will serve, before they can start the process of *applying* for release). The PRT has stated that "no future government should be allowed to preside over the decline in safety, decency and fairness that we have seen in recent years." Let me be clear: there has never been, and will never be, anything "decent", "fair" or "safe" about prison. These concepts are the antithesis of the prison industrial complex and to claim that it can ever be reformed along these lines is the most dangerous of 'red herrings'. In my mind, the only thing connecting these ideas and the PIC is that they are *all* highly problematic and concerned with maintaining a status quo which I reject and want no part in.

In response to overcrowding in UK prisons, the government relentlessly expands and outsources operational management to private companies, many of whom are multi-national security corporations. The government developed plans to build a range of so-called 'Titan Prisons', based on the maxi-prison model in America. The recently completed HMP Berwyn in Wrexham is a flag-ship for this project, and holds 2,100 inmates. It opened in February 2017[12]. This is an example of what long-term prisoner John Bowden has termed the "inexorable drive towards greater incarceration and the construction of virtual penal cities". This drive "will eventually result in whole chunks of the poor and disadvantaged population being walled into factories of repression."[13]

In March 2017, justice secretary Liz Truss published plans to construct six new 'super-sized' mega-prisons, with a combined capacity of at least 5,000. It started with major rebuilds at HMP Wellingborough[14] and HMP Glen Parva in Leicester[15], and will continue with sites in Port Talbot in South Wales, Wigan in Greater Manchester, Rochester in Kent and Full Sutton in East Yorkshire[16]. The government claims the Titan Prisons will be state run, but the reality is that the usual suspects will be operating behind the scenes. 34% of HMP Berwyn will be maintained using "private and voluntary organisations".

11 insidetime.org/newsbites-april-2017/
12 bbc.co.uk/news/uk-39347226
13 Bowden, *Return to Resistance, 2010*
14 bbc.co.uk/news/uk-england-northamptonshire-39513603
15 cape-campaign.org/leicester/
16 The second phase, of four prisons will house 5,000 prisoners

The government uses the phrase 'prison estate' to describe all its prisons (including private jails). Within the women's prison estate there are currently two private jails, Bronzefield and Peterborough. Only 18% of all those incarcerated in women's prisons are held in these institutions, but a third of all self-harm incidents, drug seizures and hunger strikes that occurred in 2015 happened within them. This is despite the fact that these corporately run establishments use nearly a quarter of the entire prison estate budget.

Apart from construction, the daily operation and logistics of the prison regime also generate big money. According to the report *Safety in Custody* (a prison led initiative), in 2015 there were 95,631 transfers between jails, and 60,896 prisoners were 'shipped out' (moved at short notice) at least once. Many of these transfers were unnecessary, and executed by a handful of companies; such as GeoAmey (or GEO), Serco and G4S. These companies also profit from many other aspects of the PIC, operating in many of the institutions outlined by Stanley and Smith:

> "Immigration centres, juvenile justice facilities, county jails, military jails, holding rooms, court rooms, sheriff's offices, psychiatric institutes, along with other spaces build the vastness of the PIC's [Prison Industrial Complex] architecture."[17]

The prison society combines these places with an arsenal of technologies, both within the physical confines of the jail, and beyond. Prison is a laboratory for the state, and procedures and legislation piloted inside get extended across its institutions. But rules are there to be broken, the PIC hasn't always existed, and it can be destroyed. As people resisting the Maxi-Prison model in Brussels have stated:

> "Power wants us to believe that we can't do anything. It wants to be invulnerable. But things are not like that. Power can be attacked everywhere it materialises: in its offices, institutions and uniforms. And this revolt depends only on ourselves."[18]

## Psychology and Prison

> "A certain feeling comes from throwing your good life away, and it is one part rapture...Innocence was no part of this. She knew her own recklessness and marvelled, really, at how one hard little flint of thrill could outweigh the pillowy suffocat-

---

17 *Captive Genders: Trans-Embodiment and the Prison Industrial Complex, 2015*
18 *The Struggle Against the Maxi-Prison in Brussels, 2014*

ing aftermath of a long disgrace."*Barbara Kingsolver[19]*

It can feel like a slow and painful attack, this "long disgrace" in prison. The state and the staff inside will do all that they can to amplify and intensify your reaction to it, but it is possible to find a clear and determined path through the violence of bureaucracy. To empower yourself and navigate the minefield that is prison life, without having to commit what Libertad termed "partial suicides"[20].

There are many examples of the ways in which the state attempts to break people in jail through 'therapeutic' interventions. Prisons are neither benign places nor therapeutic environments. These programmes, combined with restrictive periods on licence ("supervision in the community"), are deliberately designed to make people feel stressed, isolated and ashamed. The mainstream press, and the coalition government of 2010-15 (specifically David Cameron) employed and developed rhetoric related to the concept of 'Broken Britain'. This justified increasingly draconian measures of punishment, especially against those they deemed "anti-social" (and the working class). It also led to a further extension of post-crime supervision (for example, probation). This has been extremely profitable for social enterprise and private companies, and will be investigated in part two.

> "A prison might be defined as any place you've been put into against your will and can't get out of, and where you are entirely at the mercy of the authorities, whoever they may be. Are we turning our entire society into a prison? If so, who are the inmates and who are the guards? And who decides?"
> *Margaret Atwood[21]*

Rehabilitation and protection are justifications for invasive psychological programmes, sentence plans, parole knock backs, licence conditions and many other methods of control. Phrases such as "deaths in custody" hide the inherent violence of the state and brush aside the grim realities of daily life in jail. According to the 'ministry of justice' (MoJ) there were 354 deaths behind bars in England and Wales last year, including 119 which were apparently "self-inflicted". Self-harm incidents jumped by 23% to 37,784, while there were 25,049 assaults in the 12 months to September – a rise of 31% on the previous year.

---

19 Kingsolver, *Flight Behaviour, 2012*
20 Libertad, *We Go On*
21 Atwood, *We Are All Double-Plus Unfree, 2015*

England has the biggest prison population in Europe and the longest prison sentences. American prison culture has been replicated by the criminal justice system (CJS) in the UK. Bowden has repeatedly outlined this connection in his writings from jail:

> "As a model of either justice or retribution, the American criminal justice system is riddled with corruption and failure, and yet Britain slavishly attempts to imitate it, in its quest to achieve absolute social control at a time when the lives of the poor are being made increasingly unendurable, and society continues to fracture and polarise."[22]

## Abolition?

It is easy to criticise reformist organisations and the demands they make on the state. However, it is just as important to maintain a critical approach to the concept of prison abolition. The prison industrial complex (PIC) is not going to disappear quietly!

> "Prison abolition is not a call to suddenly fling open the prison doors without enacting alternatives. Nor is it an appeal to a utopian ideal. Abolition is a broad based, practical vision for building models today that practice how we want to live in the future." *S. Lamble*[23]

Many abolitionist texts, such as the example below from Critical Resistance, emphasise the need for positive alternatives to the prison system, and community resources:

> "It means developing practical strategies for taking small steps that move us toward making our dreams real and that lead us all to believe that things really could be different. It means living this vision in our daily lives. Abolition is both a practical organizing tool and a long-term goal."[24]

It is important to emphasise however that even if *none* of the examples of alternatives to prison work, that does *not* legitimise its existence *now*. Restorative and transformative justice will *not* bring an end to the prison society without aggressive solidarity and sustained attack.

---

22 Bowden, *Americanisation of the British Criminal Justice System, 2014*
23 Lamble, *Transforming Carcereal Logistics* (printed in Stanley and Smith)
24 criticalresistance.org

"There are two types of solidarity. A passive one that all too often serves only to wash away conscience for someone's own inactivity and that does not bridge the gaps between words and deeds. And then the active, concrete, real solidarity that some call revolutionary, created in silence and anonymity, where only destructive actions speak even through the words that follow. Needless to say which one I prefer." *Cospito*[25]

There are many publications and groups which outline alternatives to the prison system and PIC (see resources section). As this text is *only* concerned with surviving the prison regime in its current form they will not be discussed in detail here.

A broader interrogation of the prison system *must* include a rejection of the organisations that support it. James Kilgore argued that "a key social change underlying the advance of mass incarceration has been an increasing respect for the absolute authority of the law and those involved in law enforcement."[26] This is a critical feature of the prison society. Prisons are the end of the road for many people in a journey which is instigated and enforced by those in authority. An attack on the prison regime must therefore incorporate an attack against the police. It is not enough to resist the physical manifestations of the PIC, constant vigilance and awareness is required in order to remember how systemic and far reaching it is.

For continuous resistance to "the absolute authority of the law and those involved in law enforcement!"

"Sometimes I think this whole world
Is one big prison yard.
Some of us are prisoners
The rest of us are guards." *Bob Dylan*[27]


## Punishment

Joe Black and Bra Bros outlined the triple function of prisons[28]: deterrence (fear of incarceration), incapacitation (containment of individuals) and rehabilitation (of "offending behaviour"). They also discussed criminological theory, the increased use of thought crime within the judicial system and

25 Cospito, *2017*
26 Kilgore, *Understanding Mass Incarceration: A People's Guide to the Key Civil Rights Struggle for our Time, 2015*
27 *George Jackson*
28 Black and Bros, *The Prison Works, 2010*

prison estate, and the inconsistencies upon which the system is dependent.

> "The law does not pretend to punish everything that is dishonest. That would seriously interfere with business." *Clarence S. Darrow*[29]

Many politicians have sought to cut their teeth on the prison system in the UK, using the language of rehabilitation to create a benevolent façade whilst promising to create tougher conditions inside. During his time as secretary of state for justice, Michael Gove was outspoken in his contempt for prisoners, before then promising the world in various initiatives that never materialised:

> "Abolishing the death penalty has led to a corruption of our criminal justice system, the erosion of all our freedoms and has made the punishment of the innocent more likely. Hanging may seem barbarous but the greater barbarity lies in the slow abandonment of our common law traditions." *Michael Gove*

In the 'Prison Safety and Reform White Paper', justice secretary, Liz Truss, published plans for increased disciplinary powers for screws and prison staff including: body cameras for prison staff, greater governor autonomy, extended tests for drugs use and no-fly zones (to stop drone drop offs). She also plans to build five new "community houses" for women[30].

The prison system controls its populations using the concept of divide and rule. Issues surrounding class, race, gender and sexuality are just some of the ways in which prisons — and prison staff— play their captives off against each other and seek to perpetuate a culture of alienation. It is not my intention to get caught up too much in issues surrounding so-called identity politics. However, it *is* important to recognise and highlight the way these issues play out within women's prisons.

---

29 *Crime: It's Cause and Treatment,* quoted in *Black and Bros*
30 gov.uk/government/publications/prison-safety-and-reform  see also gov.uk/government/collections/prisons-and-courts-bill

# DISCLAIMER

"Within the war we are all waging with the forces of death, subtle and otherwise — conscious or not — I am not only a casualty, I am also a warrior."*Audre Lorde[1]*

"To be visible is to be exposed, that is to say above all, vulnerable." *The Invisible Committee[2]*

At the risk of further making my identity obvious, I am an able-bodied, middle class, white, queer, cis-woman. English is my first language. I do not have any children or dependants. I am saying this because my experience of jail was wildly different from those facing multiple forms of oppression and discrimination inside. It is absolutely *not* my intention to attempt to speak for *all* women in jail. In many ways, I had an easy ride compared to some of my mates inside. The support and solidarity I received was overwhelming (and at times frankly embarrassing!). It gave me strength, and I will never, ever forget that or take it for granted.

During the drafting of this project I read a collection from Ardent Press of historical accounts of French Anarchists. I found it refreshing in its reflection on (and inclusion of) half-formed ideas, incomplete theories, and assorted quotations:

"We approached this project not as a deformed remembrance of an idealised past that never was, nor as an exercise in nostalgia, but as an *action*: a campaign of guerilla historicism that has as its goal a paradigmal hijacking and a sweeping overhaul of existing, received doctrines concerning anarchism. Retracing

1 Lorde, *The Transformation of Silence into Language and Action, 1977*
2 *The Coming Insurrection, 2007*

the elusive rhizomes of bona fide, non-diluted anarchist though necessitated some digging, but it was delightfully dirty business - for to sort through the remains of anarchism is also to sort the viable seed for future plantings."[3]

The creation of this text has also been a "delightfully dirty business". It has meant visiting some dark corners of my mind. The quotes used may seem unusual in their randomness, but I believe in a diversity of tactics when attacking the state, and I believe in using a diversity of expressions for analysing this process. Quotes included here felt relevant to me at a particular moment. They do not mean a wholesale subscription to the beliefs of that author, nor are they an endorsement of that author's wider political views and projects.

## Language and Labels

"It is not enough to simply criticise other's actions -anarchy is drowning in critical words and empty theories -one must act."[4]

"We know that the texts aren't sufficient enough to replace the beauty of live communication, but on the other hand, we understand that the condition of confinement does not allow many options beyond the written contribution of thoughts ideas and proposals appealing to any one who believes he can get something out of them."[5]

One of the biggest challenges within these words was the selection of labels. How best to articulate myself without employing the rhetoric of the state? How to be clear in my analysis, without using damaging stereotypes? Kilgore and others have argued that many labels used to describe "formerly incarcerated people" are examples of "stigmatizing language"[6]. However, whilst I have attempted to avoid any language that is discriminatory, I have used the terms prisoner and ex-prisoner.

It is *not* my intention to imply that the main identity of the individual described as an 'ex-prisoner' is their status in relation to the legal system (though when you've first been released it can feel like this),

3 *Disruptive Elements: The Extremes of French Anarchism, 2009*
4 Wild Fire, *An Anarchist Prison Newsletter Number One, 2015*
5 CCF, *Chaotic Variables: A Theoretical Contribution in Proposal for an Informal Anarchist Platform, 2016*
6 Kilgore, *2015*

nor am I assuming they will never be prisoners again. As has been well documented, revolving door theory and analysis of so-called recidivism clearly demonstrate that once an individual has been incarcerated they are increasingly likely to be the subject of future custodial sentences.

> "Prisons remove people from their communities, isolate them from social support, and disconnect them from frameworks of accountability...As a result, people often come out of prison in a much worse state than when they went in, putting them at increased risk of the situations that landed them in prison in the first place." *Lamble*[7]

Some labels are needed to move forward with the discussion so I hope that I have chosen the least offensive, but convenient options. Personally, I have no problems with people referring to me as an ex-prisoner, however, many other labels relating to incarceration and the legal system are highly problematic. 'Offender' implies guilt, as does the word 'criminal'. The language of law is the language of domination and I do not want to perpetuate that.

> "Many people who never go to court are offensive people, and the greater someone's social power the greater their opportunities to impose their offensiveness on others." *Karlene Faith*[8]

The frustration I had with labels continued in my analysis of political geography. There is nothing 'Great' about Britain and this is hardly a 'United' Kingdom. I questioned which noun was the least offensive and decided that UK was the lesser of two evils. But it is still deeply problematic.

> "Union Jack and Union Jill
> Back up and down the same old hill
> Sell the flag to the youths
> But who swallows the bill" *Asian Dub Foundation*[9]

Angela Y. Davis stated, "we have not learned how to talk about prisons as institutions that collect and hide away the people whom society treats as it's refuse."[10] This lack of understanding, and my slightly burnt out brain, is my defence if I have written anything that is problematic. I use the

7 Lamble, in Stanley and Smith 2015
8 Faith, *Unruly Women: The Politics of Confinement and Resistance, 2011*
9 ADF, *Real Great Britain, 2000*
10 Davis, *The Meaning of Freedom, 2012*

term people in women's prisons to refer to those that the state has labelled women and then imprisoned in its gendered institutions. I do *not* assume that *all* the inmates of these miserable places identify as women. Nor do I assume that women's prisons house *all* the prisoners within the system who identify as women, as there are many trans women held captive within men's jails, Youth Offending Institutes (YOIs), Immigration Removal Centres (IRCs) and so on.

Many articles concerning women's prisons state in a strident shower of liberal outrage that women should not be in jail. Reformist organisations and criminologists claim that this incarceration destroys families, and lives, and that women have 'complex needs' that jail does not address. Let me be clear: *no one* should be in jail. Prison is poison. As Stanley and Smith have argued: "Reform is a pathway to more insidious forms of subjugation and disguises itself as humanity, hope, freedom, and possibly may end up destroying us in the end."[11]

Calls to end the imprisonment of women are dangerously simplistic and do not address the root cause of the problem. Yes, women in jail have complex needs, but so do many other people, and the impacts of these needs not being met affects *everyone*, not just those who are held within the walls of women's prisons.

> "Some of the timidity in the fight against warehousing humans in cages for part or all of their lives results from the lethal synthesis of abandoned optimism and calculated convenience.... The challenge seems so enormous that many desperately conclude it's better to save the "deserving" weak (women and children or addicts) and cross their fingers that everyone else can swim on their own." *Dan Berger*[12]

The state reinforces gender stereotypes at every level within the prison system, from the clothes and courses it offers to the punishments it imposes on those who dare to act in ways which are not deemed suitable for women. The prison system both patronises and controls its captive populations, making token attempts to promote so-called equalities. Like the locks and bars of prison architecture, discrimination enables the prison to segregate and alienate individuals inside it. People in prisons are more than numbers to be processed.

---

11 Stanley and Smith, *2015*
12 Berger,*The Struggle Within: Prisons, Political Prisoners, and Mass Movements in the United States, 2014*

"We must never forget that beyond the anecdotes and reminiscences prison consists of so many reinforced boxes that millions of people all over the world are locked up in day and night. The latter are hostages of the state and live at the mercy of a hierarchy of vile cowards 24 hours a day." *Weir*[13]

During my time inside I conducted a few interviews, and they are included here. They are *not* meant to be representative of any definable group. They are merely a small collection of voices from a corner of the prison estate. I hope they highlight some of the key issues that are commonly faced inside women's prisons.

This project was never intended to be so formal (or a book!) Like the prison industrial complex, it has expanded and undergone some reinvention. I have no interest in academia, and because of this, the text does not necessarily conform to accepted publishing and referencing norms. Hopefully it is accessible despite this. I have *deliberately* not used capital letters for some nouns because I do not want to give power to the administration of the state, or those who implement it. If an author has used capitals to refer to these positions and institutions in the title of their book, or in a quote, I have followed this convention but otherwise I have avoided using them.

I have included a glossary of terms and appendices due to the often confusing minefield of legal jargon and prison slang, so please do check the references if something doesn't make sense. In a departure from conventional lay out, I have put the glossary at the very, very back so that the reader can easily refer to it.

## Political Prisoners?

"Political prisoners occupy a crucial position in freedom movements around the world; their incarceration signals the terror of state repression, and their activism defines the principled, long-term commitments of our movements." *Berger*[14]

The label 'political prisoner' is *not* used in this publication because I reject it as a categorisation. It implies that some people inside have a supposedly higher moral dimension. The concept of the 'political prisoner' plays into a mind-set which informs activist styles of organising, imbuing

13 Weir, *A Passion for Freedom, 2010*
14 Berger, *2014*

some with a supposedly more 'principled' position than others. In employing this hierarchy of status, others are therefore implicitly renounced or looked down upon as acting (or allegedly acting) for selfish (or self-serving) reasons.

The 'Incentives and Earned Privileges' (IEP) scheme, the categorisation (and re-categorisation) of prisoners and the language of reform and rehabilitation are all used to divide the prison population, and prisoners who get caught up in these processes do the dirty work of the state. The use of the label political prisoner is just another example of how pervasive and dangerous this discourse is. Many people in jail reject authority every day, in order to survive, and thrive, despite the best efforts of the system. All these actions are political.

> "The next time we're shocked and outraged by an experience of being targeted, harassed, or otherwise mistreated by law enforcement or society in general, we should be stopping to recognize how much respect we owe to the people all around us who face much more than that every day of their lives. *Every prisoner is a political prisoner.*" Kelly Rose Pflug-Back[15]

## Statistics and Prison Service Instructions (PSIs)

> "Revolt needs everything: papers and books, arms and explosives, reflection and swearing, poison, daggers and arson. The only interesting question is how to combine them... Breaking with everything, especially with our ways of understanding the world." *Anonymous*[16]

The statistics here shave been included to provide context and a frame work for understanding the scale of the problem of women's prisons. I have tried to use the most reliable sources possible. All statistics should be viewed with suspicion, and many of the organisations included in this publication are promoting a reformist agenda. It is inevitable that there will be a tension between the broader political analysis which is a major motivation in completing this project, and the desire to impart random (hopefully useful) bits of practical information for those engaging with life inside.

In theory, prisons run according to a dense network of universal

15 Back, *These Burning Streets, 2012 italics used in original text*
16 *At Daggers Drawn with the Existent, its Defenders and its False Critics, 2007*

procedures, and legislations. "There are a number of rules, regulations and guidelines by which prisons are run. These are outlined in Prison Service Instructions (PSIs). All Prison Service operating instructions are published as PSIs. They have a fixed expiry date."[17] All jails *should* have copies of the PSIs for everyone to read, whatever your 'status', and regardless of any disciplinary procedures you are subject to. They are normally kept in the library. Please note that PSIs only apply to England and Wales. Prisons in Scotland, Northern Ireland, Isle of Man, Jersey and Guernsey do *not* have equivalents. The PSIs are all online, and all prison libraries have paper copies.

Audre Lorde famously stated in *Sister Outsider*: "the master's tools will never dismantle the master's house."[18] The use of PSIs and legal precedents will never bring about the end of the prison industrial complex. However, when you are in jail you need to utilise all that you can to challenge staff and this can mean using some random acts, figures and legislation.

**Places**

The 'prison estate' is dependent on many additional institutions, though they are often run by the usual suspects: G4S, Serco and MTCnovo. MTCnovo ran Abu Gharaib, the infamous torture unit and prison in Iraq. Abu Gharaib was built by British subcontractors in Iraq in the 1950s.

Immigration Removal Centres (IRCS, aka Detention Centres or Immigration Prisons), Youth Offender Institutions (YOIs or 'Juvie'), Secure Training Centres (also used for young people) and Closed Supervision Centres (CSCs) use many of the tactics outlined here. Many of the legal precedents cited can be applied across the prison estate, and some PSIs are the same in both men's and women's prisons, but it is not always the case.

England and Wales top the international league tables for dishing out childhood criminal records, and young people within these countries are much more likely to be incarcerated than in other countries in Europe[19]. Between 2013-2014 over 60,000 cautions and convictions were given to people under 18 in England and Wales.

According to the home office, the number of people entering detention in the year ending June 2015 increased by 10% to 32,053 from 29,122

---

17 justice.gov.uk
18 Lorde, *Sister Outsider, 2007*
19 *Standing Committee for Youth Justice* report, 2016

in the previous year. Many people held captive within these Immigration Prisons do not have any release date or legal representation. Like those in jail on IPPs (Imprisonment for Public Protection), the level of uncertainty surrounding the length of their stay within the prison system has a huge impact on people's mental health.

There are numerous connections between 'Her Majesty's Prison Service' and IRCs. All of these institutions are the brutal reality of state repression and the way it divides people into 'citizens' and 'subjects'. The status quo is dependent on such places to remove individuals who do not conform to state enforced rules of behaviour, or who do not benefit it in some way. However, it is beyond the scope of this text to go into the details of all the workings and procedures of these establishments. The focus here is specifically women's prisons in the UK.

# PART ONE: INSIDE

## RECEPTION/INDUCTION

"The current system is definitely not "mis-guided"; it's very successful in its actual goal: keeping oppressed communities in a perpetual state of chaos and agony." *David Gilbert[1]*

"Without rigorous self-reflection about your thoughts, emotions and actions you cannot be certain that you will still think and act rationally -something you took for granted before." *Klaus Viehmann[2]*

### Preparation

Before we start to talk about arriving at jail, a couple of points on preparing to get there. If you haven't been remanded straight from the cop shop, enjoy the 'luxury' of being able to bring a small selection of items in with you. If there is even a slim chance you'll get a custodial sentence, pack a bag when you go to court. Probation are *very* keen on the generic recommendation "non-custodial" in their pre-sentence reports but judges often don't listen, especially if you've got previous convictions.

Don't take anything too valuable into jail with you, or anything you are afraid to lose. Jail works on a barter economy so even if you don't use certain items (e.g. make-up) consider taking some in to trade with others for more useful stuff. The rules of every jail are different, but *none* allow hoodies or anything resembling the uniform of a screw (i.e. black trousers

1 Gilbert, *Our Commitment is to Our Communities, 2014*
2 Viehmann, *Prison Round Trip, 2009 edition*

and white shirts). It's worth researching what your local prison allows before you go to court. Courts always discharge prisoners to the same local jails, so you should be able to work it out depending on where you'll be appearing.

Carl Cattermole's *HM Prison Service: Survival Guide*[3] gives good tips on what you can take to prison. You will *sometimes* be allowed: pictures for the wall, stamps and envelopes, notepad/diary/address book, headphones, trainers (most prisons have a two pair maximum rule), list of phone numbers, addresses and dates of birth of people you'll want to visit you, basic toiletries, clothing, flip-flops (for the shower... dirty, dirty places! and also your pad if you share with someone who has chronic athletes foot like I did), stationary and books (but not too much of either or they'll make you put them all in your 'stored prop' or say 'NFI' ('Not For Issue'.)

It's also a good idea to take some cash. Cash gets put straight into your account and gets credited instantly, unlike postal orders (or cheques, which for some reason can take up to six weeks to clear in jail). However, cash is obviously riskier because the screws will often confiscate it. Whilst you're being 'inducted' you won't earn as much as the pitiful amount you'll get once you are an established member of the exploited prison work force, so having cash in your 'spends' (finances) for the first couple of weeks is really handy.

If you have any animals that you are responsible for, you will obviously need to think about them even if there is only a slim chance you will get sent down. The 'Cat Protection League' and 'Dogs Trust' can help if you have an animal who is potentially going to be without a home due to your incarceration.

Also, if you think you might get sent down, cancel all your standing orders and tidy up your life admin before court, or leave instructions with people on how to do this. It may take days or weeks for security to clear the numbers on your phone PIN. Most telephones in jail are not touch screen, and charge a fortune, so making an official phone calls is a nightmare. Doing these things before you go to jail will mean you can avoid the wing office (the place where all the screws hang out) as much as possible, especially when you first arrive. You don't want to get a reputation for hanging out with prison staff, and they *will* be nosy towards you.

Note that most of this chapter includes information for people who are new to the prison system, though if you have been 'ghosted' (transferred with no notice) or 'shipped out' (transferred with minimal notice) then

3 Cattermole, 2015

some of this will still apply.

## Reception

'Her Majesty's Inspectorate of Prisons' (HMIP) has issued guidelines on the procedure for 'processing' new prisoners[4]. The process of getting searched varies hugely. Some jails now use BOSS chairs (Body Orifice Scanning Chairs) to try to find drugs. Others will use 'passive drugs dogs'. You should only get searched by someone who the state has decided is the same gender as you. In women's jails, the dreaded 'squat and cough' and strip searches are used much less now, and staff should only use strip searches if they are adjudicating you on a specific incident. You will however have to show your mouth, take off your shoes and socks and have a thorough pat down and going over with a wand.

Everyone gets a 'reception phone call'. This will be brief, and you'll probably have a screw breathing down your neck the whole time jangling their keys (you better get used to that sound pretty damn quick). Once that's done you'll be sent down. You will be offered a 'welcome pack'. The cost of this ranges and depends on your preferred option. At the time of writing, you could still smoke in women's jails (though this will change in the next couple of years), so you could either buy a smoker's pack (containing rolling tobacco, papers and a lighter), or a non-smoker's pack (squash and over-priced biscuits). Both contain a small amount of phone credit. The cost gets deducted off your first canteen sheet so remember that when you are making your shopping list. If you are a smoker, make your baccy last. People swarm around 'fresh meat' (new people in the jail). They'll seem like your new bestie if it's mid-week and they've run out of burn, but it's most likely the baccy they are after!

Many jails have different limits on the amount of clothing you can have in possession at any one time so it's likely you will have to put some stuff into your 'stored prop'. Each prisoner is allowed one box. Make sure you watch the screws seal it, and write down the tag number, so that nothing

---

4 HMIP guidelines on reception process for new prisoners: "Although the reception process is different in every prison, an individual's typical first experiences in prison may follow the following pattern: Arrival at the prison > Led from van to reception area > Identity checked at the reception desk > Initial interview with staff > Health care interview > Searched (either rub down or strip search) > Put in a holding room > Cell sharing risk assessment (CSRA) interview conducted > Moved to first night accommodation > Access to Peer Supporters/ Listeners/ Samaritans > Meal, shower and free telephone call > Locked up for first night".

can go missing or get added in your absence. If you aren't allowed stuff, they will put pressure on you to organise it as a 'hand-out' on a visit. If you have space in your prop box, leave it in there and try again another day. Screws hate people sending in stationary and stamps, but some staff might allow it.

Once you've been searched, photographed and had all your property catalogued you will probably have an initial health care appointment. If you are on medication (meds), particularly methadone, you will need to get this sorted ASAP. If you have been transferred from another jail, your old prison should have made health care aware of this. Prisons give out meth in the mornings, so the chances are you'll have missed this by the time you eventually get out the sweat-box (prison van) and get processed, so you'll be pretty desperate.

You'll be asked lots of medical questions in your initial appointment. Be careful if they ask you about alcohol or drugs. Unless you actively want to engage with a rehab/substance misuse process play down your consumption. If you were intoxicated or high at the time of your arrest or alleged offence, or disclose that you have used anything at all, they *will* slap various rehab related programmes on your sentence plan straight away (and probably on your licence too).

Beware of the prisoners who meet you at reception. You will probably feel relieved to have made it this far, so the desire to chat to any one who isn't in uniform will be quite high. A lot of them will be genuinely nice. However, in my experience it is often the case that the girls who get the jobs of so-called 'Insiders', or 'Reception Orderlies' are quite pally with officers (same with 'Wing Reps') and work quite closely with them in processing the 'inductions'. Whatever you say to them will be around the jail quicker than you can say "shit-and-a-shave" (a short sentence) so watch out! Don't be lulled into a false sense of security by a tepid cup of prison-issue tea and some cold toast.

If English isn't your first language, request an interpreter as soon as you arrive. At the very least, basic information about the prison *should* be available in a range of languages. Be even more careful than normal about what you are signing. If you can, ask the prisoner who meets you at reception if there are any other people inside who speak your language.

## The First Few Days

"You're nervous, struggling for things to say, wanting to be normal like the other prisoners. You're careful when you look at people and make sure not to bump into anyone. you're vulnerable and careful not to make any wrong moves." *Niall Harnett*[5]

"Each prison and jail has its own set of inmate created politics and rules you must abide by in order to make it. This will often involve the way you eat, sleep, shower, brush your teeth, watch TV or even use the rest room. These are only a few examples of life in prison." *Jordan Halliday*[6]

The induction wing can be a hectic and isolating place. There is a lot of tension and uncertainty. Some will be struggling because they have just been sent down for the first time, others won't have been sentenced yet. Do *not* chat to folks about your legal business before you have put in a plea/been sentenced. Think carefully about how you want to interact with education and work. The induction can be long, bureaucratic and tedious, but it'd better than being made to do a long course that you agreed to out of boredom.

INTERIOR OF CELL.

According to the Prison and Probation Ombudsman (PPO); 20% of self-inflicted deaths in jail between 2007-2013 happened within the first three days of custody. The combination of lack of sleep (especially if you have a pad-mate who snores!), the huge amount of information to take in, and the barrage of questions can be exhausting and stressful. A lot of jails have a wing-buddy system for people who first come in. Whilst it's important to be careful how much personal information you disclose, take advantage of their knowledge. Avoid going to the wing office, but

---

5 Harnett, *Jail! An insight into prison life in Ireland, Namely Castlerea Prison, 2013*
6 Halliday, *Post-Traumatic Stress After Prison, 2014*

don't be a door mat. Make sure you demand whatever is available to you, and if staff are unhelpful (or not allowing you basic rights under prison law) then make a detailed log of their names and relevant information.

During your first few days, it is quite common for prison staff to pay extra attention to you, and test you. They may well have been briefed by security or have seen you on the telly. Screws aren't meant to look up prisoners online, but of course they do. I was followed around the exercise yard repeatedly by screws trying to be pally with me and saying some of the things they'd heard, and asking me how I felt about upcoming court dates and which way I would 'plea'.

**Bureaucracy**

There will be a centralised system for organising your daily life. For years this was run by the National Offender Management Service (NOMS) but in a classic example of the prison system re-inventing the wheel, at the time of going to press it was being scrapped and replaced with Her Majesty's Prison and Probation Service (HMPPS) -more on this later. Everything related to your time inside will be on this database, from your 'spends' (personal money allowance), to comments from prison staff will be on this centralised system. If you are waiting for a postal order or wages to clear, don't let the screws fob you off, keep getting them to check (same for visiting orders, and anything that will make your life more bearable inside).

Your 'spends' will trickle down into your account because you are only allowed so much per week. This was £12 for "standard" prisoners when I was in (and remand prisoners get less). Even if you get a lot of money sent in you'll still only get a bit at a time. If you ever have the dubious honour of becoming an 'enhanced' prisoner then you can access more of your own money each week. See sections on IEPs and work for more information on finances.

The desire to get everything organised at once can be really strong when you first enter jail (especially because you have so little control), but the wheels of prison bureaucracy move very slowly, and often stop entirely. If you want anything, from emergency phone credit to a plug for your sink, you will have to write an 'app' (General Application). Screws are notoriously bad at remembering to print these (because it generates work for them), but there *should* be copies on all wings, along with the myriad of other forms. Prisons are definitely *not* paperless. You have to write separate apps for everything. So be specific, and if it's for anything official, keep a receipt or date you sent it, as you will probably have to write several to get anything done.

## Riding Bang-up

Whilst you are on the reception wing you will probably have even more 'bang-up' than normal. Most likely you won't be able to access the gym or the library until you've been inducted. However, don't despair! *National Prison Radio* is a station that you can access through the TV in your cell, so it's really useful if you aren't posh enough to have a CD player or radio. Sometimes the public service style announcements can get a bit much (for example, endless warnings about the horrors of 'New Psychoactive Substances' and adverts for bail hostels) but the tunes are often good. Its slogan is "made by prisoners, for prisoners" and it gets broadcast from HMP Brixton. You can send in requests and do shout-outs to your mates. This always goes down well! It has a range of shows combining tunes with practical information. The listings for it are published on the back cover of *Inside Time* (IT).

IT is a newspaper concerning all things prison related which is free inside and should be readily available from the library each month. It is increasingly reactionary and often a mouth-piece for the powers that be, but it is still worth reading for up to date information about prison legislation. *Jail Mail* and *Converse* are also monthly publications. Another way to get news from the outside world is to get people outside to order you a newspaper, or just read ones that other people have ordered. Most jails have a local newsagent's who will deliver a (very limited) range of newspapers a couple of times a week. You can either pay for this from your spends inside, or get people outside to set up an order. There should be a form for this on your wing.

Prison libraries (when they are open) are surprisingly quite well-stocked places (especially if you like crime novels!). Most prison libraries are connected to their local service outside and so it's quite easy to request different titles. You can also get 'distraction packs'. These are small selections of pictures to colour in (although most likely you won't have any colouring pencils at this point in your sentence) and other puzzles to keep you occupied during bang-up. If you think looking at pictures from Disney's Frozen, and completing word-searches on topics such as 'Words for Feeling Dull' will be an antidote to thinking about your loss of liberty, family, and impending court dates, then ask wing staff.

## Observation

> "Permaculture is a philosophy of working with, rather than against nature; of protracted & thoughtful observation rather than protracted and thoughtless labour." *Bill Mollison*[7]

This principle served me well on the induction wing. You are constantly being observed and judged, so don't do anything too rash. Whilst it is obviously important to stand your ground and be consistent from the outset in your attitude to other prisoners and staff, don't be *too* quick to align yourself with any one, or any group. Pick your battles, and take time to familiarise yourself with the ways of the wing. Watch who attracts drama and 'mix up'. You can always make more friends later.

Induction involves a lot of bang-up and even when you are unlocked it can seem soul-destroying and tedious…in some jails it takes two weeks minimum! But even though you'll probably be feeling a bit lonely and bored, it's better to ride it out solo as much as possible then make informed choices about who to associate with later, especially if you are awaiting sentencing.

In 'remand jails' (for short term prisoners or those on remand) there will most likely be a lot of younger people who will often be looking for support. My advice is, be helpful and listen, but don't get too caught up in their dramas initially. Other prisoners will test you during your first few days, and how you conduct yourself during this time is critical. Even if you are feeling really low, keep your 'pad' (cell) tidy (especially if sharing), make yourself presentable at all times (even if you are wearing entirely prison issue, keep it clean). Don't hide away too much in your cell, as people won't like it if you don't make an effort.

## Sharing a Cell

If you are sharing a cell, get some ground rules established quickly, and be assertive. I got padded up with someone who smoked. This was a nightmare. Not only was our pad constantly invaded by people on the blag for burn, the room stank all the time (the air vents in most cells are pathetic). The agreement I insisted on was that unless it was the 'weekend regime' (lots of bang-up, especially during the Christmas period, up to 23 hours per day) she wouldn't smoke in our cell when I was there.

Another pad mate was convinced everyone was going to come on to

---

7 Mollison, *Permaculture: A Designer's Manual, 1988*

31

her. As soon as she arrived she asked me if I was "one of those lezzers", and said she was scared she was going to get jumped on. I politely tried to explain that I was queer, but that I also wouldn't touch her if she was the only other prisoner on the wing! As prisons are so pervasive in main stream media, everyone has preconceptions about what life will be like inside, and this can add to a general sense of doom and unease.

Sharing a cell can actually be good once you've got used to the total lack of privacy (and the worst thing for me, the constant drone of day time television). A couple of my pad-mates were older than me and had some medical needs they appreciated help with. Also, if it's going OK, then you've got someone to watch your back (and your stuff, from so-called 'Peter thieves' -other prisoners who will try to nick for your cell). I think the ideal is being civil but not too friendly with your pad-mate. I was wary of getting too close to any one person inside and this was a good survival strategy. As you can imagine, women's prisons are cliquey places and all too often 'besties' and 'prison wives' fall out massively after a few days/weeks. If you are too tight with your pad mate the potential for this to happen is obviously much higher.

You never know when you will get 'shipped-out' (transferred to another jail), so if you are dependent on someone else that will be tough. Also, prison staff *love* separating people they see working well together, often transferring one of them to another cell, wing, or another jail. So being as independent as possible can be a good coping strategy.

Some people make themselves 'high-risk' in order to avoid sharing a cell by specifying mental health issues. However, this will most likely mean being put on an ACCT (Assessment, Care in Custody and Team-work) which will involve a lot of interaction with staff, and various 'support' services such as 'Safer Custody'. Personally, I'd much rather share than have to interact with nosy staff, and have them think that I am struggling with their system.

**General Tips for 'Doin' Bird' (not gender specific!)**

-No expectations means no disappointments.

-Be consistent in your behaviour towards other prisoners.

-Never let the staff see your emotions.

-Take as much prison issue as possible. You can always trade it if you don't want it…. or recycle. For example, sanitary towels make good floor cleaning cloths, you swap prison issue biscuits for haircuts, and the rain ponchos some work details get issued make good screens for the toilet or shower.

-If you aren't having visits then save your VOs (visiting orders)... you can trade them for phone credit or the prison issue letters (O/Ls, letters the prison pays the postage on that are issued once a week).

-Shakespeare famously wrote: "Never a borrower nor a lender be". Beware of 'double bubble' (someone lending you something -for example tobacco or stamps-then expecting double back).

-Keep your cell tidy.

-Get fresh air when 'exercise' is allowed. On the induction wing we were only allowed outside for 20 minutes a day (and this was always cancelled if raining/drizzle due to supposed 'health and safety' issues). According to home office legislation, "all prisoners should be able to spend between 30 minutes and an hour outside in the open air each day." Remind the screws of this!

-Always knock before entering someone's cell. Never invite yourself in.

-Don't be nosy! A good way to deflect attention from myself whilst

FEMALE CONVICTS EXERCISING IN THE AIRING YARD AT BRIXTON PRISON.
(From a Photograph by Herbert Watkins, 215, Regent Street.)

during 'association time' is to listen. A lot of people like talking about themselves, their families/partners and their crime. A couple of well timed, open questions can keep the conversation flowing. I also found a lot of time passed outlining what my conception of anarchy meant and slagging off authority :-) However, don't be seen to be too inquisitive! Or ask specific or leading questions.

-Never share outside addresses or details of you or your friends/family with other prisoners unless you *really, really* trust them.

-Always search a new cell carefully when you move in.

-Don't lie about your crime. If you are very vague (or come in with a really long sentence for something like a supposedly minor fraud charge) alarm bells will start ringing. Prison staff take swift disciplinary action if people inside try to research new inmates but it is common practice. Prisoners will get folk outside to look up new inmates on the internet, and/or watch Crimewatch/local news/Jeremy Kyle for information about people they don't believe. If you are found out to be lying, everyone will assume you are a sex-offender, and you better watch out.

## Complaining

> "Despite fears of administrative reprisals and a lack of outside support, women in prison have found ways to individually and collectively challenge, resist and organise around their conditions of confinement.... While the processes of both verbally complaining and filing grievances may have little effect in changing the conditions of confinement, the fact that women not only utilise them but are "notorious" for doing so indicates that women do not passively accept their circumstances, but attempt to change them in any way possible."
> *Victoria Law*[8]

If you want to make a complaint, there is a lengthy process to go through. Request a 'COMP1' form, then contact the Independent Monitoring Board (IMB). Each prison has an IMB, which is made up of local volunteers. If the issue relates to discrimination or equalities, then complete a 'Discrimination Incident Reporting Form' (DIRF). The most common procedure is to then write to the Prison and Probation Ombudsman (PPO). Some people inside write letters to their MPs. I am sceptical about this as a tactic,

8 Law, *Resistance Behind Bars: The Struggles of Incarcerated Women, 2012*

but whatever works for you. There is also a Home Office process you can follow.

> "The prison complaints system is designed to be impenetrable. They know they can take the piss in the knowledge that a massive proportion of inmates are either dyslexic, illiterate or not going to have the tenacity to complain... Let them know they can't walk all over you and anyone else who might find themselves in a similar situation in the future." *Cattermole*[9]

It's also always worth investigating the PSIs, because often staff will back down on issues when presented with a piece of legislation. Other prisoners may also have experience of these issues.

Don't complain *too* much, especially if you have got a 'touch' (short sentence). For general acceptance on the wing from other prisoners remember that no one likes someone who moans all the time, especially if it's about other prisoners. Everyone will have something that is non-negotiable for them in terms of prison slackness. For me, it was being vegan and making sure the kitchen respected that; for others it's finding out information about when they can get on the Mother and Baby Unit, or get an interpreter. Think carefully, and pick your battles. So you got issued a sheet full of fag burns? Deal with it yourself!

### The Prison and Probation Ombudsman (PPO)

So you've filled in a 'General App' and a 'COMP1' form but you haven't heard anything back (or your reply was unsatisfactory.) The next phase is normally to contact the PPO. According to this organisation, "the Prisons and Probation Ombudsman (PPO) carries out independent investigations into deaths and complaints in custody."[10]

It is interesting to note the PPO's use of the phrase *"independent investigations"*. It is funded by the state. The PPO have a history of failing to act on prisoner's complaints even when they have followed the maze of nightmarish bureaucracy the system insists upon. You *must* have followed the internal complaints procedure carefully before contacting the PPO.

Bowden has called the PPO a "thoroughly compromised and discredited body". It was established in response to the Strangeways uprising in 1990. The 'Woolf Report' (named after lord justice Woolf) investigated the

---

9 Cattermole, 2015
10 ppo.gov.uk

conditions leading up to the riot, and the PPO was set up so that in theory prisoners had an independent way of getting conditions changed inside. However, both the Woolf Report and the PPO were organised by the government.

According to the PPO, it received about 5,000 complaints in 2016 but only 2,400 were accepted. 40% of these complaints found in favour of the prisoner. Complaints to the PPO tripled between 2014-2015. This reflects the worsening conditions in the UK prison estate.

If you are writing to the PPO, you must send all the relevant paperwork, with a covering letter (there is no official form), within three months of the response of your initial complaint. If your complaint is the subject of court proceedings then it is beyond the remit of the PPO.

The main recommendations the PPO will make include: an apology, financial compensation, quashing adjudication findings, changes to national policy and disciplinary measures against staff. The prison service *do* normally accept recommendations, because they don't want the bad press. Sometimes the threat of the PPO is enough to get staff to back down because prisons don't like having negative reports. But be warned, complaining isn't without its risks. If prison staff get wind of your intentions; they may well make your life even more tricky. So don't be a door mat, but do be prepared for closer scrutiny if you are following official channels.

## Categorisation

Security categories are different in women's and men's jails. This is a further example of how the UK prison system imposes different restrictions on the basis of gender. In men's prisons the structure is rigid, there are category A-D prisoners and they do not mix. People in women's prisons are not divided in this way. The main differentiation is whether someone is incarcerated in open or closed conditions. See the chapter 'Bigger Cages, Longer Chains' for information on 'open conditions' and categorisation[11] (and appendix three). The (re)categorisation of all prisoners is laid out in PSI39/2011, 'Categorisation and Re-categorisation of Women Prisoners' (updated August 2016).

For the first few months of all sentences, people in women's prisons are placed together regardless of crime or background. Prisoners with short sentences and newly convicted Lifers will all be on the induction wing and

---

11 Note that *very few* women are Cat A/Restricted. Most of the population of women's prisons are all just prisoners who are subject to closed conditions. If you are Cat A/Restricted, your cases will be controlled by NOMS/HMPPS.

this can create quite a lot of stress. High-risk individuals, such as people involved in high profile sex offence cases, will sometimes be put onto a more secure unit once they've completed the induction process (or life has become unbearable for them on the induction wing) but unlike in men's prisons, they will all be part of the same jail, and use the same facilities such as the gym and library.

## Sex Offenders

In the 1980s a new category of prisoner was born: the female sex offender. In 1988 psychotherapist Estella Welldon publicised this group, arguing that women convicted of sex offences were seen as doubly deviant: violating both legal *and* gender role expectations. According to the PRT, 14% of the total prison population are convicted of sex offences, including 42% of people over 50 in men's jails.

There are obviously a huge range of sex offences, and it is not the intention to cover them all here. The best way to avoid being labelled a 'nonce' is to be open about your conviction, even if that is just the title of your alleged offence. Nothing creates suspicion and ill feeling among prisoners quicker than someone who is being vague about why they are inside, and contrary to popular belief, people *do* ask "what ya in for?" all the time.

The main forms of alleged sexual offences I encountered inside were prosecutions for historical sex-offences, prosecutions for the taking, distribution and possession of indecent photos of children, and 'failure to protect' (a child from harm). Most prisoners in women's jails make very little distinction between being the alleged perpetrator of the crime, and those who are inside for laws relating to 'failure to protect'. The broadly accepted view inside women's prisons is that you are still a 'nonce' if you are in for failure to protect. Women convicted of this charge are often regarded as being even worse than being the actual perpetrator of the crime, because they are women, and therefore should have known better. This treatment shows the acute violence of patriarchy, and how females convicted of sex offences are indeed seen as what Welldon termed "doubly deviant".

All the stereotypical forms of attack against those convicted of sex offences occur inside, from people contaminating food to cornering people in the shower. There is a rigorous moral code on this issue and folks take a dim view of any one who does not conform to this. In women's jails the topic of sex offences is huge and gets discussed at length. My basic advice would be, unless you don't mind being shunned by the majority of the prison population, do not associate with anyone accused of being a sex offender. If you are convicted of a sex offence, watch your back and keep your head down. Prison staff will do *a lot* to protect alleged sex offenders, so be careful if you are involved in confrontation. In my limited experience screws will also often side with the person convicted of the sex offence because they tend to spend a lot of time in the office, or chatting to staff, because no one else will.

If you are a mother, no one is going to be more aware than you about the safety of your children. It's lovely receiving photos, especially seeing the speed at which young people grow. However, as has been previously outlined, women's prisons are uncategorised and as such you can never be too sure what some people are in for. One of my friends was really upset because she got moved onto a secure wing as a form of punishment after failing a Mandatory Drug Test (MDT). This wing housed many people convicted of sex offences, so she no longer felt able to display her family photos.

I was quite amazed by the number of women who were doing time for alleged sex offences. It was way higher than I had imagined. I'm not gonna lie, being inside properly tested the limits of my political analysis on the prison system and prison abolition in relation to nonces and paedophilia. However, despite hearing of some of the most pre-meditated, organised and repeat cases, I still strongly believe that prison does nothing to deal with sex offenders other than lock them away, and that there are much better models and methods for dealing with these issues.

**Phone Calls**

Trying to make phone calls inside is a minefield. Assume that all phone calls are monitored. The phones are *really* expensive, way more than calls made outside. The phones will automatically cut out after ten minutes. If no one is waiting, you can re-dial the number, but don't be one of those who are selfish and overuse the phone. One of the quickest ways to make enemies inside is by stopping other prisoners from talking to their loved ones. Everyone has such limited access to the phones. Using them during the day is prohibitively expensive, and evening bang-up comes around quick, so be aware of when you are using them and how much.

Adding numbers to your phone PIN will take several days. Write out all the numbers on the correct form (copies should be on the wing). You are only normally allowed a certain amount, so think carefully about who you want on there. Prison staff are really hot on people using each other's PINs. For example, one of my mates tried to commit suicide. Her family were contacted via her PIN when she was in hospital. Someone was adjudicated and put on basic for this.

You have to buy phone credit off your canteen sheet. It is tempting to use it all up quickly when you get it, but try to always keep a bit back for emergencies. If you run out, you can apply for emergency credit, but they will only authorise this a few times. If you are a 'Foreign National Prisoner' (FNP), they may make some exceptions (more on this later). Make sure your solicitors number is on your pin. You are normally allowed a couple of legal phone numbers in addition to the more general ones. You should be entitled to make legal phone calls from one of the wing phones if it's an emergency, but no doubt the screws will be listening very attentively to your conversation, even though they *allegedly* don't record legal conversations.

You can try to use some 'third party' phone providers such as Fonesavvy or Jail Telecom (see resources section). These enable you to phone a mobile via a land-line so it makes it much cheaper. They must be set up by someone outside. Do not let on to any one you are doing this because security will ban it. Some of my friends got away with doing this fine, but I tried and got shut down within 48 hours.

**Reception Visit**

If you are new to the whole prison system, at your 'reception visit' (your first visit) you are often allowed a hand in (*not* if you've been shipped out from another institution). Get your visitors to consider carefully what to bring. Cross reference with the maximum number of items your allowed in your possession at any one time. You are only allowed one hand in, so make it count! Be aware that if you have nice clothes they may well go missing, especially from the laundry.

A lot of people in remand jails look down on those wearing too much prison issue clothing. If you get given a load of prison issue clothing you don't want, it makes good mattress padding. Once I finally got my 'hand-in' (a parcel of clothes from outside), I tried to mix up my wardrobe by wearing a combination of prison issue and my own clothes every day. This means you never feel institutionalised, but you also don't wear out your best threads super-fast! In longer term jails it is much more acceptable to wear prison issue as many prisoners don't have money for (or want to prioritise) clothes shopping.

Be warned, your first visit will be tough. By the time you see your loved ones you will probably have already put your guard up, and be in a (most likely superficial/tentative) rhythm with prison life. That first visit can knock this bravado somewhat. But luckily people inside are generally quite good at looking out for each other after visits. Don't be shy about going to find someone you trust or at least know quite well after your visit. Sometimes this isn't possible because you may get banged-up straight after, and if you are on meds you will have to go straight to the hatch. This can be tough. You will most likely be on a hype, or sugar fuelled roller coaster after your visit and then suddenly you are confined in a small space. I always found cranking up some tunes and bashing out a load of letters a good use of this slightly manic energy.

# GENDER ISSUES IN WOMEN'S PRISONS

## INTRODUCTION

"The unruly woman is the undisciplined woman. She is a renegade from the disciplinary practices which would mould her as a gendered being. She is the defiant woman who rejects authority which would subjugate her and render her docile. She is the offensive woman who acts in her own interests. She is the unmanageable woman who claims her own body, the whore, the wanton woman, the wild woman, out of control. She is the woman who cannot be silenced. She is a rebel. She is trouble." *Faith*[1]

CONVICTS.
[From Photographs by Herbert Watkins, 179, Regent Street.]
MALE CONVICT AT PENTONVILLE PRISON.    |    FEMALE CONVICT AT MILLBANK PRISON.

The discourse around inmates of women's prisons is an ever-expanding field. Many academics and criminologists have discussed at length some of the ideological issues connected with these institutions. More women than ever are being given custodial sentences, and this is reflected in the proposed expansions of the women's prison estate (and 'approved premises' or bail hostels).

1 Faith, 2011

The aim of this text is *not* to argue that prison should be amended or re-organised to make them better places for those the state categorises as 'women'. I reject any claims that the prison industrial complex can ever be modified along these lines. As Davis has stated in *The Meaning of Freedom*, "as important as some reforms may be -the elimination of sexual abuse and medical neglect in women's prisons, for example -frameworks that rely exclusively on reforms help to produce the stultifying idea that nothing lies beyond the prison."[2]

Many advocacy groups for women inside employ the overly simplistic argument that by incarcerating people in women's prisons, the prisoner's families are destroyed. *All* families are impacted by having someone inside, regardless of their gender, and because of this *all* prisons must be destroyed.

> "Prison's don't make people safer. Quite the contrary, because of the way the criminal justice system tears apart poor neighbourhoods -especially the harmful impact on the children of prisoners- they're crime generative." *Gilbert*[3]

There are a lot of issues that are specific to women's jails, and this section will outline some of them. Patricia O'Brien, a professor of social work, has done extensive research into issues behind the incarceration within women's prisons. According to O'Brien, 54% of prisoners within women's jails are addicted to drugs before they are incarcerated, a third are sexual abuse survivors and half are the survivors of domestic violence[4].

In 2011 the cost of incarcerating someone in a women's prison for a year was £56,000 (£45,000 in men's jails). No doubt this cost has increased significantly. In the 2014-15 annual report of the 'hm chief inspectorate', 41% of the inmates of women's prisons had drug problems (28% in men's jails)[5]. Alcohol dependency was also much higher on arrival (30% vs 19%). 77% of people in women's prisons were on medication. A report by Oxford University in 2013 said there was an "epidemic of self-mutilation" in women's prisons[6].

According to the charity 'Women in Prison' in 2015 80% of women in jail got sent down for 'non-violent offences'. The report also states that <u>12,000 women </u>are sentenced each year in the UK, resulting in 20,000 chil-

2 Davis, 2012
3 Gilbert, 2014
4 O'Brien, *Making It in the Free World, 2001*
5 justiceinspectorates.gov.uk/hmiprisons/inspections
6 ox.ac.uk/2013-12-16-one-four-women-prisoners-self-harm-every-year

dren being left without mothers[7]. According to the MoJ women's prisons have the highest level of suicides[8]. In 2016 there were 119, up by a third in the previous year. There were 37,784 incidents of self-harm, and 6,430 attacks on staff. The MoJ blamed the combination of the prevalence of 'spice' and other 'New Psychoactive Substances' and a lack of prison staff (more bang-up)[9].

> "There is a real risk women's prison numbers will be pushed up as the revolving door of breach and recall to custody spins faster. Reforms that were supposed to help women rebuild their lives are leading to even more pointless jail time. The government has found £1.3 billion for new prisons, but community schemes across the country providing vital support for women in trouble battle to survive." *PRT*

## Women's Prisons in the UK Prison Estate

Women are held in 12 prisons in England[10]. There are no women's prisons in Wales. There is currently one women's prison in Scotland, and some women are held in units within men's prisons. In Northern Ireland some women are incarcerated within a male Young Offenders Institution.

> "Women become invisible as soon as they pass through the prison gates because they are subsumed into a world that is predominantly masculine and insensitive to their very differing needs". *Angela Devlin[11]*

Many feminist criminologists have argued that because prisons were historically designed by men, they do not consider the needs of women (never mind those who identify as non-binary, gender queer or trans). Within the legal system in the UK, there is a so-called 'medicalisation of deviance'. Women are often defined by biology, for example alleged offences being blamed on PMT and post-natal depression. This conveniently allows social economic factors to be ignored. Criminologists have also highlighted the

---

7 Women In Prison, *Ready Steady Go! 2015*
8 gov.uk/government/statistics/safety-in-custody-quarterly-update-to-june-2016
9 gov.uk/government/statistics/safety-in-custody-quarterly-update-to-june-2016
10 Prisons in the 'women's prison estate' (correct as of April 2017) are: Low Newton, Askham Grange, New Hall, Foston Hall, Styal, Drake Hall, Peterborough, Eastwood Park, Send, Downview, Bronzefield, East Sutton Park. Prison Service Order 4800 applies across all these institutions. Bronzefield and Peterborough are privately operated.
11 Devlin, *Invisible Women: What's Wrong with Women's Prisons?* 1998

'associated social deprivations' (poverty, racism and so on) that impact on those in women's prisons. However, I would argue that these issues impact on *all* prisoners and those supporting them.

Trying to establish a 'feminist criminology' is deeply problematic because it perpetuates the idea that 'criminality' is a *measurable* condition, and this leads to the legitimization of repressive social control rather than examining social context. This is *not* a call for a different lay out or structure of prison along supposedly more gender-neutral lines. Nor is it a call for more state based infrastructure such as bail hostels for 'women'. It is a call to attack and abolish all of these institutions. It is vital that people in women's prisons are viewed as survivors *not* victims.

## Women Prisoners and Female Offenders

> "Her crimes are the impolite crimes of the woman who lacks the resources to wrap herself in the cloak of middle-class femininity. The 'bad-girl' of cultural stereotyping is the product of class-based, racist and heterosexist myths." *Faith*[12]

'Women prisoners' are stereotypically presented as uncaring mothers and promiscuous, unfaithful partners. The pervasiveness of this stereotype means that people who are perceived as women by the state are punished for not complying with state norms, and for behaving in a traditionally unmotherly or unfeminine way.

> "For female offenders the "justice" they receive is more to do with who they are than what they've done". *Pat Carlen*[13]

The concept of the 'female offender' is highly problematic and damaging. Since the mid-1970's feminists have engaged with this stereotype and highlighted gender a social construct with deep significance for rhetoric relating to crime and punishment.

Historically, the 'reasonable person' in English law is a white, middle class male. Therefore claims that women are 'disadvantaged' by the prison system are overly simplistic. As with all aspects of discrimination, intersectionality is key here. For example, as a white and middle-class woman I had a much bigger chance of being treated like a 'reasonable person' during my court appearances. When I addressed issues around racism in jail, I was much less likely to get disciplined. When I wanted to challenge prison

---

12 Faith, 2011
13 Carlen, *Women and Punishment: The Struggle for Justice, 2002*

staff, I could make sense of the painfully bureaucratic and impenetrable complaints procedure, and use the language of oppression employed by the prison estate to gain some small 'victories'. Some criminologists have outlined the so-called 'multiple jeopardies' that exist upon those in women's prisons: the stigma attached to women as lawbreakers, their ethnicity and race, and class.

Women are expected to conform to patriarchal, middle-class forms of behaviour in order to be eligible for parole, or demonstrate their new 'pro-social' approach to life. Docility and compliance are king, and those who try to hold on to their own personality will often find themselves rejected.

The 'Incentives and Earned Privileges Scheme' was introduced in 1995. It will be discussed in more detail later in the text, but is relevant here as it so obviously appeals to a liberal approach to dealing with 'female offenders' and perpetuates this middle-class view of criminality. Individual self-governance is promoted, and women are perceived not as victims but agents in their own 'rehabilitation'. This disproportionately punishes women who are not middle class, and who do not wish (or who are unable) to conform with the accepted expressions and methodologies for addressing their 'offending behaviour'. For example, you are much more likely to get 'enhanced' status if you are well-educated, have English as a first language, and are confident. Many people within the prison system (for example, a lot of Traveller women) do not have high literacy levels, making it difficult for them to jump through the hoops required to gain this elevated status[14]. Even the PPO has said the IEP scheme provides "considerable potential for injustice".[15]

## 'Risk Management' and Sentencing

Judges and the prosecution will often use the concept of 'risk' to justify prison sentences. Perceived risk does not take into account the multiple factors that contribute to issues such as social exclusion. It is also a further way to impose and legitimise sexist approaches to punishment of women, who are often given longer sentences because they are allegedly a risk to themselves, or because their behaviour is 'anti-social'.

The violence imposed upon inmates of women's prisons is obscured by the language of risk, treatment, intervention and rehabilitation. The emp-

14 For more examples of these discriminatory practices see the PRT report *Punishment Without Purpose,* 2014
15 Nigel Newcomen, CBE, PPO *Feedback on Revised Incentives and Earned Privileges Policy Framework, 2016*

ty phrases employed by the prison system conjure up an idealised society whilst simultaneously ignoring the repression of the state and its inherent inequalities. The individual becomes solely responsible for their destiny, and the state is presented as some kind of benevolent organisation seeking to cure or improve those unruly women who have rejected its norms and moral codes.

Discourse around the concept of risk within the English legal system came into play in the 1990s. It was employed to describe the risk an individual faced to the public and oneself. This was a major justification of prison and the psychological interventions that were to become a key part of their methods of control. Putting the burden of risk on the individual is very helpful to the prison industrial complex because it justifies a privatised, 'multi-agency' approach, such as the outsourcing of specialists, for example, private security and insurance firms, and more recently, probation.

The concept of the revolving door is common throughout all discourse related to the prison industrial complex. Once individuals are inside the system, they are increasingly likely to get future custodial sentences. The bottom line -for all genders- is that *if* so-called 'social exclusion' is a factor in crime, then prison means *greater* exclusion. Some feminists have outlined the need for the penal system to address non-criminal issues of social justice. Alternative proposals to the current system within women's prisons have included a 'risk of recidivism index' (whereby the external factors likely to contribute to alleged recidivism get addressed and practically challenged) and 'therapeutic sentencing' (where therapy is still included in sentencing, but the use of 'community models' and non-custodial sentences is employed.) However, these approaches further perpetuate a sexist discourse around prisons, and fail to acknowledge the ways in which the intersectionality of oppression acts out on prisoners of *all* genders, and the families that are affected by their incarceration.

## Therapy?

Because of gendered stereotypes, women in jail are more likely to get given a 'therapeutic treatment' as part of their sentence plan/punishment, and be given courses to do upon release. The industry surrounding 'TOB' courses ('Tackling Offending Behaviour') is huge. All women's prisons (and bail hostels) promote (and often enforce) supposedly therapeutic work. As Carlen has outlined, any claims of being a therapeutic environment are undermined by the security aspect of jail, the coercive element, and the fear of being detained for longer for failure to complete these treatments (for example for parole conditions and IPP prisoners.)

It is also important to note here that *all* TOB approaches assume guilt and that the alleged offence has been committed. For many, refusal to admit guilt (or to be coerced into expressing it) means that they will never be able to apply for parole, Home Detention Curfew (HDC) or complete their sentence plan. I rejected my sentence plan because it contained a potentially unlimited number of one-to-one sessions with a police psychologist trained by the Counter Terrorism Unit. Because I had a determinate sentence, the prison could not hold me beyond my release date (my refusal just meant I could not apply for HDC). For those who have to apply for parole, refusal to engage with programmes like this can be more problematic.

The prison system also utilises therapeutic treatments as justification for ghosting difficult prisoners to other jails and separating those they can see supporting each other. It is relatively common for people to get transferred to the other end of the country when they kick off in order to be give them the 'opportunity' to engage with some state enforced psychological intervention, and separate them from those it argues are harmful to their rehabilitation.

## Elizabeth Fry and Reform

In the 1820's Elisabeth Fry campaigned for reform in order to stop the "medical and moral contagion" she saw on her 1813 visit to Newgate prison. Fry was named the 'angel of prisons'(!) and was made famous by appearing on the £5 note until fairly recently. She promoted religion (specifically Quakerism) and reform, in an attempt to stop the "blaspheming, fighting, dramdrinking, half naked women" that she encountered in jail.

In 1817 Fry created the 'Association for the Improvement of

Female Prisoners'. The aim of Fry's association was to combine activities such as domesticity, domestic routine, hygiene, literacy and religion with paternalistic forms of surveillance in order to improve the morality of lower class women. This attitude continues today in the bail hostel named after her and is outlined in part two.

> "Elizabeth Fry, of Scotland and England, an early advocate for "fallen" women who, in her view, needed to be tamed and domesticated. Above all, Fry wanted these women to learn feminine manners.. The elusive ideal of the prim, sober middle-class woman was set by reformers as the goal for all destitute, criminalized women." *Faith*[16]

Liberal outrage, and the middle-class desire to educate and transform those in women's prisons continues today. However, individual's incarcerated in women's prisons are often overlooked by feminist movements, despite being some of the most oppressed women in the country. Reformists tend to prefer making sweeping generalisations and demands for system adaptations rather than demonstrate practical solidarity with people inside.

## Staff

Many screws have a sexist view towards people in women's prisons and during my relatively short spell inside (one year) I observed time and time again the grudges and ill-feeling many male prison staff had towards those housed in women's prisons. Many male screws would frequently lament the fact that they didn't work in men's jails any more.

Many staff members regularly claimed that working in women's prisons is more difficult than men's jails. I heard several instances of staff saying people in jails I was in didn't accept authority (were too questioning), too independent, bore grudges and wanted "too much stuff" (for example, tampons and toilet roll). It is too simplistic to say this was only male staff members who employed these stereotypes. All staff members with experience of working in both kinds of institutions would often compare and contrast their experiences. The quote below from the famous misogynist physician and supposed 'father of criminology', Cesare Lombroso was published in 1895, but sums up many of the attitudes I have heard expressed by prison staff:

> "Women have many traits in common with children...their

---

16 Faith, 2011

moral sense is deficient..they are revengeful, jealous, inclined to vengeances of refined cruelty...Women are big children; their evil tendencies are more numerous and more varied than men's, but generally remain latent...The criminal woman is consequently a monster." *Lombroso and Ferrero*[17]

## FAMILY LIFE

### Young People

Whilst families are obviously impacted by the incarceration of the mother, it is simplistic to equate the imprisonment of women with the destruction of the family unit. There are many, many ways in which the state controls and separates families: from social services, to Youth Offending Institutes (YOIs or 'Juvie'), from Secure Training Centres (STC), to Detention and Training Orders (DTO). An end to the incarceration of mothers would *not* somehow bring about massive social change. What is required is not an end to women's prisons, but an end to *all* state based institutions of control and the administrative systems that support them. Hopefully some of the statistics included here will illustrate this.

The way in which young people (18-21) are incarcerated is a further example of the inconsistent gendered approaches of HMP. Those labelled 'young adult women' are held within the women's prison establishments listed in appendix two. In the men's prison estate, people who have been labelled 'young men' are housed separately, in 'Juvie' or YOIs.

In 2014, 2,000 children (people under the age of 18) were sentenced to a DTO. The average length of these was 15 weeks. Between 2013-2014, 2,000 young people were remanded. 62% were acquitted or not given a custodial sentence[18]. Children in 'care' aged ten-17 are five times more likely to end up in the criminal justice system. According to the 'Care Leavers Association', a further way in which the state controls young people prior to them entering the adult prison population is through the 'invisible minority' of so-called 'care leavers'. 49% of young men in the CJS have spent time in care. 61% of young women aged 15-18 in custody have spent time in care[19]. These statistics show that the processes of incarceration and exclusion have just as much to do with age and background as gender.

The 'Commons Justice Select Committee' report on young people in

---

17 Lombroso and Ferrero, *The Female Offender, 1895*
18 PRT, *In Care, Out of Trouble, 2016*
19 Care Leavers' Association, *Criminal Justice Project*

the CJS highlighted how neurological development continues up to the age of 25. It also recorded that rates of learning disabilities, communication impairments and autistic spectrum disorder were ten times as high within the so-called 'care system' as the general population[20].

The Traveller way of life does not conform to the model of family life and education that the state aggressively enforces through its prescriptive and restrictive definitions, approaches and institutions. Because of this, STCs are the end of the road in a long and systemic attack on young people from Traveller communities by the state. The 'Traveller Movement Charity' has highlighted the "huge over representation of GTR (Gypsy Traveller Roma) children within the youth justice system"[21]. According to research undertaken by the charity, a third of GTR children have also been physically abused by staff within STCs[22].

In 2015 the 'Howard League for Penal Reform' issued a report outlining the failings of Cookham Wood STC[23]. The report showed that violence was both endemic *and* escalating within the institution. In the six months prior to the report, there were 61 assaults and 92 fights. 15 improvised weapons were found, and "techniques to inflict pain" were used by staff *at least* 400 times (Cookham Wood admitted that not all the incidences of this had been recorded). Three young people were hospitalised[24].

**Fathers?**

> "When you incarcerate someone, guilty or not, you incarcerate the innocents who love them, and there are always such people. The most vile murderer of all time had a mother."
> *Warren Fellows[25]*

According to 'Women In Prison', 66% of those in women's jails are mothers. In the year 2015-2016, 52% of prisoners had children under 18, and 200,000 children had a parent in prison at some point in 2009[26]. The home office has stated that each year 2,200 young people were taken into 'care'

---

20 Commons Select Committee, *The Treatment of Young Adults in the Criminal Justice System, 2016*
21 The Traveller Movement, *Overlooked and Over Represented: Gypsy, Traveller and Roma Children in the Youth Justice System, 2016*
22 The Traveller Movement, 2016
23 howardleague.org/news/cookhamwoodinspection2015/
24 howardleague.org/news/cookhamwoodinspection2015/
25 Fellows, 2000
26 Inside Time

when their mother went to prison[27]. In 2009 the average prisoner was 55 miles from their home, and this will only increase with the development of the maxi-prison model (huge rural complexes such as the Wrexham institution).

The prison service often goes on about "maintaining family ties". This claim, along with their supposed interest in 'equalities' and 'safeguarding' is used to disguise the inherent violence within the system, and the way in which *all* prisons separate families. Because of the violent way in which the prison estate separates families, prisoners who have been separated from their children through the process of incarceration are much more likely to become examples of the so-called 'revolving door theory'; where by recidivism (supposedly 'relapsing' into criminal behaviour) and repeat custodial sentences are massively increased. Many feminist texts on women's prisons do not highlight the impact that prison has on *young fathers* too.

> "Maternal imprisonment has particular aspects and creates special challenges for families, policy makers and prison authorities alike, including the question of babies and young children being in prison with their mothers. However, any parental imprisonment impacts on the children. Some of these impacts may be the same, or similar, irrespective of whether the imprisoned parent is the mother or the father" Quaker United Nations Office[28] (QUNO)

The QUNO report emphasised that children with incarcerated fathers experience the same issues and exclusions as those with incarcerated mothers including: coping with loss, environmental disruption, poverty, stigmatisation, juvenile delinquency, strained relationships, health problems and all of the difficulties involved in visiting a parent in prison.

The QUNO report also outlined how the numbers of children separated from their fathers due to imprisonment is far higher than those separated from their mothers due to the vast majority of prisoners being men (globally over 90% of prisoners are male).

> "To ignore this group would, therefore, be to neglect the vast majority of children affected by parental imprisonment. Large research gaps exist regarding the needs of children of incar-

---

27 Birth Companions, *Home Office Research and Statistics Directorate, Research Findings Number 38: Mothers in Prison*
28 QUNO, *Children Need Dads Too: Children with Fathers in Prison, 2009*

cerated fathers. Not only are statistics on the numbers of children affected by paternal imprisonment lacking, but also information on how to maintain a healthy relationship with incarcerated fathers". QUNO[29]

It is a cliché but true that when you incarcerate someone it affects their whole family, and this is true regardless of the designated gender of the prisoner. This is a further example of why *all* aspects of the prison system must be destroyed, not just the women's prison estate.

## Child Care Resettlement Leave (CCROTL) and Family Days

If you are a parent inside, try to find out the procedure for applying for Family Days (extended visits within the prison), and Childcare Resettlement Leave (CCROTL). Childcare leave is *not* the same as ROTLs (Release On Temporary Licence). Whereas ROTLs are dependent on "good behaviour", CCROTLs can be applied for quite early, and is in theory available to everyone, regardless of your IEP or work status. If you are the only parent or carer for a child under 16 you can apply. This leave can be taken once every two months (see appendix one).

Having observed how long the prison takes to process these requests (and how popular they are), it is definitely worth applying even if you think that it will be too painful to see your children, or you feel too ashamed. You can always change your mind nearer the time, and neither Family Days or Childcare Leave require much interaction with (or ass kissing of) the screws. If you have any concerns or questions, then try to ask other mothers. The Prisoners Advisory Service (PAS) should have regular (often monthly) sessions within your jail where you can get independent advice. It may also be the case that you can apply for travel warrants to help with Childcare Leave costs.

A note on Family Day. In most jails, they will make some token efforts to minimise the visibility of the prison environment. During family days, prison staff should be wearing normal, non-uniform clothes. Searches of young people should be minimal, and there are various PSIs to support this. Also, you may be allowed to take your family outside the visiting hall, for example, eating together in the dining hall, or going around the grounds. This can all help make the visit feel less pressured, and can be a welcome change from the forced, hectic and sometimes oppressive nature of the visits hall (more on this later.) However, whilst this all sounds lovely

29 QUNO, *Children Need Dads Too: Children with Fathers in Prison, 2009*

in theory, it will come as no surprise that the reality is often quite different. The PPO has upheld numerous complaints of family days being cancelled for specific groups of prisoners and delays in people being brought into visits (this is a big problem across the board).

Here are a few words from mates inside with children…

> "Be strong enough to handle prison time without your children. Try to stay away from trouble inside, to make sure you can get to your kids as quickly as possible. Apply for CCROTL. The staff are not helpful. No one has ever told me about support services. My friends in here support me."

> "Being inside has affected my relationship with my son really badly. Firstly, he suffers more than me because he doesn't understand the nature of life. He knows his father is in jail but not me, he thinks I'm working and trying to get his daddy out. I don't want him to know I am in jail as well. I call him whenever I can but he lives in XXXX so it's expensive."

## Mother and Baby Units (MBUs)

"Every year, around 600 pregnant women are held in prisons in England and Wales and about 100 babies are born to women prisoners."[30] There are six MBUs in England and Wales (the national capacity is 54 beds in total)[31]. In 2015 there were applications from 173 women. According to Prison Rule 12 and PSI 2014-049, women with babies under the age of 18 months *must* be allowed to live with them in jail (see appendix two). If the mother is still incarcerated when the baby reaches this age, they will be separated.

To get a place on a MBU, prisoners should complete a general app, supported by the multi-agency admissions board to the governor. The decision is allegedly made based on the best interests of child, the "necessity to maintain good order and discipline within the MBU and the health and safety of other babies and mothers within the unit"[32]. Because competition for beds in the MBUs is fierce, prisons will use it as a way to discipline and control mothers. I saw several cases of people being terrified to question authority in case they lost their place on the MBU. Once again, social serv-

---

30 Inside Time
31 These are located at Styal, New Hall, Eastwood Park, Askham Grange, Peterborough and Bronzefield. Each unit has the capacity to accommodate one set of twins.
32 justice.gov.uk/offenders/types-of-offender/women

THE CONVICT NURSERY AT BRIXTON.

ices all too often intervene if a mother's application for a place on a MBU is unsuccessful (or if the mother does not comply to the rigid forms of expected behaviour on the unit). Sometimes the baby will be placed with a family member, but it is not a given by any means.

The campaign group 'Action for Prisoner's and Offenders Families' (APOF) has highlighted the fear and insecurity many felt about applying for a place on an MBU due to the levels of mental illness, drug and alcohol abuse, self-harm and domestic abuse among young mothers[33]. APOF also showed that many individuals eligible for MBUs were sceptical of engaging with authorities, and were all too aware of the heavy reliance the prison estate had on social services, and the repercussions this may have on

33 APOF, *Enhancing Care for Childbearing Women and their Babies in Prison, 2015*

the family life of the prisoners. In light of this, APOF called for a "whole family approach", in which release from prison is viewed as a process not an event[34].

I cannot imagine the pain of being separated from your young baby. But it is worth noting here that MBUs can be alienating and lonely places. Security is high for obvious reasons. Several of my friends in jail did not feel able to open up to other women in the MBUs due to fear of being snitched on, or losing their place. Also, because such a premium is placed on beds, they tend to only go to enhanced prisoners, or those "working towards their enhancement". Once you have been on the unit for a couple of weeks you may choose to return to work, as it is unlikely you will have had much interaction with other prisoners outside the MBU. The jail encourages women on these units to become distrustful of other prisoners. It is common for women within these prisons within prisons to become quite isolated from the broader prison population, though communal facilities such as the library, gym or chapel are possible for them to access at certain times.

The prison system routinely fails new mothers incarcerated within it. The tragic case of Michelle Barnes has been highlighted by many reform organisations to draw attention to these issues. Michelle Barnes had a history of mental health issues, drug addiction and self-harm. She was imprisoned at HMP Low Newton, and hung herself in 2016 after being separated from baby days after giving birth.

## Pregnancy in Prison

For those unfortunate enough to be doing time whilst being pregnant, the charity 'Birth Companions' drew up a *Birth Charter* in 2016 (appendix four). This demanded that pregnant people in women's prisons be allowed access to the same level of antenatal care as women outside. Prison staff are notoriously useless at processing and obtaining resources required for pregnant prisoners, so it may be helpful to quote the relevant PSI or get someone outside to contact Birth Companions if your needs are not being met. Note that in addition to the demands in the birth charter, pregnant prisoners *should* be issued with daily 'pregnancy packs' containing extra fruit and vitamins.

---

34 APOF, *Enhancing Care for Childbearing Women and their Babies in Prison, 2015*

## TRANS AND GENDER QUEER PRISONERS

"Transgender prisoners defy the institutionalised segregation of the prison system. The multiplicity of combinations of gender/sex/surgery/hormones/identification that people embody resist simplistic and dogmatic solutions. Consequently, given that no capacity (or desire) to comprehend these differences exists, transgender people are subject to what amounts as focussed repression." *Lockdown: Prison, Repression and Gender Non-conformity*[35]

"While feminist anti-prison researchers and activists have worked to make imprisoned women visible, we have tended to assume that women's prisons house only women, and that all women prisoners are in women's prisons." *Julia C. Oparah*[36]

The ministry of justice has stated that there are 100 trans prisoners in the UK. However, the reality is probably much higher than this, especially in men's jails. Incarceration is often the final, brutal expression of the systemic repression of trans people. As has been highlighted, many reformist organisations and feminist groups simplify custody arguments into a gender binary, minimising the male role in a child's upbringing, and ignoring the complexities of issues around gender non-conformity and those who identify as non-binary, trans or gender queer. One example of this is 'Women for Independence' (WFI), a group who call for a cap on the number of women in jail in Scotland, demanding that no more than 100 women are incarcerated there at any one time[37]. In making such short-sighted and arbitrary demands, reformist organisations such as this ignore the myriad of issues that contribute to issues surrounding gender in custody.

The daily life of a trans prisoner in jail can be one of constant battle. Trans people make visible the oppressions and prejudices that inmates and prison staff act out. There is increasing awareness around these issues, but it is an ongoing struggle. I observed a lot of transphobia during my sentence. The arbitrary yet rigid forms of social interaction that make up jail life mean that whilst "butch" women are massively popular, anyone who

---

35 *Lockdown: Gender, Repression and Gender Nonconformity, 2008*
36 Oparah, *Maroon Abolitionists: Black Gender-Oppressed Activists in the Anti-prison Movement in the US and Canada* In Stanley and Smith, 2015
37 Women For Indepencence (WFI), *Women for Justice, Justice for Women! 2015*

wants to actively transition is often sneered upon or dismissed as a "she-he". Trans prisoner Sarah Baker has outlined these issues in her regular column in IT:

> "I would never wish my own trauma of being beaten up, spat at, slashed twice with razor blades, raped, stabbed and scarred for life with scalding water mixed with sugar, not even on my worst enemy." *Sarah Baker*[38]

PSI 7/2011 'The Care and Treatment of Trans-sexual Prisoners' contains a lot of specific recommendations for prisons and prison staff (see appendix five). Following a report by the PPO into the discrimination involved in having to obtain 'Gender Recognition Certificates'[39], PSI 2016-017 replaced PSI 7/201. The PPO also called for individual assessments on the of needs for trans prisoners; including ACCT reviews, investigations of all allegations of transphobia, and the supervision of reasonable adjustments made to help with expressions of peoples preferred gender.

As with everyone inside, trans prisoners are theoretically entitled to the same level of health care they would expect to receive from the NHS outside (though of course the reality is totally different). For trans people this should include: access to counselling, pre and post-op care and continued access to hormone treatment. Trans prisoners should be allowed to attend their case conferences, and have the opportunity to input into planning for their needs in custody, with input from their personal officer, offender manager and wing managers.

Unsurprisingly there is an established history of prison governors persistently refusing to acknowledge their responsibilities in relation to PSI 7/2011, and the 'Human Rights' and 'Equalities' Acts. Sarah Baker has shown how many prison governors pay lip service to 'political correctness' whilst continuing to ignore transphobia in their jails, from both prisoners and staff. Despite clear instructions from PSI 7/2011, governors have refused to allow trans women to have the relevant "items to fulfil gender identity", access to showers and the NHS treatment that is routinely offered to trans gendered people outside the prison system. In January 2016, the home office committee *Transgender Equality Report* was published using evidence from the Bent Bars project[40]. It highlighted how many trans

---

38 Baker, *Transgangsta Bites Back, 2015*
39 PPO *Learning Lessons Bulletin Issue Three: Transgender Prisoners, 2017*
40 House of Commons Women and Equalities Committee, *Transgender Equality 2015-2016*, see also Bent Bars Project, *MoJ Review, Care and Treatment of Transgender Prisoners, 2016*

prisoners are "systematically denied the right to wear appropriate clothing, misinformed or lied to about their rights and not given access appropriate medical treatment."[41]

It is common practice in America for trans prisoners to be forced into seg ('segregation units') for their own 'protection'. Separation is also a fairly common occurrence within the UK prison system, and trans prisoners are coerced and forced into leaving normal location wings, as staff try to 'hide' them on more vulnerable prisoner wings (with much higher security restrictions). The MoJ has highlighted that prisons have 'duty of care' to prisoners, and as part of this they cannot segregate based on trans issues or gender. The case of Bourgass v secretary of state for justice 2015[42] highlighted issues around segregation. Following this precedent, the prison must demonstrate that any segregation is justified and proportionate.

In the process of enforced isolation, trans prisoners are doubly punished, hidden away in so-called prisons-within-prisons, while the prevailing culture of transphobia within jails goes unchallenged. Historically, the MoJ has demanded that "all prisoners should be placed according to their gender as recognised by UK law." (i.e. a GRC). However, after numerous complaints made by trans prisoners about their attempts to obtain the necessary paperwork to support their claims the MoJ *has* allowed some individuals to be moved if they are "sufficiently advanced in the gender reassignment process". This is still a lengthy procedure, and often one that involves a certain amount of privilege. It is only open to those trans prisoners with the will and money to transition, and the confidence and education required to convene a case conference and multi-disciplinary risk assessment within the prison. It also perpetuates a very limited approach to trans prisoners in terms of what are acceptable forms of appearance and behaviours.

Trans prisoners are further side-lined and marginalised in relation to prison labour, and several people have highlighted how they have been denied jobs in positions of trust, especially just after transition. Screws perpetuate transphobia by not reporting acts of violence upon trans gendered prisoners and ignoring verbal abuse from other prisoners, and their visitors.

> "There is no way that trans gender people can ever be 'safe'
> in prisons as long as prisons exist and, as scholar Fred Mo-
> ten has written, as long as we live in a society that could even

---

41 House of Commons Women and Equalities Committee, 2016
42 supremecourt.uk/cases/docs/uksc-2013-0230-judgement.pdf

have prisons." *Bassichis, Lee and Spade* [43]

The majority of trans deaths in custody relate to people seeking to be moved to women's prisons from men's jails. Jenny Swift was the third trans suicide in 2016. She had been on hormones for three years but despite this was refused medication in HMP Doncaster. Swift suffered major physical withdrawal, and was not allowed to be moved to a women's jail. She was extensively bullied by other prisoners, ultimately taking her own life. Vicky Thompson also committed suicide, in November 2015 at HMP Leeds. Despite being groomed as a child, she had been put on wing with people who were convicted of sex offences. Thompson had identified as female since her teens, but had not had reassignment surgery.

The famous case of Tara Hudson, who was held in HMP Bristol, is further example of the failings of the prison estate for trans prisoners. Despite six years of gender reconstruction surgery, Hudson was sent to a men's jail, which compromised both her mental health and personal safety. Eventually, after much lobbying, Hudson was moved to Eastwood Park. However, as Sarah Baker has pointed out, many trans prisoners never get this 'opportunity':

> "Call me cynical if you wish, but that opportunists such as Maria Miller MP, Lord Cashman, Baroness Barker, Lord Faulks, Baroness Hayter and Peter Dawson, Deputy Director of the Prison Reform Trust, should come out in support of trans issues, was shocking. Why had it taken them so long to become so vocal? Why did they decide to come out of the woodwork and jump on the Tara Hudson bandwagon? Is it because she was young, photogenic and serving a short sentence (though traumatising for any trans prisoner)? Some might say that they were only paying lip service to a cause that would increase their public profile. Would they have been so vocal if Tara had been in her mid-50s, serving a life sentence, denied trans-suitable make-up to maintain her feminine appearance, and lacked 100,000 petition signatures?" [44]

It is also worth noting here that a lot of the rhetoric surrounding Tara Hudson's case focused on her being in the *wrong* jail rather than a critique of the *whole* system as a violent extension of binary constructs. People who

43 *Building an Abolitionist Trans and Queer Movement with Everything We've Got* Stanley and Smith, 2015
44 Baker, *2015*

identify as non-binary or gender queer are often overlooked in the rhetoric around gender and prison. There is no way the prison system can deal with a non-binary model of gender, as it is dependent on putting people into 'women's' or 'men's' institutions.

Judith Butler highlighted the use of "construction as constitutive constraint"[45]. Butler argued that regimes of power produce intelligible and knowable bodies, the flip-side of this being a domain of unthinkable, abject and unlovable bodies. These are the marginalised groups who are seen as 'disposable', or what Davis labelled "detritus"[46]: human surplus, the result of sexual, psychological and physical violence, neoliberalism, heteropatriarchy, and white supremacy.

> "Most current discussions of transgender issues separate out transphobia, heterosexism and misogyny from racism, ethnocentrism, and Eurocentrism. In examining transgender identities in isolation, a white, middle-class trans gendered subject is assumed. By analysing anti-transgender violence as separate from race and class, the lived experiences and specificity of trans persons of colour are ignored." *Bassichis, Lee and Spade*[47]

In 2016 there was the first annual Trans Prisoner Day of Action, in order to acknowledge the experiences of trans and other sex and gender-minority prisoners and express transnational solidarity. This has become an annual, international event. Solidarity with trans and gender queer prisoners!

> "The survival of trans and other sex and gender minority people is not a quaint conversation about awareness, but a struggle for us to live in a world so determined to marginalize, dehumanise, and criminalise us...Once incarcerated, trans people face humiliation, physical and sexual abuse, denial of medical needs, and legal reprisals... Just as our lives are violently repressed on the outside, trans people experience extreme suffering and death within the walls of jails, prisons, youth facilities, and immigrant detention centres." *Transprisoners.net*[48]

---

45 Ellen Samuels, *Critical Divides: Judith Butler's Body Theory and the Question of Disability, 2002*
46 Davis, 2012
47 *Building an Abolitionist Trans and Queer Movement with Everything We've Got* in Stanley and Smith, 2015
48 *Trans Prisoner Day of Action Zine, 2016*

Please note that if you are a trans prisoner and you would like a pen-pal then Bent Bars can help, see resources section.

## SEXUALITY

> "To those whose bodies have forgotten the rhythms of the earth, and to those who cannot let yourselves cry. And those whose bodies have been used as though you had no hurt, and to those who feel you must hide your true selves, and to those who have been hated or hurt because of who you are, may we all find our ways back home -back to ourselves and back to each other." *Wildflower*[49]

Issues around sex and relationships within women's prisons are frankly a minefield. My basic advice would be, if engaging in this, watch your back, and be prepared to get some shit (the two best ways to find yourself in a spot of bother inside are through drugs and sex.) Prison is *not* a safe environment to have relationships in, for a whole litany of reasons... However, if you find someone you like, enjoy it! Having a relationship inside definitely makes your sentence go faster, and it feels like a small victory in the face of institutional repression and grimness.

People in women's prisons have invariably come from a huge variety of backgrounds, and are often survivors of trauma. Be aware of this when chatting, and if any one discloses stuff to you about their sexual orientation *always* keep it to yourself unless they are 'out'. In my experience, the second most popular topic in jail after talking about sex-offenders was speculating about so-called 'pussy politics', and this can be extremely damaging to those involved, especially any one people perceive as being too 'easy' or having multiple partners.

> "If we rely on the prison system to solve the problem of homophobia, we are relying on a system that is complicit in the process that has rendered homophobia socially acceptable....The prison is one of society's major institutional gendering apparatuses, and encourages and relies on homophobia." *Davis*[50]

As with many sections of this text, I am mindful of issues around language. The vocabulary around sexuality is always developing, and no doubt the

---

49 Wildflower, *Pieces of Self: Anarchy, Gender and Other Thoughts, 2005*
50 Davis, 2012

words and labels I use here will quickly seem clumsy and outdated (but hopefully not offensive). I sincerely hope that I do not alienate or offend anyone. Please get in touch if this is the case.

During my time inside I noticed a definite confusion/conflation between issues around sexuality and issues around gender. This was also perpetuated, and encouraged by prison staff. Experiences of trying to engage with people around queer issues inside made me see what a sham the concept of 'equalities' is in prison. Prisoners and staff bristled and said that I was being offensive when I used the word 'queer', and one person refused to write it down when they asked me to define my sexuality for a prison survey.

My attempts to promote the 'Bent Bars Project' within prison resulted in people saying that I was a man, and so-called 'he-she' (I called people out on this and explained that being queer and being trans were different things -and that both were fine!) The so-called Equalities Officer declared that the organisations use of the word 'bent' was offensive and not inclusive to him as a straight, married man (!?!?!). One of the jails I was in also refused to allow letter-writing to pen-pals through Bent Bars as they argued that if they allowed letter writing for LGBT people (I am deliberately omitting the QIA as they refused to accept it) then they'd have to allow it for all 'equalities groups'.

Being a queer prisoner can be a lonely place at times, especially if you don't fit in with the accepted norms of prison beauty. One of the things I like about being queer is that it applies to my gender *and* my sexuality. I've never really paid much attention to 'butch' and 'femme' categories. I've just been me. But prison has rigid codes of behaviour and appearance. Even butch girls shave their legs inside, so when I rocked up with hairy armpits it was the talk of the jail.

"And all but lust is turned to dust, In humanities machine."
*Oscar Wilde*[51]

There is so much drama and gossip in prison about whether you are a 'jail gay', 'gay for the stay' or not. The high speed aggressive shag in the shower and inevitable post-match analysis (often shouted through windows across blocks after bang-up) left me cold. I think part of the reason there is so much drama and nosiness around sex/sexuality in prisons is that people don't question the broader social picture. People inside often feel unconfident, awkward, and lonely. There is an ever-pervasive sense of competi-

51 Wilde, *The Ballad of Reading Gaol* 1904

tion. As a queer, I believe that we are all on a fluctuating spectrum of sexuality. I don't care how someone identified before they were inside. What I do care about is respect, and healthy relationships.

A great coping mechanism for jail (regardless of your sexuality) can be to get yourself a 'prison wife'. This does not need to be someone you are shagging! But someone who will have your back, and who you can cuddle up to before the long weekend bang-up. I generally found the best way to ride my sentence was to be mostly autonomous, but having a couple of very close mates who I could rely on and respect was a life saver. A word of warning though, beware of making someone much younger than you your wifey! Lots of the younger people in jail can throw themselves into relationships very hard, wearing their hearts on their sleeves and desperately craving physical intimacy and validation. This is a heady combination and can lead to lots of 'mix-up', jealousy and heart ache.

If the prison suspects you are in a relationship they will separate you. Jealous girls inside are often known to report people in relationships to 'Safer Custody' to try to get lovers separated. In a system reminiscent of the witch trials, any one can go and report 'suspicious behaviour' to screws in the Safer Custody Team and the onus will be on the accused to prove their innocence of the allegations. If someone is accused of bullying, or supposedly being a 'bad influence' on someone else, they will often be shipped out (or at least transferred to a different wing or work detail) without any formal investigation being made. In a process that is both patronising and oppressive, the prison often uses the guise of rehabilitation to legitimise these separations; arguing that individuals do not have the mental health to engage with relationships.

It is *not* against prison rules for prisoners to take part in sexual acts as long as it is *not* in front of third party. However, prison staff often claim that hearsay of the alleged sexual act is enough to offend, and use legislation such as the 'Tackling Anti-Social Behaviour' policy (TAB) to justify disciplinary action and separate inmates who are allegedly in a relationship. As with many forms of discrimination in jail, it is nearly impossible for the accused to challenge this, as staff do not follow the official 'nicking' process (adjudications).

When I was in a relationship in jail we kept it our hidden from most people and this enabled us to get away with a lot. Use what materials and spaces you can. Find camera blind spots. Write love letters. Some people even manufactured strap-ons out of various bits of prison-issue equipment (respect to your lovely, feisty, self... you know who you are!!).

As I have argued, the myths and oppressions promoted by the prison system around queer and trans prisoners show how the prison system promotes ignorance and ill-feeling around these issues to distract individuals from the inherent homo/transphobia within the prison industrial complex. The campaign group 'Justice Now!' Clearly outlined some of these issues in their publication *Prison Abolition is a Queer Issue* (appendix six). It is not the intention here to make demands of the prison system, nor to become too bogged down in the mire of identity politics. However, some of the points are very pertinent in relation to LGBTQIA prisoners.

"In the recognition of loving lies the answer to despair."
*Lorde*[52]

If you can keep your head, and enjoy the ride without losing your spirit then falling in love in jail can be a brilliant, emancipatory experience. However, a note of caution based on recurring issues I saw (and experienced) inside. I am yet to hear of a relationship which started in jail but which survived once one of the individuals was released. Jealousy and an active imagination can understandably negatively impact on the person who is still in jail, and it is inevitable that the newly released individual will drift away from them, however much they try not to. It is also increasingly common for individuals to have restrictions slapped upon their licence or parole conditions which specifically stop them from interacting with their partner. For more information on relationships and licence conditions see part two.

For those in women's jails who have a partner 'on road' be aware that you may be disappointed if you ever get ROTLs. Unsurprisingly, people in jail spend a lot of time dreaming of the glorious day when they will be reunited with their lover. However, it can be a bit of a minefield. The time pressures of temporary release, plus the different realities that individuals inhabit in their daily lives do not make for a very satisfying or nurturing experience. One of my dear friends inside spent months dreaming her first night with her lover for years, only to find that in her absence he had become a total spice addict, and could manage no more than a very sweaty fumble. She came back fuming!

---

52 Lorde, *Zami: A New Spelling of my Name, 1982*

# RACE, RACISM AND INTERSECTIONAL OP-PRESSION

## RACISM

> "If you are legally against enslavement, how are you for pris-
> on?...By linking slavery and prisons, the concept of abolition
> also highlights the interaction of racial and economic dynam-
> ics in processes of mass incarceration." *Oparah*[1]

The black community and people of colour are massively over-represented in jail, because they are disproportionately excluded from society. Individuals from these groups are more likely to be arrested, harassed by
the police in the street (especially using 'stop and search' powers), plead
not guilty (and therefore get longer sentences) and be victims of crime.
According to the Equality and Human Rights Commission, there is now
greater disproportionality in the number of black people in prisons in the
UK than in the United States.

   According to the PRT, despite accounting for only one in ten of the general population, black people are the largest number of 'minority ethnic
prisoners' (49%) in jail, (21,937 prisoners in 2017)[2]. In June 2016 "usable
operational capacity" of the prison estate (the name the government gives
to describe and include all prisons in the UK) was 86,288[3]. It is both offensive and inaccurate to state that such a large group of people are a 'minority', but I guess that's symptomatic of 'democracy'. These labels and statistics give an insight into the systemic and targeted attack on black people
and people of colour that is integral to the PIC.

1 *Maroon Abolitionists,* in Stanley and Smith, 2015
2 PRT, *Projects and Research: Race, 2017*
3 *The Statistics Portal statista.com/statistics/283475 2017*

As with all aspects of racism, media stereotypes perpetuate a culture of difference. Criminology has traditionally focused on white males, with 'feminist criminology' focusing mostly on white women. Emma Goldman, one of the most famous female anarchist prisoners, has been criticised for ignoring questions of race in her writing, instead focusing on peoples' rebellious value as workers[4]. It is critical to analyse these issues. Intersectionality isn't just a mathematical formula, it's a contextual, compounded issue and exposes the CJS for the farce that it is. The jury system, courts, prison and the police force in the UK all oppress and misrepresent black people and people of colour.

The examples below have been selected to show that racism is both endemic and inherent within the prison estate and legal system in the UK. The quotes from interviews I conducted in jail are *not* meant to be representative of any group, nationality or race, but are rather examples of a *specific* moment in time within the prison estate. This section includes language that is both offensive and discriminatory.

> "We cannot let the illusion of freedom
> Endow us with a false sense of security as
> We walk the streets
> The academies and the super cops
> Struggling to define institutionalised racism
> As we continue to die in its custody" *Benjamin Zephaniah*[5]

## Criminal "Justice" and Colonialism

> "Law-and-order discourse is racist; the existing system of punishment has been deeply defined by historical racism. Police, courts, and prisons are dramatic examples of institutional racism." *Davis*[6]

Ruth Chigwada-Bailey has outlined the impact the CJS in the UK has on black women and people of colour[7]. A shift in the types of crimes executed by women, a general move towards the concept of 'equality' in punishment, changes to sentencing patterns and types of sentence means that there are more women of colour imprisoned in the UK legal system than ever before. Chigwada-Bailey argued that race, class and gender are all

---

4 Kathy Ferguson, *Emma Goldman: Political Thinking in the Streets, 2011*
5 Zephaniah, *What Stephen Lawrence Has Taught Us,* from *Too Black, Too Strong, 2001*
6 Davis, 2012
7 Chigwada-Bailey, *Black Women's Experiences of Criminal Justice, 2002*

"structuring forces affecting behaviour", and that these are used as forms of domination and oppression by those who have the power to define, label, legally enforce, organise and control other people[8].

Social exclusion, police harassment, 'guilt by association', and imprisonment all combine in a toxic mix of racism in the UK. The increased use of remand against those perceived to be black women combined with longer sentences clearly demonstrates this.

Many writers have connected the expansion of the PIC to a continuation of slavery. Michelle Alexander has stated that there are more black people in prison than there were enslaved at the height of slavery[9]. Continuing this analysis, Imarisha has argued that:

> "The plantation haunts us, a living spectre, not just a past dead
> and buried. The foundations of our justice system are rooted
> in enslavement, in the concept of white supremacy as law."[10]

Several writers, including Davis have applied this analysis to the relentless expansion of the prison system in America[11], but less has been written about it's application in the UK. It is an unavoidable truth however that the penalogical system in this country is a direct descendent of both the mentality that gave birth to slavery, and the lack of critical engagement with it that allowed it to continue.

> "The modern prison grew out of, and continues to be deeply
> embedded within the European colonial project and the lega-
> cy of slavery." *Biko Agozino*[12]

One clear example of the way in which the 'colonial project' continues to perpetuate the prison estate is the development of a new British prison in Jamaica. In October 2015, the British government announced it was spending £25 million on this new jail, in order to deport hundreds of 'Foreign National Prisoners'[13]. There are currently at least 600 Jamaican people incarcerated in the UK. Under British law, individuals cannot be 'repatriated' due to the human rights issues in Jamaica. However, the UK government

---

8 Chigwada-Bailey, 2002
9 Alexander, *The New Jim Crow: Mass Incarceration in the Age of Colour Blindness,* 2012
10 Imarisha, *Angels With Dirty Faces, Three Stories of Crime, Prison and Redemption,* 2016
11 Davis, 2012
12 Agozino, *Counter-Colonial Criminology* (printed in Stanley and Smith, 2015)
13 bbc.com/news/uk-34398014

planned to deport many people with long sentences to the prison in 2020, which was to contain 1,500 people. In a further example of how the prison industrial complex and colonial control/development often go hand in hand, in exchange for the building of the new British prison, David Cameron pledged £300 million of 'aid' funding into infrastructure in Jamaica (to be spent on roads and bridges), to be 'overseen' by the Caribbean Development Bank[14]. However, despite this blatant bribe, the plans were ultimately rejected by the Jamaican government.[15]

## Architecture and Race

"Prison sitings themselves are the outcome of powerful spatial and social relationships, highlighted by the processes funnelling prisoners from metropolitan spaces to non-metropolitan prisons...This expansion of prisons into rural communities is commonly framed as an issue of economic development, a perspective that is generally devoid of any discussion of the undeniable fact that more prisons necessitate the continued mass incarceration of people of colour and the poor." *Anne Bonds*[16]

Most women's prisons are in rural locations, and this will only increase with the closure of urban jails and the development of maxi-prisons. Many of my mates preferred being at HMP Holloway (now closed and sold off for development) to any other jail, because it was the one prison where screws came from culturally diverse backgrounds and had experience of (or were) black women. As someone I interviewed said: "Many white screws don't realise that what they are doing is racist, then they dismiss challenges as people 'overdoing it', because only a few have the confidence to point stuff out. This means that ignorance often goes unreported."

The physical architecture of the jail acts upon it's subjects and creates hostility between its inhabitants. Access to resources inside is scarce, and this also leads to animosity between groups. To quote some of my mates inside:

"Issues around racism are much more acute in jail because

14 caribank.org/programmes/uk-caribbean-infrastructure-fund
15 jamaica-gleaner.com/article/news/20170113/why-govt-rejected-uk-prison-offer-jfj-demands-answers
16 Bonds, *Building Prisons, Building Poverty* (in Lloyd ed, *Beyond Walls and Cages: Prisons, Border and Global Crisis, 2012*)

you are in a small environment where you cannot escape it. Outside you can Walk away."

"We are in a confined space -we live, sleep and eat together. It's easier for people to stick to their own and a lot of girls aren't educated."

I found it quite common for white girls to moan that black women dominated communal spaces on the wing. The main examples of the behaviours people on my wing moaned about in relation to the association room were: spending hours doing each other's hair, using the microwave to make curry on canteen day, and being too loud generally. All these examples show racist attitudes towards the black prison population.

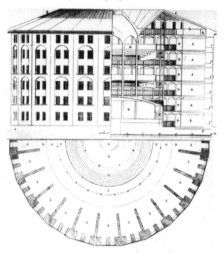

## Daily Life

"The prison is not some building "over there" but a set of relationships that undermine rather than stabilise everyday lives everywhere." *Ruth Gilmore[17]*

Mistrust, competition over resources (encouraged by screws), precarity, ignorance/lack of understanding, fear and forcing people from very different backgrounds to live in close proximity all create a culture of animosity and misunderstanding. Prison exacerbates and perpetuates a culture of racism. One of the most common declarations you will hear before some

17 Gilmore, *Golden Gulag: Prisons, Surplus, Crisis and Opposition in Globalizing California (American Cross Roads), 2007*

tirade of frustrated discriminatory language inside is "I ain't racist but *they always...*" Prisoners oppress each other in their languages and behaviours, and this is one of the most depressing aspects of prison life.

Prison staff actively contribute towards this culture of racism within jails, and it is no wonder that inmates with already discriminatory views become more vocal in expressing them when it becomes acceptable to verbalise oppressive language and stereotypes. The quote below is an account of an incident that occurred at an 'equalities' meeting to talk about racism when I was inside.

> "In the BME meeting I was told by staff that there were "no go areas" in the jail due to the high concentration of black girls. This was supposedly intimidating. Apparently there were areas that were 90% BME so they [screws] had to move people around. Staff also call a table in the dining hall the 'black table' and make an issue out of it,  even though the other 19 tables are majority white. I don't think the staff realise they are being racist."

**Random Examples of Racism**

To demonstrate the breadth and depth of racism within women's prisons I have included examples below of stuff I witnessed:

-Doing a Sieg Heil/Nazi salute as a joke (several times)
-Offensive language ('Paki' is commonly used inside)
-Generalised comments: "blacks always play the race card" "white girls always comment on how noisy/intimidating we are".
-Impressions, and laughing at someone without their knowledge (for example, laughing at Chinese women for their "funny accent").
-Chanting: "deportation not immigration" and "I hate blacks and Pakis".
-Using someone's perceived nationality as a way to identify them: "Hey Africa!" "Where you going Albania?"
-White girls talking in a psuedo-Patois language. I lived next door to one girl who would get wrecked on the perfume and hairspray you could buy from the 'salon' and then become a right 'window warrior'; shouting her violent intentions against other prisoners using phrases and accents adopted from Jamaican culture across the block as soon as we had been banged-up for the night.

-Resistance to relationships between people of different skin colours (several people made comments about me and my girlfriend).
-Lack of beauty products/magazines and 'international food' on canteen sheets.
-A white person knitting a 'golliwog' and giving it to a person of colour.

## Reporting Racism

As with challenging any aspects of discrimination inside, you have to be a bit selective, you can't fight it all. It is *always* better to fight your own battle in jail. It may seem scary; but the chances of success will be much higher if you can stand it, and girls will respect you more. If you don't feel able to confront the perpetrators of racism on your own, then get a crew, but be *really* careful of how you manage this. Many people in women's prisons may not appear to be racist, but it's amazing (and downright depressing) how quickly people revert to stereotypes and crude generalisations in the heat of conflict. If you think stuff might get physical, think carefully about where you might challenge the individuals. One of my mates gave some good advice on confronting racist behaviour: "Calmly, verbally confront the person. Quote their behaviour and explain how that makes you feel. Impotence feeds bullying and greatly affects your self-esteem. If you've been a victim all your life it doesn't take much to trigger this."

As has been previously outlined, reporting racism is not without its risks. Firstly, and most importantly, if you aren't the 'victim' but you are advocating for someone else, or reporting something you witnessed, *always* check with the individuals who have been targeted. There are various allegedly anonymous ways in which you can report racist incidents. You can make a report to the Safer Custody/Wing Rep. You can also complete a 'Discrimination Incident Report Form' (DIRF). However, this is rarely successful, and will often result in informal disciplinary action on the individual complaining[18]. As one of my mates argued:

> "DIRFs are allegedly anonymous but you have to collect one from an officer. Two people have got moved off the wing after completing one of these forms. A lot of girls complain to me because I am the BME rep which is hard."

18 Only one in 100 prisoners who made an allegation of discrimination against prison staff had their case upheld by, compared with 76% of staff allegations of discrimination by prisoners (Zahid Mubarek Trust, *Tackling Discrimination,* 2017).

You can also submit a generic 'COMP1' form instead of a 'DIRF' if you prefer. These are used for all complaints. As ever, keep a record or copy of all the documents you submit.

For all its claims of 'equalities' and 'zero tolerance on discrimination' many screws equate complaints with being a trouble maker, and the administrative system does little to challenge this. Because of this, many people in women's jails don't speak up about racist incidents for fear of jeopardising parole/TAG, or getting shipped out. Screws do not like any one who generates paperwork for them; or risks getting them unwanted attention from their superiors, and jails do not like any paper trails that give them negative statistics; such as issues of racism, or drug use. The case study below from someone on my wing shows how systemic these issues are:

> "I had to resolve a racist incident myself which made a complete farce of their paperwork and the signs they put up about discrimination. This sent a bad message: it's allowed to happen with no consequences. If I was a self-harmer they would've acted differently. I have a degenerate brain disease so it affected me badly. The incidents triggered all the PTSD from the bullying and racist attacks I had in the 1970's. I have experienced arson due to racism so this is quite acute. The 'Offender Management Unit' even wrote to prison staff who did nothing, they just said log it all down. When I challenged the bully, it was me who was investigated. I have been bullied, had phone credit stolen, been punched in the head. But it was never investigated or put into my paperwork. There is an institutional cover up. Everything logged by me was omitted but the one time I kicked off went onto my parole paperwork. Also, because I am cheerful I often get ignored. I am strong. I have picked up the pieces. People are too quick to judge."

## Race and PSIs

For more information see PSO 2510 and PSI 32/2011 'Ensuring Equality'. In 2011, PSI 32/2011 replaced PSO 2800 ('Race Equality') in order to "harmonise anti-discrimination policies" within the Prison Service:

> "The main purpose of this instruction is to promote equality within prisons. It sets out a uniform framework for anti-discrimination policies relating to the eight protected character-

istics in the Equalities Act. Unlawful discrimination by prison staff on the basis of colour, race, nationality or religion is prohibited, as is any racially abusive or insulting language or behaviour. Prisons are under a positive duty to take steps to actively eliminate discrimination."[19]

Before October 2010, civil claims for race discrimination were brought under the 'Race Relations Act' (RRA) 1976 (as amended). The 'Equality Act' 2010 (EA) unified the existing anti-discrimination legislation covering eight 'protected characteristics': age, disability, gender reassignment, marriage/civil partnership, race, religion/belief, sex and sexual orientation. Whilst the act has changed the provisions regarding race discrimination are largely the same. PAS has drawn up an overview of the main manifestations of racism in jail (see appendix seven)[20]. The quotes from friends below show how prevalent these methods of overt and indirect racism are inside:

"Racism manifests itself within prison in different ways. Inmates will use verbal, whilst from officers it's more about general attitude. The staff aren't directly racist, but they do take the racists side by not putting a stop to it. If you don't act you are part of it. There is a difference between disagreeing and saying, "no you cannot do this".

"Racism goes hand in hand with bullying. You find that the person who is the victim feels isolated, paranoid and anxious. A dangerous situation in jail is with warring factions, and a popularity contest. More freedom to move can mean more "she said, she said" and gangs."

"Issues around race don't get discussed enough in jail. People are scared to talk about it; scared to be called out on it, and scared to call other people racist. It would be better if it was discussed more with people who do want to understand. If people don't want to understand there's no point. Jail is old school: it's all about appearances. For example, they do 'equalities' training for a couple of hours as part of the induction process but it's a total box ticking exercise."

---

19 PAS, *Information Sheet: Complaints About Racist Treatment in Prison,* updated 2015
20 PAS, 2015

## FOREIGN NATIONAL PRISONERS (FNPs)

There are about 10,500 'Foreign National Prisoners' (FNPs) within the UK. According to WIP, foreign nationals make up 13% of the women's prison population. The home office has stated that in the last ten years the number of FNPs has doubled and now represents over 14% of the total prison population in England and Wales. These people are demonised by media and often receive a 'double whammy' of punishment; being given custodial sentences *and* threatened with deportation. Legal aid has been removed for most immigration cases, and many Foreign Nationals often do not know their rights. Unless they were living in the UK before getting sent down, FNPs cannot access ROTLs/HDC (tag) and often have parole issues. Because they are held so far from their families, most FNPs do not have visits, and it is harder for them to speak on the phone as it is so expensive (especially if they do not have money sent in from outside).

Since the Brexit vote, anxiety among many Foreign Nationals inside has increased, as there is a large amount of uncertainty as to what legislation will occur once England leaves the European Union. Many FNPs come from European Economic Area (EEA) countries and so they will obviously be greatly affected by the UK leaving the EU. In relation to Irish prisoners, legislation is emerging around 'The Early Release Scheme' (TERS)[21]. This means that potentially all Irish passport holders can opt to get deported if they have parental links to the Republic of Ireland. If you think you would like to do this, act now, because it is uncertain how this will be affected by Brexit.

Legislation around deportation and repatriation is constantly changing, and FNPs experience extra levels of isolation, stress and suicides in custody, as they are trapped between two nation states, and the negotiations and wrangling this involves. About half of FNPs are released at very short notice and are sent back to their country of origin with no attempt at resettlement. For more information see PSI2011-052 'Immigration, Repatriation and Removal'. There are numerous PSIs that relate to FNPs (see appendix 17). The 'Hibiscus Initiative' can provide support in understanding these, and other information for FNPs. Hibiscus aims "to empower foreign national, black and minority ethnic groups, affected by the social, criminal justice and immigration systems"[22].

---

21 Inside Time, *Calling All Irish Prisoners, 2017*
22 hibiscusinitiatives.org.uk

## Context

During his time as Home Secretary, John Reid made deportation *mandatory* for FNPs serving sentences of over a year (except those with a 'valid' asylum or human rights claim), which caused a five-fold increase between 2005 and 2008. A secret policy was devised, involving the detention of all time-served FNPs for as long as it took to deport them - which could be years - regardless of their mental state. The policy was ruled illegal in March 2011, but in the meantime, thousands of offenders were rounded up and detained, and those already in prison stayed there. By January 2011 over 1600 FNPs were stuck in prison beyond their sentence, a quarter of them for over a year[23].

## Language

One of the most obvious ways in which the prison system controls and discriminates against FNPs is through the use of language. It is often down to other inmates to try to help FNPs understand the minefield of prison bureaucracy, especially when they first enter jail. I cannot imagine how confusing this avalanche of bureaucracy must be to someone who does not have English as their first language. It did my head in and I'm used to dealing with officious admin!

If you are a FNP, try to access the library as soon as possible, and if it does not have a dictionary for your first language, request this or get it sent in. Some screws reluctantly agreed to use Google Translate to help make sense of some of the PSIs used to control FNPs but this is obviously woefully inaccurate. The *Information and Advice for Foreign National Prisoners* guide published by the home office should be available across the prison estate[24]. It is published in 22 languages and contains information on issues including: prison regimes, support organisations and contacting families. If you have access to someone outside jail but within the UK it might be worth getting them to contact your embassy/High Commission to see if they can help access any resources.

FNPs can be massively isolated and various organisations have outlined the 'prison within a prison' that exists for them. ESOL ('English as a Second Language') classes are often not available, or are massively oversubscribed. The Bell Foundation promotes language and learning with-

---

23 Institute of Race Relations, *Hidden Despair: The Deaths of Foreign National Prisoners, 2015*
24 justice.gov.uk/offenders/types-of-offender/foreign

in prisons, and in 2015 they launched an initiative called 'Language for Change'[25]. This programme will run until 2018 and if your prison does not provide adequate resources for ESOL then contact them. The Bell Foundation currently work with St Giles Trust in developing their 'Peer Advice for Foreign National Prisoners', through which prisoners are trained up to NVQ Level Four to support fellow prisoners who are foreign nationals and have English as a second language[26]. They are also working with the Hibiscus Initiative to provide language and support to migrant women in the criminal justice system.

If you know someone is a FNP, try to help them access the resources inside such as 'Turning Pages'[27] (the peer-reading programme), and the Listeners service if they are depressed (though obviously there are potentially major communication/language barriers here.) If you know other people in the jail with a common language, try to encourage them to support each other. Help people make sense of their legal paper work, and get people outside to research for you.

**Family and emotional life**

"Missing my son is the hardest thing about my sentence. Having friends ask me about him is good, and talking about him helps. I am worried I will be deported and he will lose his home. More support is needed for being a mother. They should let me have more credit for calling my son (who is currently living in XXXX while I am inside). You do get a O/L [postage paid] letter for overseas if you are a FNP which is good. I am unsure of the translation services. I am lucky because I find it quite easy to make friends, but a lot of girls are very shy, especially about talking about their lives or crimes. This can make you feel lonely." *A friend in jail*

If you have the misfortune to have a partner in a men's jail and you are both FNPs it is worth noting here that on top of all the difficulties involved in making an inter-prison phone call, you will have to conduct the call in English (for 'security' reasons.) This is extremely upsetting for women inside, and is yet another way in which FNPs are penalised. Inter-prison phone calls are difficult to organise, time limited, and use your own credit, so if

---

25 bell-foundation.org.uk/Work/LanguageforChange
26 bell-foundation.org.uk/Work/Offenders/PeerAdviceProject/
27 Project run by the 'Shannon Trust' (turningpages.shannontrust.org.uk)

you are emotional and stumbling over language it can make for an even more frustrating experience than the standard phone call.

A final practical note on supporting FNPs relates to weekend bang-up. Many people struggle with the extended time in isolation over the weekend. If you are a FNP, or know someone who is (especially if they are in a single cell) then try to help them get through this by accessing art materials, a radio or CD player, a pack of cards (even if they are on their own, playing Patience will kill a bit of time) or puzzles. All these things should be available from 'Safer Custody' or the Chapel. For people who cannot lose themselves in books or TV during the weekend regime due to language barriers, they can be really helpful.

## Detention Services Orders

FNPs from women's prisons deported are from the 'Hub' at HMP Peterborough. People in men's prisons can get deported from a few different locations because they make up most of the prison population. For more information see PSI 01/2015 'The Allocation of Prisoners Liable to Deportation or Removal from the United Kingdom'; and PSI 52/2011 'Immigration, Repatriation and Removal Services'.

It is worth repeating here that there are thousands of people held captive without release dates in 'Immigration Removal Centres' (IRCs) (aka 'Detention Centres' or 'Immigration Prisons') as well as those inside the women's prison estate. Much of the legislation used to control Foreign Nationals is also employed in IRCs. The Detention Services Order (similar to a PSI) is applied across the prison estate. One particularly abused piece of legislation is 'Removal from Association' (DC Rule 40) for individuals who are deemed to be "stubborn, unmanageable or disobedient". The means that individuals can be placed in seg for up to two weeks. It can be very difficult for Foreign Nationals to challenge this due to the lack of resources outlined above.

## Deportation and 'Early Release'

There has been increased collaboration across the prison estate between jails and the UK Border Agency over the last 18 months. The UKBA is currently 'transferring' a greater number of time expired prisoners from prison service establishments to Immigration Removal Centres, and researching whether or not FNPs should get deported at the end of their sentence or not.

In addition to the normal removal at the end of sentence, a prisoner can return home up to 135 days early by the 'Early Removal Scheme'. Many FNPs are repatriated to serve the remainder of their sentence in their home country. The 'Facilitated Returns Scheme', launched in October 2006, means that FNPs from outside the European Economic Area return to their country of origin. The UKBA and the prison service further incentivise this by waving the possible carrot of 'financial assistance' for 'reintegration' to those who 'volunteer' to go back to their country of origin. Many FNPs have opted for this scheme, but have returned in a *much* worse position than when they left, and have been instantly detained at the airport upon arrival.

## Operation Nexus

In 2012 the Metropolitan Police launched Operation Nexus, which uses deportation as a sanction against *unconvicted* people it claims are 'criminals'. The stated policy of the Met is to target "more serious or prolific offenders"[28]. The reality is that this is a rationalisation for immigration checks on just about every Foreign National who is arrested, including EU citizens, whether or not they have been charged with any offence. Over an eight-week period in 2012 checks were carried out on 41,712 individuals. This is a huge operation, and continues today. Many charities are also complicit in its execution.

> "We know that 28 per cent of all people arrested in London are foreign nationals, which reflects the population of this international and hugely diverse city, and emphasises why this operation is so important. We will continue to explore every tactic to make London safer for everyone." home office[29]

Note that this statistic only says *arrested* it does not say how many people were *charged*. As with more draconian and discriminatory stop and search powers, Operation Nexus provides a rationale for the deportation of many individuals *before* they have even allegedly committed a crime. Many people deported or sanctioned under this operation are removed just because they are deemed "undesirable" such as those who are street homeless.

As with the proposed construction of the UK prison in Jamaica, Operation Nexus is also an example of how the prison estate in this country has expanded into other countries, as it is dependent upon the recruitment and

28 gov.uk/government/news/operation-nexus-results-in-more-than-175-removals
29 gov.uk/government/news/operation-nexus-results-in-more-than-175-removals

involvement of police from other countries (see appendix eight).

## TRAVELLERS

The Traveller community is massively over-represented within the UK prison system, and for Traveller women there are multiple ways they are discriminated against in jail. According to the Traveller Equality Project, Irish prisoners constitute the third largest ethnic population of prisoners in the CJS in England and Wales. Since the 'Equalities Act' of 2010, Travellers have been a protected group, and are now included in the Census as "Gypsy, Romany or Traveller". Travellers are the smallest ethnic group in UK (0.1%).

One in 20 inmates – or 5% – told HMIP that they considered themselves to be Gypsy, Romany or Traveller in 2012-13[30]. This is a a very high percentage given how small the Traveller community is nationally compared to other ethnicities. The grim reality is that the number of Travellers incarcerated is probably also much higher due to an understandable reluctance to engage with state monitoring.

> "Alongside the over representation of Gypsies and Travellers in the prison system...the Inspectorate found that Gypsies and Travellers experienced poor levels of health, well-being and safety...it also identified disproportionate numbers of Gypsy and Traveller young people in Secure Training Centres."[31]

In 2015, in keeping with the current rhetoric with supposed 'equalities', NOMS created a new code 'W3 Irish Travellers/Gypsies'. Many reformist organisations called for this to be added, but the reality is that unsurprisingly it has *not* improved life for Traveller prisoners, as one of my friends inside argued:

> "The new W3 code in prisons is just another way to find out who Travellers are without giving out benefits. No one wants to register because it means you are much less likely to get TAG/ROTL due to a "lack of suitable address" and have licence problems/restrictions. Prisons and probation say Travellers are "flight risks" or "in danger of absconding". This means you are much less likely to be allowed out on hospital

---

30 HM Inspectorate of Prisons (HMIP) *People in prison: Gypsies, Romany and Travellers, 2014*
31 HMIP, 2014

appointments or funerals. You are also much less likely to get put on an enhanced wing if you say you are W3."

In relation to Travellers in women's prisons, it is important to note that class and gender issues create anxiety and uncertainty. Any one who has been to jail will know that you have to constantly fight to get your basic "rights" met, and that screws will never do anything for you unless they have to. This means that if you are confident, and middle-class you have a much higher change of accessing resources successfully. It is also important to note that many individuals in jail are motivated to challenge authority because of the contrast between jail and their normal life. Liberal outrage is based on this discrepancy, however, as my mate said:

> "There is a common misconception that loss of freedom equals loss of rights. But we Travellers don't have rights even when on road. Therefore we don't question the prison system as much as other people because we aren't used to having the rights many take for granted in the first place."

**Support Services**

There are various resources for Travellers inside. 'Open Road' is a weekly show for Travellers on National Prison Radio, the Travellers Times is a sporadic publication that should be available in prison libraries and *On Road* is a compilation created by people at HMP Parc.

The Traveller Equality Project is the main support organisation for Travellers, and they run the Irish Chaplaincy Prison Outreach (ICPO), providing a specialised response to the needs of the Irish prisoner in Britain (see appendix nine). The resources section lists information and resource for Travellers, including 'The Traveller Movement' which is an advisory and advocacy organisation[32].

**Literacy?**

> "Problems with literacy are especially noticeable among women Travellers because it's a patriarchal culture. Women are encouraged to look after children and avoid education. Many women drop out of school. When Travellers engage with programmes to help with literacy it's often done in a very patronising way." *A friend from jail*

---

32 For contact details see resources section 'Traveller Support Organisations'

Due to a combination fear and mistrust of authorities, and systemic repression the prevailing attitude among many Traveller prisoners is to "just keep your head down". People I interviewed during my sentence who identified as Travellers repeatedly outlined how the prison system used the IEP scheme to divide the prison population. Because of a reluctance to engage with authority, and low levels of literacy, Travellers within women's prisons are unable to access many of the more popular jobs and cannot get enhanced.

### 'Equalities'

There are now 50 groups led by Travellers in UK prisons. These groups each have a designated Rep, organise events such as Traveller History Month, and promote focused support services such as Traveller literacy programmes. However, these changes are tokenistic, and ineffectual in the face of a systemic attack against Travellers, and many are understandably reluctant to engage with this initiative. People I spoke to also acknowledged that being a Traveller Rep is a very difficult position as Travellers are used to being put down and have a lot of issues interacting with authority due to the system being so biased against them.

Traveller women I interviewed made some very specific demands that they said would greatly improve life for Traveller prisoners:

- Buddies for health care appointments: many Travellers inside women's prisons are frightened to go to health care as they often don't understand what the Doctor is saying. Individuals I spoke to emphasised the need for guidance, reassurance and clear explanations.
- The recognition of Traveller culture, such as a 'celebration day'; the opportunity to make traditional food; such as bacon pudding and cabbage, and having country and western music in the library.
- Allowing Traveller women two bowls (you are given one when you enter jail and it is a punishable offence to have more than this in your cell). It is traditional for Travellers to have one bowl for washing clothes, and one for dishes). (Note: everyone would benefit from this; it's basic hygiene!)
- Help writing letters.
- Listener service needs to include Travellers so individuals can get support from someone within/with knowledge of their community. Because of issues around literacy and confidence, it is quite difficult for Traveller women to complete the Listener training.

## Health

> "Gypsies and Irish Travellers are among the most marginalised groups in society and there is research evidence that both physical ill health and suicide are more prevalent among this group than in the wider community. Research also suggests that Travellers may receive poor treatment in the criminal justice system and in prison." *Nigel Newcomen*[33]

Because of the history of repression that Travellers have faced, many are reluctant to access health care. This means that many people have a low life expectancy rate. Common health problems are angina, asthma and mental health. Unsurprisingly, the prison system (and the inadequate medical services it provides) exacerbates these conditions.

The PPO report found that Travellers are nearly three times more likely to suffer from anxiety and twice as likely to be depressed compared to the rest of the population. HMIP found higher levels of mental health difficulties among Travellers compared to other prisoners (27% compared with 13%)[34]. Out of the Travellers whose deaths were investigated, over half had at least one recorded mental health issue. Depression and schizophrenia were common, and Travellers whose death was self-inflicted had either attempted suicide before, or had self-harmed. When suicide and self-harm procedures (ACCTs) were in place, they were often not implemented fully.

## Family Life

One of the most important features of Traveller life is the importance of family. As one of my mates said: "Traveller: you are born into it, you can't just become one." Traveller families are very large; and the prison estate uses this as another way to discriminate against people from this background. Visits in jail are very strict, and only three adults maximum are allowed to visit at any one time. As family support is very important within the Traveller community it really impacts on the mental health of both the prisoner and the family outside.

> "All prisoners are affected by the separation from their family. However, for Travellers, this separation is often a particularly difficult aspect of imprisonment. Travellers are high-

---

33 PPO, *Deaths of Travellers in Prison, 2015*
34 HMIP paper *People in Prison: Gypsies, Romany and Travellers, 2014*

ly family orientated, often marrying young and having large families. Although not all have nomadic lifestyles, Traveller families often do not have land-line telephones, resulting in extra cost to call a mobile. Irish Travellers, in particular, are more likely to have family in the Republic of Ireland. This combination of factors can lead to expensive calls to mobiles charged at an international call rate." PPO[35]

Travellers that I spoke to reiterated the issues with telephone communications to families. For those who were not particularly scrutinised by security, some could use third party telephone providers, such as 'Jail Telecom' and 'Fonesavvy', but this doesn't always work. Before being shut down, HMP Holloway allowed Traveller women a 'Gypsy PIN' where they could put more money from their private spends into phone credit each week to reflect the lack of access to landlines from this community.

One of the most obvious ways in which prison life is traumatic for Travellers is in the process of bereavement. Rituals and practices around mourning are really important to Travellers. Theoretically if a close family member dies and there is sufficient time for the prison service to organise an escort, then the prisoner should be allowed to attend the funeral. However, as with many rules, this procedure is applied very inconsistently. One Traveller mother was not allowed out to her own child's funeral[36]. Screws routinely cite "intimidation" in relation to Travellers, using this as an excuse for not allowing attendance at hospital appointments or funerals.

35 PPO, *Deaths of Travellers in Prison, 2015*
36 Case study taken from an interview conducted with a friend inside

# MANUFACTURING OBEDIENCE (OR TRYING TO)

## SCREWS AND STAFF

"Approach with caution
They are programmed to obey,
The robots of the future are living here today." *Zephaniah*[1]

"being captured is beside the point,
the point is no surrender."*Hikmet* [2]

In 2012 there were 29,660 'operational staff' in the prison estate. This figure fell to 23,080 in March 2016, meanwhile, the prison population has expanded rapidly[3]. The result of this is a lot more bang-up, and a lot of bad-tempered screws. In 2010 HMP extended the weekend regime, and instigated Friday afternoon bang-up to save costs (about £60 million in 2010). The number of screws was cut by 28%. This section is *not* a call for more prison staff (or staff from a wider diversity of backgrounds), or less prisoners. It is stating the case for *no* prisons.

"Do you want to talk to someone who locks you up during the day and who is ready to shoot you if you attempt to escape during the night?"[4]

1 Zephaniah, *The Robots of the Future* in *Too Black Too Strong, 2001*
2 Nazim Hikmet, Turkish political prisoner 1948 (reprinted in Gilbert)
3 Harm and Evidence Research Collaborative (HERC) (Criminology Research at The Open University) *Blood Baths and Prison Staff: Considering the Actual State of our Prisons, 2016*
4 Viehmann, 2009

In my angry (dogmatic?) mind the distinction between prisoners and everyone else in jail is clear and rigid. Screws have signed up to inflict misery on those they control for poxy pay and the other staff are just as bad. Some people volunteer in jails, hoping to make life better for those inside. But this legitimises the prison estate and any one who has keys or a security pass has in some way complied or collaborated with its repressive regime. Volunteers who come into the jail can help distract prisoners, but their intentions can also be suffocating. One of the most pitiful things I have ever seen is the queue -and anticipation of- the monthly 'Card Club' organised by the 'Mother's Union'. People battled it out to claim scraps of old Christmas and birthday cards. The cost of picking up these stationary items was a bunch of patronising questions about life inside and your alleged offence, and how you were trying to make yourself "better". The volunteers clearly had good intentions, but it was very challenging to engage with them.

"There are many demons with men's faces. It is wrong to join hands with everyone." *Rumi*[5]

In jail, the screws ('officers') are the lowest of the low in terms of rank. Above them comes an 'SO' or 'senior officer'. These people wield much more power, so if you want to challenge something a screw has done then sometimes it can be worth taking this up with the SO. The *only* time I would personally advocate this was in a serious incident of mental health issues, such as if one of your mates is suicidal and has been put on basic. Even in these incidences, it is highly unlikely that talking to the SO will make any difference; they tend to stick together. If a screw thinks you've talked to their SO they will most likely make your life hell.

Screws love to exert their power, playing with their radios and keys at every available opportunity, and issuing (or threatening people with) 'negative IEPs'. As has been previously outlined, they will often talk in discriminatory language, using sloppy generalisations, making claims that women prisoners are "manipulative", "bitchy", "complainers", or more "unstable".

Because prison is such an intense and artificial environment, it is impossible to be in a prison environment for any length of time and not get caught up in its dramas and 'prison politics'. This is partly why some screws end up shagging each other (or the prisoners). It is not uncommon for screws to have sex with prisoners. This has been labelled 'tampering' and happens a lot more in women's prisons than men's. Preoccupation with

5 Rumi, *Story II. The Oilman and his Parrot*

the daily inter-personal dynamics of life inside applies to both prisoners and screws, so be careful what you discuss within their ear shot, and do not be fooled by their patronising language when they ask casual sounding questions. I have this to say to them: I ain't no lady. You can't call me girl. Jog on and go to hell.

> "You must never allow them to persuade you that there are no clear front lines and that "big brother" is your friend. Ulrike Meinhof's declaration that "the fight of the people against power is the fight of remembering against forgetting" sums this up perfectly." You have to figure out how to survive with your personality intact." *Viehmann*[6]

You can tell how high up the ranks someone is by the number of stripes they have on their epaulettes. A 'three stripe' is high up and they can override all kinds of decisions. Screws generally live up to their stereotype; most of them are lazy. This can work to your advantage, but it also means you do have to get them to check fairly regularly that you have been paid (many work parties are rubbish at processing wages) and that your VOs (visiting orders) or telephone PINs have been updated.

In order to keep a beady eye on inmates, HMP has a 'personal officer' scheme. Each prisoner is allocated one and they will sporadically collar you for a general chat. They will also write reports about your "progress". They often have favourite prisoners and will generally be even more nosy than normal screws because they have pressure from above to find out information about you. Do not be fooled by their polite inquiries or "general catch ups"!

Body warn cameras are also being introduced for screws as part of a "violence reduction strategy". There are already cameras everywhere inside, but these are a further method of control that individual screws can wield.

In jail *who* you talk to and associate with is just as important as *what* you say. Screws delight in writing their end of day reports speculating about the relationships you have and with whom. Throughout my sentence, the 'personal officers' assigned to me often asked why I chose to hang out with so many people on drugs when I clearly didn't use, and tried to use emotional blackmail (for example, that I would never get enhanced) to discourage me from associating with my mates. Once they realised I had no intention of asking for their poxy privileges they eventually left me alone.

6 Viehmann, 2009

In *Discipline and Punish: The Birth of the Modern Prison*[7], Foucault described jail as a "series of excesses"; useless acts of violence perpetuated by wardens and "a despotism of administration". Screws use this administration to control and this can have big impacts on your applications for parole/release/licence. They write reports everyday about you. They have a smart comment and judgement for everything, and they don't like it when prisoners treat them with contempt or withhold information.

The prison system also has a lot of governors for different things. The main governor (or "number one guv") is normally supported by an army of minions, such as governor for security, for regimes, for equalities and so on. In private prisons the label 'director' is used instead of governor, but it means the same thing. Governors are normally fairly elusive, busy creating the bureaucracy and implementing the strategies and 'initiatives' that make prisoners lives hell.

## Corruption

> "There are only two types of screws... firstly those who are malevolent from the start and secondly those who are quite reasonable with you but then show their true colours. The former is preferable because at least you know what you're getting. Never ever trust a screw." *Cattermole*[8]

Corruption is rife within prisons. Despite hysterical media reports of endless drone drop-offs and sneaky prisoners getting stuff in through visitors, there is no way that the amount of "contraband" (mainly unprecedented levels of drugs inside and mobile phones) would get through security without some staff involvement. Screws are also often the source of leaks to the media about high-profile prisoners and life inside.

In March 2017, the BBC conducted an investigation into corruption within the prison system. The old head of the 'Anti-Corruption Unit' John Podmore stated that corruption is an "inconvenient truth" which has far more of an impact than the well-publicised problem of drones, which deliver packages to prison cell windows or drop them inside perimeter walls[9]. The 'Corruption Intelligence Unit' claims the prison drugs problem has got so out of hand that individuals are joining the prison service just to supply,

---

7 Foucault, 1975
8 Cattermole, 2015
9 bbc.com/news/uk-39616399 *Drones Flying Into Prisons to be Examined by New Police Team, 2017*

but in an attempt to deflect 'blame' from the staff he oversees, Podmore has argued that screws become corrupt because they are manipulated by inmates[10].

> "One well-informed source with extensive knowledge of the prison system told BBC Radio Four's *File on Four* there was a working assumption that between three and five staff in every jail were corrupt, which equates to around 600 across England and Wales."[11]

A word of caution if you are trying to get favours off a new screw. A lot of staff will join the prison system with some misguided belief that they can actually make it better. Approach this group with extreme caution. Faith has outlined the issues with this attitude among staff:

> "There is a particular pattern of behaviour that occurs among new prison staff who bring with them a social-worker orientation, especially those assigned to youth or female institutions. They enter with a high degree of idealism and they want to "help" the prisoners, especially for those for whom they feel great sympathy... In time, these staff become distrustful and authoritarian."[12]

**Class, Race and Screws**

Quite a few studies have been done on class issues and prison staffing. It's not rocket science, and you don't need to be an academic to see how it plays out in jail. A lot of screws come from a working-class background. A lot of 'old school' screws I encountered (especially older men who resented working in a women's jail) were against education in jail, or anything that could be interpreted as a "soft touch", endlessly droning on about the glory days when they had an even freer rein at making the lives of prisoners hell.

A lot of people inside women's prisons, especially those serving longer sentences, get pally with prison staff generally. It was quite depressing to see how the healthy dislike and mistrust of screws was not applied universally to prison staff, with many people being far more amenable -and even

---

10 bbc.com/news/uk-39616399 *Drones Flying Into Prisons to be Examined by New Police Team*
11 Danny Shaw, *The Prison Contraband Crisis File on Four -BBC Radio 4, 2017*
12 Faith, 2011

actively seeking the approval of- those of a higher ranking/class. Whilst a lot of screws are working-class, the probation service is rife with middle-class do-gooders. In jail, you have an 'offender manager' (OM) inside who is your link to your probation officer outside. My OM was a classic example of this demographic: a liberal, middle-class, middle-aged, nosy individual who always told me to be more 'pro-social' (and join Greenpeace!) OMs are slippery characters and they will do all they can to lure you into believing they are not part of the problem.

## DISCIPLINE

> "Raised by ashes in the dirt and dust
> Cutting teeth then flesh on rust
> They come to teach me what is just -
> The oppressors' fists to kiss me" *Sean Swain*[13]

Women's prisons in the UK generally employ much less overt forms of control than that outlined in Swain's poem. The use of force is (mostly) negated by the execution of calm, efficient, observations. Power is exerted through architectural features, such as the physical arrangement of bodies, and the individual watching and controlling does not require much training.

As with all aspects of the CJS, women's prisons rely on what Foucault called a "swarming of disciplinary mechanisms" which are both flexible and adaptable, and an "anatomy of power"[14]; whereby the state has a whole arsenal of techniques, institutions and targets. Foucault described this as "apparatus intended to render individuals docile and useful, by means of precise work on their bodies"[15].

In Foucault's analysis; prisons are an example of "juridicio-economic and technico-disciplinary" procedures; where the traditional use of force and violence is replaced by the "gentle efficiency of total surveillance"[16]. The individual may never really know why they are the subject of a disciplinary procedure, or where it has come from. Screws relish using the dreaded phrase "information received...." to legitimise all kinds of punishment in jail and many a prisoner has been disciplined using this vague terminology.

---

13 Anarchist prisoner Swain, *The Wretched of the Earth, 2014*
14 Foucault, 1975
15 Foucault, 1975
16 Foucault, 1975

## Incentives and Earned Privileges Scheme (IEP)

Black and Bros have outlined the development of the IEP scheme in their text *The Prison Works*[17]. The 'Prisons Act' of 1952 was amended after the Strangeways riot of 1990 and this led to the introduction of the 'Incentives and Earned Privileges' (IEP) scheme in 1995. In the ongoing process of 'dynamic security' prisoners police their own actions. The scheme exists "to encourage and reward their constructive participation in the regime of the establishment"[18]. Thus, prisoners become complicit in their own oppression and control. Mother's in women's prisons are especially fearful of the repercussions of the IEP scheme, as failure to comply can often mean they are denied the 'privilege' of access to their children.

The IEP scheme encourages a sense of division and competition between prisoners. It is used to discipline prisoners based on a 'loss of' system of punishment. The scheme operates on a four-tier process. Prisoners are 'basic, standard or enhanced' depending on behaviour, or at 'entry level' while they are on induction (this fourth level was added in 2013). The scheme relies on prisoners policing themselves (and in this process; often snitching on others) in order to comply with what the prison system deems to be 'good behaviour'. You move up or down the system depending on the work you do; and the number of 'positive' or 'negative' IEPs (comments) you receive.

In order to become 'enhanced' the individual is required to go "above and beyond" what the prison expects of them as a bare minimum in terms of behaviour. This often means completing courses, doing voluntary work, and applying for higher grade jobs within the prison. All these activities require a level of literacy and confidence which many people lack. It's depressing how quickly prisoners who have been 'enhanced' or given ROTLs become snobby and quick to judge and condemn. Once someone has been enhanced, they are expected to continue to demonstrate their "enhanced behaviour". Again, this acts as a depressingly easy way for staff to control this demographic of prisoners. Screws have often been heard to tell someone they are not behaving like "an enhanced prisoner" and the individual in question will then frequently modify their behaviour to demonstrate their compliance.

If you get three negative IEPs within 28 days you will get put on basic (but you can also be put straight on it if you commit an 'Offence Against

---

17 Black and Bros, *2010*
18 NOMS PSI 11/2011, *Incentives and Earned Privileges*

Discipline' (see appendix 12). Basic lasts for seven,14, 21 or 28 days, depending on your behaviour. It can really drag if you are not mentally prepared. Some good words of advice from a mate who was constantly 'riding basic', but refused (and refuses!) to be beaten:

> "I think to myself: whatever I want is outside prison. Nothing I want is in here in this situation. So, if they want my telly, let them take it. I don't care. My unlock time counts for a lot so I can see my friends. I am very spiritual so that helps. I sleep a lot less because I'm not using energy (you can only go to the gym for 30 minutes once a week at best). Catch up on letters, doing legal stuff helps. Most people crack and grass after seven days."

The prison dresses up the IEP scheme in all kinds of ways. As with many aspects of prison life, the theory and reality of life inside are very different. The quote below from the PRT shows how complicit reformist organisations can be in promoting and implementing the regulations of the prison regime.

> "It promotes conforming behaviour through rational choice. Enabling people to earn benefits in exchange for responsible behaviour encourages prisoners to engage with sentence planning and ensures a more disciplined and controlled environment which is safer for staff and prisoners. Other outcomes include a reduced risk of self-harm and improved staff prisoner relationships"[19]

During my time inside there were countless examples of people being put on basic or segregated for anything but "rational choice". As for encouraging "responsible behaviour", if the behaviour of prison staff is deemed responsible, then as ever, I embrace my anti-social and irresponsible tendencies.

If you are enhanced prisoner you will get more visits as one of your 'privileges'. If you are on basic you are still entitled to visits. However, screws often 'forget' to unlock people until after the final entry time for a visit. People on basic are often not allowed to attend work or education.

The PPO found that the number of prisoners who have committed suicide and were on the basic regime was a higher proportion than those on other levels. The ministry of justice found that black prisoners were more

19 PRT, *Incentives and Earned Privileges, 2011*

likely to be on the basic regime than white prisoners[20]. There isn't available information to prove whether people with a learning disability might be over represented on basic. However, it is highly likely that those with literacy, mental health issues or impairments are disadvantaged by IEP scheme.

If you are on basic you will lose most of your weekly earnings, and will not be allowed access to your private spends. When I was inside you got £3.50 of wages per week only. You will also lose that great pacifier of the prison populations; the television.

> "One reason that televisions were introduced into cells was because there was so little activity available to prisoners."[21]

For many people loss of TV is the worst aspect of basic. But you should still be allowed a radio/CD player (ask Safer Custody or the chapel if you don't have one) and access to the library. Staff will try to isolate you as much as possible from all other inmates. They will try to stop people coming to your door (if you are in a double they may well move you to a single). For the first few days at least will normally be given your meals in your cell. Then you might be allowed to go to the dining hall, but accompanied by a screw(s).

For more information on basic read PSI 2013-030 and PSI 11/2011[22] If you are riding basic here are some words of advice:
- Demand your 30 minutes 'exercise' (fresh air) per day. Note however that at some jails where food is served in a dining hall/canteen they will try to claim that counts.
- Check if the gym is available (some prisons have specific gym slots for people on basic to avoid 'association'.)

---

20 MoJ, *Race Review,* 2008
21 PRT, *Incentives and Earned Privileges, 2011*
22 According to Miscarriages of Justice UK, "The scheme aims to encourage good behaviour and participation in interventions to reduce re-offending and challenge poor behaviour and non-compliance. The scheme works by offering key earnable privileges including extra visits, higher rates of pay and in-cell television. These privileges are removed if behaviour deteriorates. Prisons are expected to avoid demoting prisoners directly from enhanced to basic level, except in the most serious cases of misconduct, for instance assault. Prisoners at basic level should have their level reviewed within seven days and be informed of the steps they must take to return to standard level. Following this review, adult prisoners who remain at this level must have a monthly review. Young offenders should receive a review at least every fourteen days." 'Prison Rule 8', 'YOI Rule 6' and 'PSI 11/2011', state that all prisons and YOIs, are required to provide a system of privileges in addition to the minimum entitlements detailed in the rules of each institution.

- Save and collect dog ends if you are a smoker.
- Get mates to order you stuff off canteen. Get friends outside to send in stamps you can trade (limited spends allowed)
- Stay positive: do in-cell work outs, listen to tunes and catch up on your letters.
- Don't let them rile you, especially towards the end. They will try to push you to keep you on basic.
- Use the library, read trashy books to distract you and check the PSIs in relation to your charge/adjudication (also in the library). In theory, you are only allowed one 15 minutes escorted library trip per week if you are on basic but you can make this last longer by taking time over the PSIs.
- Borrow CDs off mates. Be warned; they can slam you with more time on basic if they do a cell-spin and you have items that ain't on your 'prop card', but it's generally worth the risk to keep you sane. Beware, some people on basic get properly stuck on a song and play/ sing it 24/7. I never, ever want to hear 2pac's 'Ghetto Gospel' or the theme tune from Disney's 'Frozen' again.

> "To think of untamed mountains and seas puts your own problems into perspective...Books can take you to a different world when the one you are facing is intolerable."[23]

You can get put straight back on basic if you receive one 'negative IEP' within 28 days of your stretch ending. It's because of this that many people end up being perpetually put on basic. Screws love to exert their power on individuals they perceive to be 'acting up' or 'causing trouble' or not bowing down to their authority.

If you are inside and someone you know is on basic, here are some words of advice to help them:

> "Write me cheeky letters and put them under my door, or a joke. Chat by my hatch, wish me good morning or good night. Offer to order stuff for me on canteen. Take risks and come to my door. When I'm low, friends will talk to Safer Custody for me to get me unlocked for longer. Any physical contact is good."

If you are outside supporting someone in jail who is on basic; then take time to write them longer letters. They won't be able to use the phone much

23 Viehmann, 2009

(if at all) so mail becomes even more precious. Send in nice pictures, cards, poems and stories. Anything that will keep fire in their belly and distract them!

## Disorder

In recent years the combination of over-crowding, staff cuts, and the prevalence of New Psychoactive Substances has led to an increase in unrest within the UK prison system. According to the PPO, between 2015-16 there were 13 prisoner inflicted murders in the UK prison estate. There was a 27% increase in assaults (almost 4,000 reported incidents) and a 31% increase in serious assault incidents in prisons in 2015, compared with the previous year[24]. The PRT issued a 2015 report alleging that assaults by prisoners on staff had risen by 28% per week (3,637 assaults in 2014)[25]. The PPO report stated that almost one in five assaults in 2015 involved the use of weapons, compared with one in ten in 2010[26].

## Revolt?

"Solidarity is the worst thing a prison guard fears. They can understand a prisoner that fights for his or her own rights, but when a prisoner fights for the rights of another it has to be punished. But inevitably, solidarity will endure." *Mark Barnsley*[27]

"No significant reform of the prison system has ever been achieved by anyone other than prisoners themselves, usually as a result of collective direct action."[28]

In *Return to Resistance*, Bowden outlined the steady decline in large scale prison unrest, and called for a return of working-class solidarity, and a united front in the face of Tory divide and rule tactics. He argued that the so-called "millennium prisoner" (someone incarcerated after 2000) has no memory or knowledge of the history of prison revolt in the UK, and accept the dogma, control and liberalisation of the prison system.

"What happened to the spirit of revolt that used to periodi-

24 PPO, *Homicides: Fatal Incidents Investigations volume 12, 2016 (Learning Lessons Bulletin)*
25 PRT, *Putting Prisons Right, 2015*
26 PPO, 2016
27 Barnsley, *If It Was Easy, They Wouldn't Call It 'Struggle, 2005*
28 Bowden, *2010*

cally shake the British long-term prison system and engender a philosophy of prisoner empowerment and solidarity, a philosophy that situated the struggle of prisoners at the very forefront of the universal struggle for human rights and even social revolution?"[29]

The political landscape Bowden described in his essay was bleak. But there is reason to be hopeful. In 2016 there was a well-documented spate of riots within the men's prison estate. In Birmingham, Bedford, Swaleside, Erlestoke, Moorland and other prisons, hundreds of inmates attacked the prison system. Many wings were taken over. Physical and administrative infrastructure was destroyed. It was heartening to hear of the failings of G4S and other security operations to 'control' their captive populations and on several occasions unrest only ceased when the 'Tornado' task force (the government's rapid response unit in jails when all else fails) was drafted in. The ministry of justice reports a steady increase in prisoner unrest. According to the MoJ, the 'national tactical response group' (NTRG) was involved in 223 prisoner disturbances last year, double the number in 2010). This number is increasing all the time. The NTRG provide "security" for private and public institutions. Their funding massively increased under the coalition government.

Recently released figures claim that in 2016, at least 20,075 mobile phones and SIM cards were seized in UK jails[30]. Because of the amount of contraband phones within the prison estate (especially in men's jails), people during the riots were able to get footage out of the conditions inside and events as they were unfolding. Social media was also used. Obviously, there are major security implication for this, and the CJS wasted no time in trying to secure convictions and adjudications for those allegedly involved. After the riots, the boss of NOMS, Michael Spurr, outlined plans to recruit 8,000 new screws over by 2018[31].

The riots last year show that even in the face of pronounced oppression and control, there is always the capacity for resistance and organisation. The use of mobile phones has enabled prisoners to plan with people outside despite prison security and new technologies. Screws now routinely use BOSS chairs and phone scanners on landings, but record numbers of mobile phones are being smuggled into jails in the UK. Liz Truss has

29 Bowden, 2010

30 MoJ figures quoted in the Telegraph, *At Least 20,000 Mobile Phones and SIM Cards Discovered in Prisons Last Year* 2016

31 mirror.co.uk/news/uk-news/jail-boss-reveals-8000-prison-9358880

outlined plans to install 'phone jammers' ("denial and disruption technol-ogy"[32]) which would block mobile phone signal within prisons. However, this procedure is prohibitively expensive.

32 The Sun, *Prisoners will Have Their Phones Cut Off as Justice Secretary Liz Truss Launches £550m Bid to Tackle the Prison Crisis, 2016*

Why did the riots last year only happen in men's jails? It is interesting to note that historically most of the *large-scale* unrest in the UK has happened within men's prisons. My limited experience inside was that there were many acts of rebellion and solidarity that occurred on a small scale. In the prisons I was in mobile phones weren't that prevalent, and I wonder if this a lack of "recognition of female agency"[33] outside jail (for example in the mainstream media) are factors that combine to make women's prisons appear more orderly than men's prisons.

> "Researchers, scholars and activists often do not search for acts of defiance among the growing female prison population, often assuming that the silence around women prisoners' agency and activism signifies passive acceptance...They also overlook the instances in which women *do* riot and initiate litigation."[34]

The IEP scheme has been highly effective in separating prisoners and encouraging a culture of disapproval and disdain. Methods of resistance that are traditionally attributed to men were definitely dismissed as being "juvenile", "showing off" or resulting from an "attitude problem". I cannot speak from experience, but I'd imagine in men's jails these expressions of revolt are much more encouraged (and applauded) by other prisoners.

In the women's prisons I was in, there *were* overt displays of aggression towards authority and public spectacles. However, they were often criticised by the more compliant population within them. One example of this occurred during a noise demo that happened outside the gates. Some women were quick to condemn those of us who ran outside and used the opportunity to vent some anger. But for most of us it was an uplifting and empowering occasion.

## Prison Rule 051: Offences Against Discipline (OADs)

There are currently 25 'Offences Against Discipline' (OADs) (appendix ten) that a prisoner can now be accused of[35]. OADs carry the threat of a number of 'governor's punishments'. For adult prisoners these can include: loss of privileges for up to 42 days, up to 21 days cellular confinement, stoppage of earnings for up to 84 days, or deduction from earnings of

---

33 Law, 2012
34 Law, 2012
35 Note the use of "he" throughout the OADs as a further example of the gendered aspects of, and assumptions relating to, discipline within the prison system.

an amount not exceeding 42 days earnings. As with licence conditions, the CJS will include many specific conditions, and then a catch all clause that is suitably vague in order to give them the capacity to take indiscriminate legal action against a prisoner.

## Adjudications

Adjudications occur when the prisoner is accused of not complying with the OADs or PSIs. For more detailed information see PSI 47/2011. Adjudications *should* happen the day after the charge has been made (unless it's a holiday or Sunday). Prisoners are entitled to legal representation if they wish (though in reality this can be difficult to organise). If you request legal representation the case should be adjourned. You may be allowed a 'McKenzie Friend' (an unqualified 'lay person' who can be your legal advocate.)

You *must* be allowed to look at the relevant documentation for your case before the adjudication; and you should also be allowed access to the library to see the PSIs. "You must also be able to look at other reference books if you wish so that you can properly defend yourself against the charge, and you should be allowed at least two hours for this."[36]

Don't let the screws stop you doing research, even if you are on basic! Also make sure they give you all the paperwork they will be submitting. In order to trigger the adjudication process, a screw *must* complete a 'DIS1' form, setting out brief details of the alleged incident and the relevant Prison Rule, and telling you when the case will be heard. Don't let them get away with not giving you a copy; it's your legal right (for what it's worth!).

In your adjudication you will be asked if you understand the charge; and if you have had time to prepare a defence. You will have to enter a plea of guilty/not guilty. You may call witnesses. The governor can defer the adjudication to the police if they claim the alleged incident warrants a police enquiry. Most adjudications will result in extra days being added to your sentence if you are found 'guilty'. There are two types of adjudication: governor's adjudications and independent adjudications. If the case is not referred to the police or there is no prosecution, the governor or director will decide whether it should be referred to an independent adjudicator, who can give a punishment of additional days. If you are serving an indeterminate sentence such as life or IPP this would not happen. If the charge is not referred, the governor or director will continue to hear the adjudica-

---

36 justice.gov.uk

tion. Legal representation is rarely allowed in cases heard by governors or director, but you *are* entitled to be legally represented if your case is referred to an independent adjudicator.

Common reasons cited for extra days in adjudications are: assaults, possession, failed MDTs, damage to property. If you are accused of any of the above, *always* check for technicalities: incorrect procedure followed, paperwork not in order, wrong charges, misleading witness accounts and so on can give you enough leverage to get the case thrown out, and staff will sometimes back down if they see you are building a solid case. If you are waiting for parole, or HDC it is even more important to write everything down. Even if your case is dismissed, in the oppressive logic of jail the very fact that there was an adjudication in the first place may be enough for a parole knock back.

If you are charged with possession then the prison must demonstrate the individual had presence, knowledge and sole control over the item. The adjudication must fulfil this. In law, ownership is not necessarily important. Possession is.

The maximum number of extra days a governor can give is 42. In 2014 the total number of extra days added by private prisons was 27,176. Public (or state run) jails added 132, 321[37]. Adult sentencing guidelines on adjudications vary. See *Prisons Handbook*[38] for more information on this (there should be a copy in the library with the PSIs).

A final note to Foreign National Prisoners. Obviously, the legal process in jail is designed to mystify and confuse and adjudications are no exception. Make sure if you don't have access to a solicitor that you request copies of all the paperwork relevant to your adjudication and go through it with someone trusted on the wing. You are allowed to take notes during the hearing, so try to write down as much as possible. Try to recruit a 'McKenzie Friend' to help fight your corner.

**General Alarm/Roll check**

Some screws love general alarms; they get really psyched and start shouting at the radio, attempting to run or grapple with anyone who stands in their way. The general alarm will ring for all kinds of nonsense. If it does, you will normally be stranded and locked in for quite some time until they have worked out what's going on. The prison will also sporadically 'cease

---

37 *Jail Mail,* 2014
38 *Prisons Handbook 2016*

movement' just because it can and it likes to flex its muscles, or if the administration thinks a prisoner has escaped. If movement is ceased, again, you will be contained where you are. There will normally be a 'stand fast roll check' of the whole jail. You can imagine how long this takes.

Roll call happens several times a day and you better get used to hearing it hollered out across the wing. It happens normally in the morning, lunchtime, afternoon and night time (when it's lock in). You are meant to stand by your door and be counted. Screws will often use roll-check as a way to try and be chatty to prisoners who avoid the office, enjoying the captive audience they have on the landing, especially if some exciting bit of prison gossip has happened that day.

## 'Deep Custody'

The total segregation capacity of prisons in England and Wales was 1,586 cells in 2015, including 60 places in 'close supervision centres'[39]. Some prisons have a designated segregation wing; where inmates get moved once they have been issued this form of punishment. Seg wings exist in both men's and women's prisons. CSCs are only used within male prisons and so are not analysed much in this text. In women's prisons without a seg wing, they will use basic, and 'CC' ('Confined to Cell') as ways to punish prisoners.

> "Each actor is alone, perfectly individualised and constantly visible."[40]

The aim of CC is to isolate the prisoner as far as the physical architecture of the prison will allow. You will be escorted to collect any meds you take (you may even have to take them before everyone else is unlocked) and you will eat in your cell. If you are on CC you might also be on 'three man unlock' (or even more if you've really kicked off). This means whenever you are outside of your cell you will be surrounded by screws. Three man unlock is normally used as a pre-cursor to shipping someone out.

> "There is no end and no beginning: there is only one's mind, which can begin to play tricks." *Nelson Mandela*[41]

Unsurprisingly, all forms of isolation have an impact on people's mental

39 Dr Sharon Shalev and Kimmett Edgar, *Deep Custody: Segregation Units and Close Supervision Centres in England and Wales, PRT, 2015*
40 Foucault, 1975
41 Mandela, Nelson *The Long Walk to Freedom, 1994*

health. *Deep Custody* by the PRT highlights some areas of segregation practice which do not appear to meet international standards, including standards found in the 'European Prison Rules' (2006) and the 'UN Standard Minimum Rules for the Treatment of Prisoners' (or so-called 'Mandela Rules') [42]. The 'Convention Against Torture' is also relevant, particularly as it covers conditions or treatment which, while not necessarily amounting to torture, are inhuman, degrading, or cruel. The 'European Prison Rules' suggest that segregation should *not* impose social isolation or long hours of inactivity. As with many aspects of prison life (and the CJS in general) this legislation is totally incompatible with the forms of discipline it claims to police. Social interaction and isolation *cannot* exist simultaneously.

For more information see PSO1700 ('On Segregation') and PSI 64/2011 'Management of Prisoners at Risk of Harm to Self, to Others and from Others (Safer Custody)'. Individuals being placed on seg should have an Initial Segregation Health Care team and Segregation review boards. An Assessment Care in Custody and Teamwork (ACCT) should also be implemented and it should clearly state the alleged reason for the segregation. If you are on seg you won't be allowed to attend education or work.

## 'Ship Outs' and 'Sweat Boxes'

The prison estate often transfers (or 'ships out') prisoners. In 2015 each transfer cost £1,500 per prisoner, so there is a tidy profit being made out of

42 According to PAS; seg should only be last resort, used for a maximum of 14 days after adjudication. However, unsurprisingly it is used increasingly as a way to to control and hide those who do not comply with or conform to the prison regime. A working group of 24 international 'experts' drew up the 'Istanbul Expert Statement in 2007' to address the increasing use of solitary confinement. *The Use and Effects of Solitary Confinement*, called on states to limit its use to very exceptional cases, for as short a time as possible, and only as a last resort. The statement outlined that up to 90% of prisoners have "adverse effects" from segregation including insomnia, confusion, hallucinations and psychosis, and that in many cases this was not reversible. The report states that seg over 72 hours *should* be approved by the secretary of state, not just the prison, that prisoners *must* be given valid reason, and alternatives must be considered; such as being transferred to a different wing/unit, or 'Close Supervision Centre' (CSC) (basically a different name for the same regime). CSCs are only part of the men's prison estate so won't be discussed here. For more information see the Bristol Anarchist Black Cross publications: *Close Supervision Centres: Torture Units Across the UK (Parts One and Two)* As long-term CSC prisoner Kevan Thakrar has argued, CSCs are the logical extension of the IEP regime; the last step for those who do not comply with it. In the PPO's 2014 report *Learning Lessons*, the Ombudsman outlined the details behind the suicides of eight prisoners on seg. Four of these individuals were at risk of self-harm prior to segregation. Because of this, the PPO stated that those at risk of self-harm should not be put on seg.

the human cargo who are moved arbitrarily around the UK…

> "The sight of a large, white prison van or 'sweat box' moving through the traffic on its way to or from court is a familiar one. But most of us know little about who is inside or what is happening to them. There are over 820,000 of these journeys a year: between October 2013 and September 2014 there were 818,168 escorted journeys of men, women and children provided by Prisoner Escort and Custody Services (PECS) at a cost of £128.2 million, and 3,962 escorts of younger or more vulnerable children to or from STCs, provided by Secure Escort Services for Children and Young People (SESCYP) in a four year contract costing £9.1 million. PECS are currently provided by GEOAmey and Serco Wincanton and SESCYP by Serco." HMIP[43]

There are numerous reasons ship outs tend to happen: if you are going to court or get given a sentence longer than six months, if you have a course put on your sentence plan that they don't provide where you are, if you need hospital treatment, or if they just want to mess with your head. Never be fooled by promises from your work party that grafting for them will put

43 HMIP, *Transfers and Escorts within the Criminal Justice System, 2014*

you 'on hold' (i.e. stop you being shipped out) the reality is, the governor decides.

It is common for prisoners to be given minimal notice of a ship-out. You are often told the night before. Screws enjoy issuing the papers after evening bang-up, denying phone access to anyone outside (in case you try to organise an escape). It is also quite common practice if you are an alleged 'high risk' prisoner that you won't be told where you are going.

'Ghosting' is basically a ship-out but with even less notice than normal. Ghosting normally happens as a form of punishment; or if staff suspect the prisoner might kick off if they found out they were going to be 'ghosted'. If you are to be ghosted you will be given as little as 30 minutes notice to pack all your belongings, and you won't get to say goodbye to anyone.

Moving jails can be quite daunting, especially if you are given no notice or new to the regime. It will take several days for all your numbers to get transferred onto your PIN (and many might get lost in the process). You will have to do a whole new induction process.

Being shipped-out can make daily life a bit more bearable. The jail I ended up in had better courses and facilities than where I was on remand, and it mixes up your sentence a bit. A lot of Lifers chose to transfer jails a few times to mix-up the tedium of prison life, especially if you are approaching parole, as sadly it is quite common in women's jails for people to deliberately wind up those with a hearing looming.

When you are being transferred you will be subjected to all the usual searches and 'volumetric control' (putting all your stuff into two boxes). Be careful if you have stuff in possession that isn't on your 'prop card'. Being transferred can be a good time to sneak through a few extra items of clothing etc; but it is a risky business! If you are vegan or have special dietary needs ask the prison to phone ahead to alert the catering staff in the new prison. As the HMIP report highlighted, sweat boxes are an all too common feature on the roads in the UK. They are a bumpy ride. Because of alleged concerns about 'self-harm' individuals being transported are not allowed seat belts. In the 12 months to October 2014, there were 36 road traffic accidents involving the 'escort vehicles'.

> "Adult detainees were routinely cuffed on and off the vehicle, regardless of risk, and even children were routinely handcuffed on and off vehicles at court, although not on arrival to STCs or YOIs. The disproportionate use of restraints was a

particular concern on hospital escorts."[44]

Sweat boxes live up to their name; they are all plastic inside and you will be locked into a small perspex cage. There are normally 14 cells. Some people I was shipped-out with managed to share fags on the ride (once they got you locked in they normally leave you alone). Be warned; don't drink too much before you start the journey; it'll be a long, bumpy ride! Also, if you are on methadone then expect to be pretty desperate by the time you get to your new residence.

## Cell Spins

No analysis of discipline in jail would be complete without reference to 'cell spins'. These are searches conducted by screws and/or security. As with 'Mandatory Drugs Tests', there are two types: random and targeted. In reality, very little is random about either one. The prison is required to complete a certain amount of searches each month; but who is searched is often much more considered than they would have you believe. If you ever hear the phrase "information received" then you'll know someone's been snitching. If any of your 'in possession property' goes missing, check PSI 12/2011: 'Prisoners Property'. Always get a 'Cell Clearance Certificate'. Also, check any seals on property they take away and always sign for volumetric controls.

Cell searches vary in length of time depending on what they are hoping to find. You won't be allowed in your cell during your search (and quite often it might happen when you are out anyway). When you return to your cell, it will feel a bit like a violation and they will have undoubtedly made a right mess. Look carefully for any missing items when you are putting your house back in order, and as with everything, keep copies of the paperwork.

## Women and Discipline

A lot of people I was in jail with feared any kind of disciplinary procedures because 'loss of' spends would mean loss of phone credit; and for those with kids this is obviously extremely difficult. A lot of women on basic with children developed serious mental health issues. It is also worth noting that the prison system rarely takes into account 'extenuating circumstances'. For example, who wouldn't 'act up' if their child was about to be

---

44 HMIP, *Transfers and Escorts within the Criminal Justice System, 2014*

taken into 'care' and they had just seen them for the last time? I absolutely reject the argument that it is *only* those in women's jails who have issues surrounding their families, but it definitely true that *a lot* of inmates in the women's prisons estate fear disciplinary procedures because of these issues.

All prisoners are expected to strive towards modifying their behaviour, reintegration, redemption and inoculation into social norms. Therefore, the emphasis is on so-called 'progression'. Those who resist this are viewed with suspicion and this is especially the case with people in women's prisons, especially mothers.

Frances Malloch has outlined how women's prisons are "structurally located in patriarchal society"[45]. Women who comply with the IEP regime are seen as "deserving" of treatment, and touted as "successes". They have been contained, controlled and reformed. However, those who then resist the scheme are therefore stigmatised and villainised. The IEP scheme acts upon prisoners in many little ways every day, and through this normalisation process, compliance becomes the expectation. A depressing number of prisoners become 'officer no keys', being all 'extra' and obsessing over the daily details that maintain the prison regime and doing the work of the screws for them.

The concept of the 'deviant woman' is reiterated throughout the CJS. Men administer and define 'justice', and this supports the status quo and is biased. Women are not treated as equals, rather as criminals/offenders or victims. Criminology has historically theorised the relationship between production, marginalisation and punishment but not the relationship of reproduction. Individuals are faced with a deluge of bureaucracy; which reproduces itself and has a very physical impact on their conditions inside.

## 'Extremism'

> "Something needs to be done to change your perceptions of the police, and encourage lawful campaigning. There is a suspicion that you might act behind closed doors...How will I convince probation this is not the case?" *My offender manager in prison*

If the prison system has decided you are an 'extremist' and 'anti-social' then you will be given a whole heap of bull-shit courses to engage with *if* you want to pander to the prison staff and get enhanced; or apply for HDC.

45 Malloch, Margaret *Women, Drugs and Custody* 2001

You also better prepare yourself for an avalanche of licence restrictions and a spell in a bail hostel when you are 'released' from jail (more on this in part two).

The 'Thinking Skills Programme' was historically used as a last-ditch resort to get prisoners who did not demonstrate so-called 'pro-social behaviour' to comply and bow down to authority before release. The government is constantly changing and re-inventing the wheels of 'treatment' in this process. The 'Thinking Skills Programme' has been replaced by the 'Offending Behaviour Programme' RESOLVE, a group therapy course based on Cognitive Behavioural Therapy (CBT) which looks at issues like 'Understanding My Violence', 'Lifestyle and Relationships' and 'Becoming a New Me'. The aim of all these courses is to change the individual, and they are based on the assumption that it is the individual, not any aspect of the state which has created the conditions in which their alleged 'offence' occurred.

A further course they commonly try to slap on any 'extremists' who have the misfortune to be behind enemy lines is the so-called 'Extremist Reduction Guidelines (ERG)'. The ERG is a risk assessment tool carried out over an unspecified period of sessions/time depending on the whim of the psychologist.

**Surveillance**

> "CIA FBI
> All they tell us is lies
> And when I say it they get alarmed
> Tappin' my phone, they never leave me alone
> I'm even lethal when I'm unarmed
> 'Cause I'm louder than a bomb"
> *Public Enemy*[46]

Various methods of surveillance have been outlined here. It is impossible not to feel paranoid in jail. Never get complacent about this. There are cameras everywhere and roaming drug dogs. Every day you get comments added to your OASys report (sadly, it's not the tropical retreat the name implies but a detailed analysis of your behaviour and compliance with the regime). All of your personal post will be opened, read, and sometimes photocopied. Much of your legal paperwork will be too. So, get used to it,

---

46 Public Enemy, *Louder Than a Bomb, 1988*

and have constant vigilance.

PSI 22/2012 relates to surveillance in jail (see appendix 11). Note that there is an extension to this which only governors are privy too, making the PSI for the prisoner virtually worthless: "A restricted PSI is being issued to governors, which contains more detailed instructions. Governors must only share that PSI with staff engaged in or likely to be engaged in the use of 'secret' surveillance."[47]

As one prisoner outlined in a letter to IT, this use of surveillance is extremely dodgy in relation to remand prisoners, or prisoners maintaining their innocence[48]. The use of blanket secret surveillance and cameras shows what a farce the concept of innocent until proven guilty is. It also shows how surveillance is used as an integral tool in punishing prisoners and exerting control over them. The prison service is far from neutral, and each prison contains a police liaison officer. Apparently, in the case of the Birmingham Six, and other high-profile cases, police officers masqueraded as screws.

---

47 PSI 22/012 part 1.3
48 Keith Rose, *Secret Squirrels at Work, 2013, IT*

# REHABILITATION?

"Rehabilitation, as a modern concept, is metaphorically derived from the ancient practice of banishment, whereby the individual lost his dignity by being cast naked into the wilderness to contemplate his anti-social behaviour...The French word 'habiller' means "to dress" or "to wrap up"; to be rehabilitated is to start life anew, once again fully "clothed" in the garb of respectability with one's dignity restored."[1]

David Cameron promised a so-called "rehabilitation revolution" in prisons. Governors were to be given greater autonomy over budgets, prisoners were to be not seen as "liabilities to be managed" but "assets to be harnessed"[2]. Michael Gove also talked of an "unremitting emphasis" on "reform, rehabilitation and redemption", quoting Winston Churchill's "treasure in the heart of every man" speech[3]. In a wildly irresponsible and unrealistic claim, Gove also promised an 'Earned Release' scheme in August 2015. This was to create opportunities for early release on 'Home Detention Curfew' after the completion of "serious educational activity"[4]. Many people I was inside with (especially mothers) were very excited about the prospect of this. However, unsurprisingly, the reality was further cuts to the prison system and early release was replaced by extended bang-up.

The concept of rehabilitation places all emphasis on the individual and negates the impact of broader social issues. Rehabilitation was a driving force behind reformist initiatives such as those led by Fry and other Victorian liberals. Quakers promoted rehabilitation in the UK and America. In

1 Faith, 2011
2 bbc.co.uk/news/uk-politics-20022794
3 gov.uk/government/speeches/the-treasure-in-the-heart-of-man-making-prisons-work
4 gov.uk/government/speeches/the-treasure-in-the-heart-of-man-making-prisons-work

1790, they built the Walnut Street Jail in Pennsylvania.

> "The Quakers believed that rehabilitation would occur through silent, solitary reflection, so everyone in the jail remained in solitary confinement. The idea was one of seeking penitence (sincere and humble regret for one's misdeeds). From this notion of penitence comes the modern word *penitentiary*."[5]

'Tackling Offending Behaviour' (TOB) courses are classic examples of this, where the 'offender' is required to lament at length about the motivations behind their crime and expected to take 'responsibility' for their actions (past and future). Kathleen Kendall has argued that "cognitive behaviourism is a governmental technology which obscures the pains of social exclusion and imprisonment."[6] The government emphasises the importance of readjustment and rehabilitation, whilst denying the inherent aspects of punishment and restrictions which are the back bone and main rationale for the existence of jail.

## WORK

> "The aim of Prison Industries is to occupy prisoners in out-of-cell activity [and wherever possible] to help them gain skills, qualifications and work experience to improve their employment prospects upon release...The desired outcomes from prison industries are: (i) to ensure dynamic security by providing purposeful activity at relatively low cost; and (ii) to support education, training, and employment (ETE) outcomes on release." *Prison Industries*[7]

As with many aspect of the prison society, England is leading the way in developing the tools of oppression and exploitation required to perpetuate its economy. Bros and Black have outlined the liberalisation of the more punitive aspects of the prison regime: "It is no coincidence that the introduction of IEP also coincided with the beginnings of the Prison Industrial Complex in the UK." Davis has further outlined this phenomenon, arguing that "corporations that are not directly involved in the punishment industry have begun to rely on prison labour"[8]; as a way to exploit a captive labour force without having to outsource labour to other countries. As Davis

5 Kilgore, 2015
6 Kathleen Kendall (in Carlen, 2002)
7 In Bros and Black, 2010
8 Davis, 2012

stated, the PIC is dependent on expansion to survive, and "prisons play a central role in the process of manufacturing crime and manufacturing criminals."[9]

9 Davis, 2012

## Context

> "Prisoners are on the front line of wage slavery and forced slave labour where refusal to work while in prison results in inhumane retaliation and participating in slave labour contributes to the mechanisms of exploitation."[10] *The Incarcerated Worker*

> "The labour by which the convict contributes to his own needs turns the thief into a docile worker."[11]

The average wage for a prisoner in 2016 was approximately £10 per week. When I was inside, our work party (the gym) was notoriously bad at remembering to pay us. In theory, for a full day's graft we should have got about £2.50. However, the reality was often much more like 85p. A few jobs offer slightly more pay. For example, my mates in Holloway (now shut down) worked as 'Specialist Cleaners' (aka 'Biohazard'). They would go in and clean up after incidents of self-harm, suicide, and medical emergencies, and could get paid around £10 an hour. If you are a 'Lifer' then you can apply to do 'Fine Cell'; a sewing initiative prisoners can complete in their cells. Fine Cell is a classic example of the exploitation of prison labour. According to the Fine Cell website, each piece takes a prisoner about 100 hours to create (the canvases I saw inside were very large and intricate); however each prisoner only gets about £20 for completing it. The Fine Cell charity website makes much of the "dignity in work and through this, dignity in life". The transformatory power of sewing is emphasised by the charity in the claim that "when a man gains self-respect he may start addressing his offensive behaviour."[12]

Most prisons require prisoners to do the daily grunt work of keeping them operating. This means they normally have job 'opportunities' (especially for non-enhanced prisoners) in the following areas: kitchens, gardens/maintenance, laundry, cleaning, gym. One jail I was in claimed to be a 'working jail', which meant it prided itself on having most prisoners allocated to a work party. When you arrived, you were put straight in gardens or kitchens. I played the vegan card, refused to work in the kitchen and made it straight into the gym. A lot of girls love working in the kitchen because you can get extra food. Personally, I hated going there even for meals

10 *The Incarcerated Worker (Volume One, Number One), Industrial Workers of the World, 2015*
11 Foucault, 1975
12 finecellwork.co.uk/

never mind working there every day. Also, you had to work weird shifts, and never got let out before a visit so you'd have to go stinking of the deep fried offal that permeated the dining hall and surrounding area.

> "If prisoners didn't cooperate with prison officials in maintaining and keeping this muthafucka up and running the days of prison will be over with. Prisoners do everything: cooking, cleaning, maintenance, cutting grass, painting, clerical work, loading and unloading trucks, manufacturing, instructing classes, farm work,etc."[13] *Michael Kimble*

Whilst jails are *dependent* on prison labour to keep them operating (and for their statistics and funding), there are often too many prisoners for the limited range of jobs they are allowed to do. This meant for example that on one small wing I was on (40 people) there were 20 wing cleaners! This worked out well for people who didn't want to do much work but still get paid, though it does mean you are 'behind your door' a lot.

## Corporations and Prison Labour

According to an article published in March 2017 by that bastion of Tory opinions, the Telegraph, prisoners currently bring in about £5.4 million for the government from work contracts. The Telegraph cited a report published by the 'Trades Union Congress for the UN International Labour Organisation', which includes examples of various corporations and companies who would have taken their business abroad if they hadn't been able to capitalise on the use of prison labour. There are currently 13,000 prisoner workplaces in 130 prisons. This is big business.

> "Prisoners are paid between £10 and £20 for a full working week... Many more leading companies are also relying on cheap prison labour to manufacture their goods. Sub-contractors for Virgin Atlantic, the airline, and Coca-Cola, have placed contracts with jails. Figures show that the turnover of prison industries and farms rose by more than ten per cent to £52.9 million in the 12 months to April this year, compared with the same period last year...Inspectors preparing the UN report found that inmates at Blakenhurst prison cleaned out concrete mixers for HSS Ltd and SES Ltd, two plant hire

13 Michael Kimble *'Up the Ante', in Wildfire An Anarchist Prison Newsletter NumberTwo, 2015*

companies. They also made trailer boards and lighting for roadworks for Maypole Ltd."[14]

As has been previously outlined in this publication, prison labour is yet another example of the ways in which the state reinforces gendered lines. In 2015 the ministry of defence secured a ten-year contract to use inmates of men's jails to create sandbags, fence posts and kit bags for the armed forces[15]. Lamble has highlighted the institutional use of this gendered labour and how it plays a key role in 'correctional' efforts at behaviour modification: "Historically women's prisons were designed to transform "fallen" women into better wives, mothers, home-makers, and domestic servants, whereas men's prisons were designed to transform males into disciplined individuals, productive workers, and masculine citizens."[16]

These patterns of control continue today, through the educational courses offered, and the types of work available to inmates within the prison system. Where those in men's jails are put to work doing fabrication and labouring, women's prisons offer such 'opportunities' as packing ear-phones and sewing for Top Shop. Charities also utilise prison labour *and* perpetuate gendered forms of exploitation. Those operating in women's prisons tend to only offer call-centre work, whereas Life Cycle UK have run an 'initiative' for years from HMP Bristol (a men's prison) which uses prisoners to rebuild and refurbish second hand bikes it can then sell on.

Argos, Topshop, Tesco, DHL, Virgin, Timpsons, Greggs, Boston Tea Party, Max Spielman and the Ministry of Defence, are just some of the examples of companies who profit from prison labour. As anarchist prisoner Sean Swain has observed: "prison labour is now an integral component of the global economy"[17]. Companies love to dress up the cheap labour they benefit from in the language of opportunity. Probation and the job centre will tell you repeatedly how difficult it is for ex-prisoners to find work. This is the rationale behind Prison Industries.

In 2012 the department of justice has re-branded the old 'Prison Industries Unit' as a new body called 'One3one Solutions'. They aimed to increase prison revenues to £130 million a year by 2021. One3one, which was named after the number of prisons in the UK estate at that time, has continued to develop, offering contracts to companies on every aspect of facilities management, from wood work to washing, engineering, printing

14 telegraph.co.uk/news/uknews/1368417/Top-names-rely-on-prison-workforce.html
15 politicshome.com/news/uk/home-affairs/news/64360/armed-forces-profit-prison-labour
16 Lamble in Stanley and Smith, 2015
17 Swain, in IWOC, 2016

and textiles. One3One is part of NOMS. Their website was last updated in August 2016:

> "We have over 100 locations across England and Wales, utilising a workforce of many motivated prisoners. Work helps prisoners to pay back their cost to society. We create high quality products and services for a whole range of businesses, including some household names as well as other government departments. We help businesses by working with them on a whole range of products and services. Our prices are set fairly with reference to the market with no element of public subsidy. We want to continue to support UK businesses, and we do not take work which results in the loss of jobs in the community."[18]

## Is It Worth It?

As with many aspects of prison life, I felt conflicted between my ideological position, and my daily life. Many anarchist prisoners have refused to work. However, I wanted to study fitness, and that meant working in the gym. The benefits of this were also that I could train much more, and most importantly, I could see my girlfriend. By using the opportunities that can arise from engaging with the prison labour system to your advantage, you can avoid discipline whilst staying true to your principles.

> "Prison work is slavish work; and slavish work cannot inspire a human being with the best inspiration of man – the need to work and to create. The prisoner may learn a handicraft, but he will never learn to love his work. In most instances, he will learn to hate it." *Peter Kropotkin*[19]

## Enhanced Jobs

In women's prisons, certain jobs are only available to those who are enhanced and this adds to the sense of a hierarchy of prisoner. Beware 'officer no keys'. Examples of jobs which are only available to those who are enhanced are being an 'Insider' (the name says it all; you have to work closely with screws to welcome the 'fresh meat' off the 'sweat boxes' and see them through the induction process), working for support services such

---

18 one3one.justice.gov.uk
19 Peter Kropotkin, *Prisons and Their Moral Influence on Prisoners,* 1887

as St Giles (the housing trust) and the National Careers Service, working in the chapel, the Peer Mentor jobs for the Rehabilitation and Addiction (RAPT) unit, and most jobs in education. One of the most problematic enhanced jobs I encountered was the 'Keep Out' initiative. Keep Out is a supposed "crime diversion scheme"[20]:

> "The first crime diversion scheme to be delivered by dedicated teams of serving prisoners – managed by civilian staff – inside UK prisons. Prisoners are trained by Keep Out to run intervention programmes for young people that inform, support and divert those between 13 and 17 who are either at risk of entering the criminal justice system or are already involved in criminal activity."

Keep Out was founded in 1996. The project works with 1,500 young people each year, and aims to change young people's attitudes and behaviours: "Prisoners on the Keep Out team share their personal experiences with the young people who attend the workshops. This helps them to reflect on their own previous offending behaviour, reinforces the lessons they have learnt and enables them to give something back to the community. Since the scheme started in 1996, over 500 prisoners have benefited from the Keep Out experience."[21]

As with many interventions aimed at modifying people's behaviour, Keep Out places the onus on the individual for their alleged 'offence' and uses peer pressure, guilt and shame as methods to get young people to think about their so-called 'anti-social behaviour'. Keep Out works closely with external agencies such as Youth Support Groups to select "the most suitable prisoners" for their projects.

As with many examples of reform the prisoners involved in delivering Keep Out sometimes had a slightly evangelical air about them, especially in relation to their 'crimes' and backgrounds. There was a definite sense from many involved in the programme that they had moved on from the situations that led to their crime, and into a place of 'pro-social behaviour'. This was also very clear in relation to the RAPT Peer Mentors who really got into the 'diseased vs clean' model of drug addiction treatment.

**Wages**

Labour contracts seen by the investigative website Exaro News show com-

20 crimediversionscheme.org.uk/
21 crimediversionscheme.org.uk/

panies are typically paying prisons the equivalent of around £2 an hour for prisoners' labour[22]. Of course, the prison takes a cut of this, and so the prisoner sees even less than this on their spends account (normally on average about £2 *per day*). Bowden has written extensively on this topic:

> "Prisons now replace factories where the new underclass are increasingly concentrated and forced to work as cheap labour for multi-national private security operations that now own and operate a significant portion of the American prison system. This new prison industrial complex is laying its roots in the UK too, and it is from the poorest industrialised communities that it draws its sources of cheap labour and human commodities."[23]

IN THE WOMEN'S WORK ROOM.

22 independent.co.uk/news/uk/politics/plan-for-cheap-prison-work-may-cost-thousands-of-jobs-7815140.html
23 Bowden, *Americanisation of the British Justice System, 2014*

## EDUCATION

Gender is imposed on individuals within the prison system at every level, and one of the more obvious expressions of this is the approach to 'education' commonly employed within women's prisons. In the remand prison I was in, most of the courses on offer read like something out of a 1950's women's magazine: nail art, beauty, family life, cookery and textiles. It is true that some of these courses are popular among people in jail. However, it is definitely *not* representative of the diversity of backgrounds and interests within the women's prison estate.

There are various ways inside to try to complete education without signing up to formal courses. Prison libraries have a wide range of reference books, and if you can wait a couple of weeks, staff will normally help reserve titles from local authority libraries. If you want to practice reading there is the 'Six Book Challenge' and The Shannon Trust have recently updated the old 'Toe-by-Toe' scheme to make it more appropriate for adult learners. 'Turning Pages' was launched towards the end of 2016 and it aims to help prisoners teach each other how to read, by doing small amounts of study every day.

There are often sociable less formal educational activities and these can be a good way to avoid bang-up and see people from other wings. During my sentence I studied Arabic. This was interesting and got me off the wing when it was early bang-up on Fridays. If you are artistic then the Koestler Prize might be worth entering. This is an annual exhibition of prisoners' art, from poetry to sculpture.

If you are musical (and don't mind interacting with the chapel) you may want to look up 'Changing Tunes' (they organise events such as the most terrible 'concert' I have ever been to -a Michael Jackson themed tribute). Changing Tunes "uses music teaching, rehearsing, recording, performance, improvisation and composition to aid the rehabilitation of prisoners and ex-prisoners."[24]

> "The common purpose of making music creates an environment for prisoners to improve self-esteem, build healthy relationships, and engage in an activity where hard work and perseverance brings rewards. These factors are major steps towards rehabilitation."[25]

If you are in a longer-term jail, you can sometimes do quite in-depth courses (up to NVQ level, A-level or equivalent); for example in catering, fitness, horticulture, textiles or hair and beauty. Most women's prisons don't offer many practical trade based courses at any in depth level. This is an ongoing bone of contention for many prisoners. Most jails offer access to Open University courses. There is normally a designated staff member who coordinates this. Be aware however that the OU application process can take *ages* inside.

If you want to do an education course there are various organisations who will help with funding. The 'Prisoners Education Trust' (PET) is the main one, but 'Women in Prison' and a few others also provide support. PET can help with grants for books and resources, and 'Women In Prison' funds more extended courses, as long as there is at least six months before your release date. See resources section.

**Mutual Aid**

There are strict rules inside about working with other inmates, see PSI 2015/017 'Prisoners Assisting other Prisoners'. Prisoners can write out apps and complaint forms for other prisoners. However, according to this PSI prisoners *must not* be relied on to provide support that staff should provide, and they *must* be appropriately selected and trained. Annex B of this PSI states that prisoners *can* provide assistance where "appropriate": with

24 changingtunes.org.uk
25 changingtunes.org.uk

transportation (for example helping on a ship out, or with moving wings), tidying someone's cell, accessing training/work, general moving and handling, and reading. Prisoners *cannot* help with intimate care (for example, assisting with food and drink, oral care, washing, dressing, toilet support or cleaning). Obviously, these rules get ignored on a daily basis, especially when helping support elderly or disabled prisoners who would otherwise be left to rot in their cells most of the time.

Unsurprisingly, prison staff don't like it when people inside become too autonomous or organised. We had a good outside training crew at the weekend when the gym was closed, but that quickly got shut down due to 'health and safety issues'. The concept of 'health and safety' in jail is a huge stick to beat inmates over the head with and legitimise the end to all sorts of prisoner-led initiatives, as is the potential for 'bullying'. Bullying does occur inside, especially in relation to alleged sex-offenders. It isn't unheard of for prisoners to demand some perks off canteen, or guilt trip others into ordering stuff for them, especially if drugs are involved. However, this manipulation doesn't happen that often. That said, as with all aspects of prison life, it is important never to get complacent and if English isn't your first language always get someone to double check what is being done for you, especially if it is legal support.

You will earn money through attending education courses, though as with work it will be a negligible amount. Failure to complete a course, or attend, is disciplined in the same manner that work is, so you should expect all the usual 'loss of...' restrictions if you decide a course is not for you. Because of this, it is important to think carefully before signing up to a course (especially a long one). Prison staff will not make it easy for you to quit a course (they hate anything that makes their statistics look bad) especially if the course isn't popular. Before you sign up to anything, ask people who've already completed it what they thought.

## PSYCHOLOGY AND PRISON

"It is often precisely when the prison medical and psychiatric apparatuses are "working well" that they are mobilising some of their most fundamental violence against people's already fragile sense of bodily integrity and emotional well-being." *Dylan Rodriguez*[26]

---

26 Rogriguez, *Forced Passages: Imprisoned Radical Intellectuals and the U.S. Prison Regime*, 2005

> "Psychological torture is extremely painful and, some may say, worse than the physical kind. Orders are barked and failure to jump high enough leads to further abuse and, often, assault." *Kevan Thakrar*[27]

Being in prison is a form of ongoing psychological warfare. 'Safety in Custody' is an initiative which supposedly promotes mental health inside. In women's prisons, the 'Safer Custody' team wield a huge amount of unspoken power. They can decide issues around seg, basic, ACCTs, transfers and so on. The *Safety in Custody* report 2016 makes for grim reading, and it is important to note that as this is a governmental report, the reality is probably much worse[28]. There can be *no such thing* as safety in custody. The prison system and all the apparatus that supports it are inherently violent.

> "The act of putting people in cages is a form of violence in itself. Such violence leads to extremely high rates of self-harm and suicide, both in prison, and following release. These problems are neither exceptional nor occasional; violence is endemic to prisons."[29]

According to the PRT, in 2015, 10% of prisoners (9,458) self-harmed in 2015. This practice was especially acute in women's prisons. In 2015 women accounted for 23% of self-harm incidents of self-harm despite only representing 5% of the total prison population[30].

The jargon around mental health in jail has major repercussions on people's sentence plans, parole hearings, IEP status and the physical location they are situated in within the prison. The Department of Health stated that about 21,000 people – nearly a quarter of the total prison population of –have bipolar disorder, depression or personality disorders. Other studies show that around a quarter of women and 15% of men in prison have experienced "psychotic episodes". The rate of this among the general public

---

27 Thakrar, long-term CSC prisoner, Open Letter, 2016
28 *Safety in Custody* report overview 2016 (gov.uk/government/statistics/safety-in-custody-quarterly-update-to-june-2016) Deaths in custody were up 38%, self-harm was up 26% with 37,784 recorded incidences; nearly one incident for every two prisoners within the estate. Prisoner on prisoner assault was up 28% (18,510 assaults), and assaults on staff were up 40%. 19 women died in UK prisons up to September 2016, the highest rate in over a decade (this included eight suicides; six of these were incarcerated for minor convictions such as shoplifting or breaching a community order).
29 Stanley and Smith, 2015
30 PRT, *Bromley Briefing, 2015*

is about 4%[31].

In a chicken and egg type situation it is sometimes unclear if people are inside because of their 'disorder' or if their incarceration has caused this. Post-Traumatic Stress Disorder (PTSD) majorly impacts on people's health in prison, and will be discussed in part two of this publication.

People with learning difficulties are massively over-represented within the prison estate, as are people with autism and Asperger's syndrome. Prisoners with autism can be particularly affected by conditions inside due to their heightened sound awareness and need for strict routine. The prevalence of autism spectrum disorder is much higher in the prison population than outside, and research has shown that juries are often prejudiced against those with ASD. Matt W, prisoner at HMP Rye Hill has outlined the conditions and issues for people with Asperger's inside:

> "Very few staff, let alone prisoners, understand or even believe in Asperger's and its effects on an individual. Within the current state of prisons, I constantly battle with anxiety from one day to the next, not knowing if my routine will change unexpectedly...Quite often I am branded a nuisance by staff, and a 'difficult prisoner' or 'serial complainer'. I just get so confused by my environment."[32]

**Treatment**

> "It is important that there is wider public recognition of the impossibility of delivering adequate health care in many prisons at present." *Royal College of Psychiatrists*[33]

As has been outlined in the chapter on drugs inside, the treatment model within women's prisons is inherently damaging. People are forced to comply with residential 'therapy' programmes as part of their sentence plan, and this often involves segregation and isolation.

The history of medicine and criminology are full of examples of ways in which medicine in the UK has a class based offensive. Cleanliness has long been associated with discipline and order; and in contrast to this disease becomes an expression of physical disorder. Within this context, criminality is viewed as an example of social disorder, a contagion that must be stopped. The medical model of female deviance promotes stereotypes,

31 gov.uk/government/policies/mental-health-service-reform
32 insidetime.org/please-try-to-understand-me/
33 rcpsych.ac.uk/pdf/TheMentalHealthPrisoners2007.pdf

especially around sex-work. The contradiction of women's prisons is that inmates are vilified for their criminal cunning, whilst being patronised as examples of female feeble mindedness.

*The CJS is not* a benevolent system. It is not uncommon to hear of people dying after repeatedly asking for help and staff failing to respond even when people have been on an 'ACCT'. In Bronzefield someone had been ringing their bell for two and a half hours after overdosing but wanting help. In 2006, the Corston Report famously investigated HMP Styal after six women died there between 2002-2003[34]. The report made 43 recommendations surrounding "prisoners vulnerabilities", none of which have been implemented.

## Self-harm and Suicide

"The MoJ is presiding over a blood bath of assaults, suicides and self-injury in prisons." [35]

According to research conducted by Lord Falconer, a Labour Peer, every four days someone in prison takes their own life[36]. This does not account for the 'deaths in custody' which are an extreme expression of the violence of the prison estate.

Cutting up (slashing) is the main form of self-harm that occurs in women's prisons. But DSH (deliberate self-harm) takes many forms: injuries, swallowing toxic substances, scratching and scouring (especially the face) are common occurrences in jail. These practises are often reactions to the loss of control and stress that people face; especially when on remand or waiting parole, and are an outward expression of the pain of the prison population. Nothing the prison can do will *ever* alleviate this. It is *because* of the prison system that these behaviours occur.

## Shame

"It may be somewhat paradoxical to refer to shame as a feeling, for while shame is initially painful, constant shaming leads to a deadening of feeling. Shame, like cold is, in essence, the absence of warmth. And when it reaches intensity, shame is experienced, like cold, as a deadness. In Dante's In-

34 justice.gov.uk/publications/docs/corston-report-march-2007.pdf
35 Deborah Coles, Inquest (inquest.org.uk) and Howard League for Penal Reform, *Prison Statistics Reveal a Bloodbath of Assaults, Suicide and Self-injury, 2016*
36 Howard League, *2016*

ferno the lowest circle of hell was a region not of flames, but of ice, absolute coldness." *James Gilligan[37]*

Feelings of guilt and shame are high within the women's prison estate, and this is why so many people turn to self-harm and drugs. The prison encourages a culture of dependency through an over-reliance on staff and a total lack of autonomy. Some individuals constantly seek the approval of the screws and are dependent on them for much of their emotional wellbeing. Of course, staff do little to discourage this, especially if it means individuals are working harder; or snitching. Even if you are an anarchist and strongly disagree with authority; constant vigilance is required to keep your guard up in jail in the face of the continuous psychological onslaught. As Weir described in *A Passion for Freedom*:

> "Prison is a microcosm of the world outside, a kind of caricature that you're stuck in. There's nowhere to hide, so you become socialised to some extent whether you like it or not... The times that I came within inches of this participatory oppression were the worst for me, and the kind of reality they are aiming for filled me with disgust. You'd like to spit in the screws eye and tell her to wipe the smile off her face when she comes to unlock you in the morning, but you can actually end up saying "good morning."[38]

Many women are often too ashamed to prepare their kids for the idea of them going to jail. This happened to my pad-mate who was in for shoplifting (mainly to get money to support her children). Her duty solicitor had told her it was highly unlikely she would get a custodial sentence, so she didn't tell her kids she was going to court because she didn't want to scare them. She then got a three-month sentence.

## Support Inside?

> "We, who live in prison, and in whose lives there is no event but bitter sorrow, have to measure time by throbs of pain, and the record of bitter moments." *Oscar Wilde[39]*

The 'Listeners' are fellow prisoners trained by the Samaritans[40]. You

37 James Gilligan, *Violence: Reflections on a National Epidemic, 1997*
38 Weir, 2010
39 Wilde, *De Profundis, 1897*
40 Note that Samaritans call centre volunteers now have to agree to pass on information to the police.

should be allowed to call them any time day or night, just press your cell bell. The Listeners have been active in jails since the 1980's when suicides in custody increased. The scheme runs in most jails. Listeners can't provide advice, but they can provide emotional support, and a friendly ear. Sometimes they might also give you a fag if you smoke and are desperate (though prisons increasingly discourage this!). A word of caution: do not assume everything you say to a Listener will remain confidential. As with all aspects of prison life; it's about finding a balance between maintaining a distance and security, with the need to occasionally off load/mouth off. A further word of warning; some of the Listeners I knew in jail were solid, reliable and caring people. But some who did the training were not. The Listeners seem to attract quite a lot of people who are looking to get (or maintain) their enhancement or who are just plain nosy.

If you don't want to call out a Listener, but you would like a general chat then 'Safer Custody' train wing-reps to do 'walkabouts' around the jail. These are other prisoners who can listen to your issues. They should only take matters further *if* you instruct them, but again, the reality is that this post (a voluntary position within the prison) is often filled by people who are looking to get their HDC/tag or become 'enhanced' so, as ever, never assume confidentiality. Safer Custody Reps can help with things like 'distraction packs' (colouring in and sudoku), puzzles and board games if you want something to take your mind off the grimness of prison life for a few minutes.

Another support service which you can access via healthcare is a 'Sleep Clinic'. Unsurprisingly, many people develop insomnia inside. The combination of stress, artificial lighting, being locked in, having a pad mate who snores (or even someone across the landing if they are that noisy!), thin prison issue mattresses, and the clumsy night staff shining lights in through your hatch and jangling keys does not make for a good night's kip! Some people seemed to get a lot out of the Sleep Clinic, though I'm not sure what it involves exactly.

In some jails, there is a new network called 'Hearing Voices'. According to the network, hearing voices is a common experience inside. 25% women and 15% men in jail hear voices. "The Hearing Voices Network hold staff facilitated discussions, and encourage peer support model." 1,000 screws have been trained in this programme.[41]

If you have mental health issues and you want to go down an official route you can get put on an ACCT. This will mean you get a hell of a lot

41 hearing-voices.org/

more attention from screws. You will be subject to cell observations, suicide watch and 'quality conversations'. The sad truth is that some people get a lot out of these conversations (which are meant to be an extended look in to how the individual is feeling.) A word of warning if you are thinking about going on an ACCT. If it's conversation you're after, the screws often don't bother fulfilling this requirement, unless they are trying to get 'intelligence'. As with any aspect of mental health services inside, once you have been put on an ACCT, it is difficult to go back under the radar of the prison staff. The same is true if you get put on a 'WAVE' book (the anti-bullying book).

> "Prison is a site of pain, and unnecessary psychological games justified by the need to "keep the inmates on their toes, so they don't know what's going on". It is like a vase, jarred by running careless hands, toppling to the floor and spraying a pattern of heartbreak underfoot."[42]

There are many other random ways to try to improve your mental health inside without talking to the screws:
- Go outside; get some vitamin D
- Do a cell work out or go to the gym (see 'Health')
- Listen to loud music
- Chat to your mates (inside/phone/visits)
- Write a letter/poem/story or draw a picture
- Have a wank!
- See if there are any activities coming up (sometimes the prison will organise a movie screening/bingo/card club etc...all fairly tedious but passes a bit of time and can be good way to see other people off your wing).
- If you are over 50 your jail may have a project called 'Rubies'[43] (though one of my mates went and said it was an hour of women fighting over knitting needles!)
- Put a general application in to see the 'PAT' dog (Pets As Therapy) warning, the one who came into our jail was lovely but he *stank!* I ain't fussy about smells and I love dogs but it was almost suffocating in the sealed classroom.
- Do some yoga or meditation in your cell (National Prison Radio do guided sessions twice a week)

42 Imarisha, 2016
43 insidetime.org/the-rubies/

- Clean your cell/room/yard
- Take some drugs/hooch if you can find some
...Basically *anything* is better than talking to the screws about your mental health.

It's a cliché but true that prison teaches you to savour really simple things in life. Even if you are on basic there are always little things; a kind note or silly joke from a friend, the sound of the wind outside, sunlight through your window. For all the days that drag on interminably in a fog of predictability and frustration these moments are so precious.

## Programmes

There are two main 'prisons within prisons' aimed at 'behaviour modification' in the women's prison estate: 'Psychologically Informed Planned Environments' (PIPEs) and the 'Therapeutic Community' (TC). A lot of longer term prisoners will get one (or even both) of these programmes slapped on their sentence plan. Both TC and PIPEs involve a lot of group work, and therapy activities such as drama or art therapy. TC is a much more secure unit; it really is a prison-within-a-prison, with survivors of abuse locked up alongside *a lot* of people convicted for sex offences (because the wing is much more secure this is where the jail tends to shove high-risk prisoners). Inmates doing TC have to eat on their wing; and it is very difficult to get on or off there. Because of this, it can all get very personal. TC members can use the gym. They can also use the library; but under closer supervision than most prisoners. Speaking to people doing TC, it seemed really invasive to me. All the sessions of therapy are led by screws, who people tend to become much closer to than on other wings (there is a certain amount of 'Stockholm Syndrome' that occurs with these programmes). People graduate from TC after varying amounts of time; anything between six-18 months. Because some girls are desperate to get off it (and people are forced to live in such close proximity) there can be a lot of bitching and snitching.

PIPEs is also residential, but the wing is not locked off like TC. The aim of PIPEs is to help prisoners towards the end of their sentence to consolidate what they might have 'learnt' in jail. "PIPEs are specifically designed contained environments. Professionals in PIPEs work with the residents to consolidate learning and to form and maintain positive pro-social relationships.. A PIPE unit is designed to provide a socially encouraging environment that may not otherwise be available in a prison estate".[44]

The PIPE unit is allegedly a bridge between prison and the 'community'. It has extra wing staff (specially trained), psychologists and structured group sessions. It combines the types of activities people chose to engage in their leisure time (for example cooking, music), with programmes aimed at developing confidence and relationships for release. People with 'personality disorders' are often referred onto PIPEs[45]. In theory, the referral *must* come from the prisoner; it cannot be forced on by staff. However, the reality is that many people have it added to their sentence plan, or coerced into it. PIPEs last anything from six months to two years.

A word of caution. If you think that you might want to do TC or PIPEs, think *very* carefully before you sign up. It is notoriously difficult to get out of education in jail, and these two courses are the worst for this. Once you've been issued a place, it is very difficult to get off, and any attempts to do so will be taken as evidence of how deep-rooted your supposed "offending behaviour" is, and may well end up in disciplinary action.

Another (non-residential) course that gets slapped on most people's sentence plans is 'The Sycamore Tree'. This is a 'restorative justice' programme:

> "Sycamore Tree is a victim awareness programme that teaches offenders the principles of restorative justice. The course is a powerful rehabilitative tool that can initiate change and encourage an offender to desist from crime."[46]

The Sycamore Tree Project is an accredited course delivered in prisons across the UK. The course is made up of six sessions of two-and-a-half hours, culminating in meeting the 'victim' of a crime.

> "Sycamore Tree gives participants the opportunity to think about their lives, using knowledge and experiences to inform their attitudes and underpin a change in behaviour. It is intended to be a turning point that encourages change of direction."[47]

The reality is that Sycamore Tree is yet another tool used by the prison to

44 Tully, *Forensic Psychology* (tullyforensicpsychology.com/)
45 Note that the use of the label 'personality disorder' is also a gendered term, and is often used to describe people the state perceives to be women who do not conform with acceptable gender norms.
46 Sycamore Tree (prisonfellowship.org.uk/what-we-do/sycamore-tree/)
47 Sycamore Tree

get inmates to repent and lament their 'crime'. I refused to do the course because I had no intention of dealing with my 'offending behaviour' but my understanding; based on seeing the faces of friends who were completing the programme, is that it is just a protracted and painful way to basically get prisoners to feel like they are terrible people.

## REFORM

> "Liberation rather than reform, and the abolition of genocide rather than genocide management." *Rodriguez*[48]

As has already been outlined, many reformist organisations exist along gendered lines. 'Women in Prison' (WIP) is the most obvious example of this. WIP provides funding for inmates in women's jails, and raises awareness on some of the issues facing people within this part of the prison estate:

> "Women in Prison supports women to avoid, survive and exit the criminal justice system and campaigns for the radical changes needed to deliver justice for women. Our vision is of a world without women's prisons. A world where the abuse, marginalisation and poverty at the root of so much of women's offending is addressed before women come into contact with the criminal justice system...Women that pose no risk to the public should not be in prison. For the very few where prison is deemed absolutely necessary, women should be incarcerated in specially designed small units, close to the communities in which they live."[49]

WIP offers support to individuals engaged within the women's prison system throughout their sentence, from legal advice to 'through the gate' assistance. Women in Prison also runs three Women Centres -Women Matta in Manchester, the Beth Centre in Lambeth and the Women's Support Centre in Woking.

> "The key to what we do is that our support for women is holistic; our Women Centres are one-stop-shops for women to access all the services they need under one roof. WIP's staff are gender-specialist practitioners, providing support across

---

48 Rodriguez, *Suspended Apocalypse: White Supremacy, Genocide, and the Filipino Condition*, 2009
49 womeninprison.org.uk/about/who-we-are.php

all the difficulties and barriers commonly experienced by women affected by the criminal justice system -domestic and sexual violence, poor mental and physical health, addiction, homelessness, debt, and unemployment."[50]

It is undoubtedly true that many women within the criminal justice system face a complex matrix of issues, as outlined above. Many women inside are the survivors of abusive relationships and sexual violence. But any attempts to address these issues by working with the state-or supporting it's so-called 'therapeutic interventions' are doomed to failure. WIP perpetuates the discourse around women as victims, and does not operate within men's jails, therefore ignoring the trans people housed within these walls. WIP consistently refers to the issues individuals face in relation to their families as being one of the main driving forces and rationales behind the organisations existence. This is highly problematic as it negates the impact that *all* custodial sentences have on the families of the individual in custody. It also implies a hierarchy of suffering, whereby mothers are given greater status than those without children.

> "The prison itself was born from early reformers' calls to replace corporal and capital punishment with the extended loss of liberty. Imprisonment, reformers argued, would provide the opportunity for those convicted of crimes to reform themselves through hard work, silence and solitude." [51]

Like hate crime legislation, reformist agendas merely perpetuate the issues they supposedly try to resolve. There is *no* safe way to reform the prison system. Gender specific institutions have just led to the expansion of the PIC, and this has led to more women being banged-up. The answer is *not* more prisons, better prisons, or different types of prisons. But no prisons at all.

> "Prison reforms, however well-intentioned, have tended to extend the life and scope of prisons. So-called "gender-responsive" prisons are a prime example; reforms intend to address the needs of women have led to an increased punishment and imprisonment of women, not less."[52]

Lamble has outlined the dangers of the LGBTQIA community becoming

50 womeninprison.org.uk/about/who-we-are.php
51 Law, 2012
52 Lamble, in Stanley and Smith, 2015

complicit in prison expansion, highlighting how the 'criminal justice system' fails to protect women from domestic violence. The prison/police will never keep us safe. Even a former senior Home Office Researcher, Carol Heddermann has noted: "Prisons will never be an effective crime-control tool because the evidence clearly demonstrates that it actively creates or compounds the factors that contribute to offending."[53]

53 independent.co.uk/news/uk/home-news/womens-prison-numbers-rising-faster-than-men-2022887.html

# LONG-TERM PRISONERS

## 'Indeterminate Sentence Prisoners' (ISPs)

"Stacked life upon life, year upon year,
Rising upwards in four tiers,
Landings and centre like a giant clock wheel,
Stands the warehouse of lost years."[1]
*Mark D Lawless*

"It is time we opened our eyes. Our prison system is geared to
torment it's human stock, to lock us away in concrete tombs
and cages, degrade us, strip us of our identity, punish us mentally and physically, and leave us to rot and die a thousand
deaths." *John Steele*[2]

There are many types of sentence and this chapter will explore some of
the differences between them; mainly 'Lifers' and 'IPP' (Imprisonment
for Public Protection) prisoners. Most prisoners are 'determinate' or 'fixed
term prisoners', (i.e. they have a release date) and do not have to sit a parole board before being released. However, there are various categories of
prisoners who are serving longer sentences.

All prisoners subject to Life imprisonment or IPP are now, for the purposes of their management, classed as indeterminate sentence prisoners
(ISPs). ISP people have *no* automatic right to be released, instead they are
given a 'tariff'. The parole board are responsible for the decision on the
release date of ISP people. A key document for both IPP and Lifers is the

---

1 Lawless, *Ode to Strangeways*
2 John Steele, *The Bird that Never Flew: The Uncompromisng Autobiography of One of
the Most Punished Prisoners in the History of the Btitish Penal System, 2002*

*Indeterminate Sentence Manual*[3]. Many of its chapters have been cancelled and replaced (see appendix 12), but it is still the legal backbone of these sentences. Also, PSI 36/2010 'Serving the Indeterminate Sentence' provides detailed information.

## Imprisonment for Public Protection (IPP)

In 2005 David Blunkett introduced IPP sentences for "violent or sexual offences". The rationale was that individuals would be kept away from the public as long as they posed a threat. As with many aspects of the CJS this is a total contradiction: IPP prisoners are allegedly "too dangerous to be released" yet category A prisoners get released every day. IPP prisoners were given a 'tariff' and could then apply for release, much as a Lifer does, through the parole board. IPP prisoners were supposed to be too dangerous to be given a fixed sentence, but not so serious as to warrant a life sentence.

There are currently 11,178 people in prison are serving a life or other form of indeterminate sentence[4]. This is roughly 16% of the total prison population. Of these 3,859 are serving an indeterminate sentence of Imprisonment for Public Protection (IPP). 81% of IPP prisoners are held over tariff, by an average length of 44 months (but many for *considerably* longer). For example, one of my mates got a 14-month tariff for robbery but has now been in for *12 years*. Unsurprisingly, IPP prisoners have the highest level of self-harm of any group in the prison system, with 550 incidents for every 1,000 inmates. Being an IPP prisoner is *extremely* stressful, as a friend outlined:

> "We can't plan for the future because we don't know where we will be. Not only that but even when we are released we still have to do a minimum on licence, such as ten or more years. I got a four-year tariff on my IPP sentence for arson. I don't know why there's a tariff because everyone goes over."

In IPPs were abolished as part of the 2012 'Legal Aid, Sentencing and Punishment of Offenders Bill' (LASPO). The case of R (Guittard) V Secretary of state for justice was successful and some IPP prisoners were transferred to open conditions outside of the parole process, if their 'dossier and review' were in place. This precedent became known as the 'Guittard Prin-

---

3 justice.gov.uk/offenders/psos/pso-4700-indeterminate-sentence-manual
4 prisonreformtrust.org.uk/PressPolicy/News/ItemId/375/vw/1

ciples.'[5]

Technically, as of November 2016, IPP prisoners can be released by the parole board *without* an oral hearing. However, as with many aspects of law, the onus seems to be on the individual to flag this up and remind the parole board of this new legislation (most cases still rely on the old fashioned methods of oral hearings and there is a massive backlog). Despite the use of IPP being scrapped, there are still *huge* administrative delays with the process of releasing IPP prisoners.

In 2012, the European Court of Human Rights stated that it was a violation of prisoners' human rights if they were subject to continued detention beyond expiry of minimum term of sentence without access to rehabilitative courses[6]. However, in 2014, a Supreme Court ruling said that the state has duty to provide this *but* this does not affect the lawfulness of detention. All the 2012 ECHR ruling meant is that Lifers and IPP prisoners have to complete loads of ridiculous courses that get put on their sentence plans to 'prove' they are ready for release and parole. One of my mates who is an IPP prisoner had done 'Dialectical Behaviour Therapy', an analysis of 'Dangerous Serious Personality Disorder', PIPES, and 'Sycamore Tree'. She was a reliable worker, and didn't kick off (in order to attempt to get parole). However, despite all this, she then get a two year parole knock back for cutting her hair. Apparently this sign of "impulsive behaviour" meant she wasn't ready to go back into the 'community'. Another person was given a knock back and put on basic for chewing a tablet at the meds hatch in the wrong way. These examples show that there is no end to the number of hoops IPP prisoners have to jump through, and even when they are released, this continues. As the campaign group 'Smash IPP' has argued:

> "Even if IPP prisoners manage to jump through the hoops and convince the parole boards that they are no longer a "danger to the public", the sentence carries a 99 year license, meaning that they face arbitrary conditions on their freedom and can be recalled to prison at any time for something that's not even considered a crime. Even politician David Blunkett, whose idea the disastrous Criminal Justice Act of 2003 was, admitted that "we certainly got the implementation wrong".[7]

Ken Clark (the former secretary of state for justice) has called for a re-

5 insidetime.org/guittard-applications/
6 theguardian.com/law/2012/sep/18/strasbourg-judges-indeterminate-sentences-unlawful
7 smashipp.wordpress.com

view of IPP prisoners, saying their incarceration was a "stain on the justice system". The whole CJS is a stain! In 2015, a briefing paper entitled *Sentences of IPP*[8] was heard in the house of commons. It outlined the main concerns in relation to IPP prisoners:

- 'Offenders' given very short tariff then kept in way beyond
- Administrative delays created uncertainty and stress
- IPP increase contributes to prison overcrowding
- Provision is too broad
- Strain on parole board due to many short tariff IPP prisoners having to access specifics to demonstrate no longer a risk
- More than three quarters of IPP prisoners are now post-tariff
- IPP and Life sentences increased by 6% and 31% respectively

**Lifers**

'Lifers' have been given a mandatory life sentence. The *starting* point is 15 years if not for financial gain (30 years if financial). This then increases depending on the number of alleged victims the prisoner had. The 'financial gain' clause covers a huge range of 'offences'. One of my mates has experienced the sharp end of this legislation:

> "I got 30 year start because £20.00 was taken from the victims bank account after their death, despite me handing in six credit cards. The £20 was for a key metre in his flat. The judge took six years off because I didn't take more (the victim had £1.6 million in his accounts). I am up for parole in 2032 but I won't get it because I am not guilty so I refuse to do programmes like Sycamore Tree or deal with my supposed "offending-behaviour".

As with IPP prisoners, it's really a daily challenge for Lifers to get through their sentence and fair play to any one doing this without resorting to snitching and bitching. Some advice from a beautiful, fiery lifer I love:

> "Surround yourself with positive people. Keep in contact with those you love on the outside. Inside-build relationships with a few people but avoid drama/mix up. It's important that people will understand that you'll have good and bad days and who listen don't just off load and judge. Read for escapism. Sing and dance like you are on your       own.   For   some

8 researchbriefings.files.parliament.uk/documents/SN06086/SN06086.pdf

people, it's the gym. Take care of yourself and your room, decorate it, make it personal. Spend as much time outdoors as possible. Always listen to others even the dull, ignorant and judgemental as we all have issues, and sometimes they just need an ear. Go to bed at night time with a clear conscience, know that you have done all that you can in that day. Don't dwell on the stuff outside your control. Ignore staff and their silly games and attitudes. Most of all: laugh and smile."

There is a further category of prisoner called a 'Two-strike Lifer'. This was used by Chris Grayling for "people who commit "the most serious" violent or sexual crimes more than once"[9]. During his time as justice secretary, Grayling used LASPO to introduce this regime where those given two prison terms lasting more than ten years would be upgraded to the greater punishment, an automatic life sentence. There are currently 3,000 two-strikers in jail over their tariff. Many of these individuals are housed in 'Dangerous Personality Disorder Units'. ECHR has stated that the two-strike act is inhumane as prisoners have no release date and very little chance of getting out.

### Extended Determinate Sentences (EDS)

In December 2012 LASPO was also used to introduce 'Extended Determinate Sentences' (EDS). These replaced IPPs. EDS sentences are used where the defendant has been convicted of specified offence (sexual or violent as listed in CJA 2003) and the court deemed them to be a substantial risk of harm through re-offending (using the same frameworks and tests as IPP)[10]. However, the court is *not* required to impose life sentence.

EDS prisoners face a long custodial plus an extra-long licence period. There is no minimum or maximum; the broad guidelines are five years for violent offences and eight for sex offences. EDS prisoners can apply for parole after two thirds of sentence served. This is at the discretion of the individual prison when they work out your release date on sentencing. Like IPPs used to be, release from an EDS is determined by an oral hearing to the parole board[11].

---

9 bbc.co.uk/news/uk-politics-19887793

10 converseprisonnews.com/the-legal-aid-sentencing-and-punishment-of-offenders-laspo-act-2012/

11 gov.uk/government/uploads/system/uploads/attachment_data/file/317735/guidance-on-laspo.pdf

## Parole and Re-categorisation

Because *so* many people have to apply for parole, the parole board is a bottle neck for prisoners trying to get released. In 2015 the back log was 3,163 cases. In 2017 this went down to 2,030 but it's still a clear example of how this system does not work, and many of the people waiting parole clearance are over-tariff IPP prisoners. The parole board is also incapable of dealing with the high volume of prisoners who are recalled (it oversees cases of "fixed term recall" and conducts oral hearings for them)[12].

Prisoners hoping to get parole must make a dossier to show they have addressed all risk concerns connected to their 'offence' and demonstrate clear benefits to being transferred back into society. So, it basically involves total and utter compliance with whatever the prison system and CJS throw at you. You can currently get legal aid for parole board.

> "Prisoners may also have their security category reviewed whenever there has been a significant change in their circumstances or behaviour that impacts on the level of security required, whether negative or positive, e.g. a key piece of offending behaviour work or a detoxification or opiate substitute maintenance regime is completed." PAS[13]

Life and IPP sentence prisoners can only be transferred to open conditions following a recommendation by the parole board and/or a decision by the secretary of state to grant them open status. If you have an indeterminate sentence you can potentially be categorised at the 'Sentence Planning and Review' meetings which occur every 12 months of your sentence. If you have a determinate sentence of over four years, this review will also be every 12 months (becoming bi-annual two years before release date). For all other prisoners, these should happen roughly every six months.

## Appeals and Maintaining Innocence

ISP prisoners who maintain their innocence/not guilty status will potentially never get out of jail, because the whole process of applying for parole is based on admitting guilt and repenting for your crime. If you are an ISP and you refuse to complete your sentence plan, the jail will do all that it can to bring you down. You may well get shipped out, given the worst jobs, and persecuted by prison staff. The prison system *hates* any one with

---

12 nao.org.uk/wp-content/uploads/2017/02/Investigation-into-the-Parole-Board.pdf
13 PAS, *Information Sheet Categorisation – Women Prisoners, updated 2016*

a rebellious heart, especially if you are an ISP. Going for an appeal can be hard, but you have no choice if you want to get out of the dump. One of my mates gave this advice for people embarking on the appeal process:

> "Never lose hope. Find fresh evidence that wasn't bought up during trial. Go through all legal documents to prove a wrongful/unsafe conviction; find loop holes yourself (don't rely on solicitor), find a friend inside you can trust (beware most girls). Get friends     inside to help with legal aid forms. Have a good support network inside and out. Try to find other prisoners also going through the appeal process that you can trust. Learn your legal paperwork inside out and keep it with you, even if they try to get you with "volumetric control". Don't let OMU or officers know about your appeal. Don't trust them, especially personal officers."

If you consistently deny your offence, in theory the parole board *must* consider this. 'Denial' is a heterogeneous issue. You will need specialist assessments to explain why you haven't completed your sentence plan.

The MoJ uses a 'Seven Pathways Model' for those 'deniers' who are going for parole. This is meant to show other ways risk can be reduced without an admission of guilt. For example, engaging with education, giving up drugs/alcohol, changing attitudes and so on. Maintaining innocence *shouldn't* impact on IEP status in theory, though as I've said, nothing winds screws up more than those who refuse to comply, so don't expect to get many 'privileges'.

PSI 39/2011, 'The Re-categorisation of Women' outlines how individuals *can* refuse to do offence-related work without being penalised, provided their 'risk' is reduced sufficiently to be re-categorised. In theory, the parole board is concerned with *risk* not *guilt,* and the PSIs state that the board *cannot* refuse to release someone due to maintaining innocence. However *risk* still implies *guilt*. It is highly problematic to say that someone who has not committed a crime is still a risk to society. PSI 36/2010: 'Serving the Indeterminate Sentence' also states that it is unlawful for the parole board to refuse to consider the question of release solely on the grounds the prisoner denies guilt.

If you are convicted of a sexual offence then it will be more difficult to get parole if you maintain your innocence. PSI 19/2014 outlines sentence planning. The 'Sex Offenders Treatment Programme' requires an admission of guilt from the outset.

Preparation for the parole board is epic. You must also complete a member case assessment [MCA] before your case is heard, and a MCA member must know all about your case. For more information see: *A Guide to Help with Your Parole Review* (Easy Read Guide)[14]. Also *Preparing for your Parole Oral Hearing*[15]. Please note, I have deliberately *not* included too much information about conducting an appeals process, or too much information about sitting a parole board because these are massive topics and vary from prisoner to prisoner. Please get legal advice on these issues from a solicitor.

> "The emotional process of preparing for parole is hard. You have to be really careful not to get any negative IEPs or put on basic. I have to be really careful of what my mates are doing and my partner because it has an impact on me. My girlfriend was really naughty when we got together, now she finds it hard to be good." *A mate serving an IPP sentence*

## Supporting a Long-term Prisoner

If you are inside there are basic things you can do to support someone who is ISP. Try to help them stay positive, and don't go on about your release date. If they are struggling with their mental health, remind them how strong they have been to get this far. Don't try to fill them with false hope, they are undoubtedly cynical about the system and have witnessed all its grotesqueness before you even got sentenced. Try to listen and encourage them to maintain some connection with the outside world). Keep them distracted, and keep their rage directed at the poxy system rather than themselves. Here are some thoughts on support from an IPP prisoner:

> "I have support from my family, on visits and so on. Girls in here help too. There are a few women in this jail who are IPP. A lot of my friends are Lifers. Last year I had a two year parole knock-backs and a lot of psychological reports. This was tough. You have to prepare a lot of reports as an IPP: for OMU, for psychologists."

> "Friends outside are great at helping with legal stuff, espe-

---

14 gov.uk/government/uploads/system/uploads/attachment_data/file/444706/A_guide_to_
help_you_with_your_Parole_Review_-_Easyread_Booklet_2015.pdf
15 gov.uk/government/uploads/system/uploads/attachment_data/file/444707/Preparing_
for_your_Parole_Oral_Hearing_-_Easyread_Booklet_2015.pdf

cially stuff you don't want to come into the prison and get read by the screws. Chase up legal phone calls. Visit you. Write to you. Chat on the phone and provide financial support. Friends in jail can be there for you, keep confidences, look out for you, give massive hugs (and massages when you can get away with it!). Get into bed with you at the weekends for a cuddle when unlocked."

> Eric King, *A Poem about Freedom*[16]
> One day the water that feeds
> the grass
> Will wash away the stain
> of captivity off me
> The clouds will open their arms in a
> Warm embrace
> Years of hurt and abstract existence
> will be wiped clean
> I can't smell freedom but one day
> we all might
> Day's can't be bought on the free market
> But they can be stolen at gun point
> Trees can't grow in a day, but we clean
> our forests in mutilating seconds…
> One day the water that feeds the world
> will purify my soul.

---

16 2015  Eric King is a long-term anarchist prisoner in America

# EVERYDAY LIFE

## PHYSICAL HEALTH AND IMPAIRMENTS

> "People in prison are more likely to have high cholesterol, high blood pressure, diabetes and smoke a lot more than people in the general population...The bodies of prisoners age more quickly than the general population, putting them at greater risk of getting dementia." *Alzheimer's Society*[1]

Prison healthcare is often a bonkers place, especially if you are in a remand jail. Initially you will have to go a lot (for various vaccinations etc.). Lots of people will be detoxing, and there are likely to be many self-harmers. You will be asked about your medical history including vaccinations. If you haven't already had your hepatitis B jabs then this is the main one. To complete this in jail you need three shots over a one month-six-week period, then a final one a year later. If you have a long sentence you may be given a booster after five years. Due to the sharing of needles for tattoos and drugs, self-harming, and sexual health issues, Hep B is *really* common in jails. It mainly affects the liver, and cause cirrhosis and cancer.

As with everything inside, prison healthcare is very, very slow so you need to think ahead and never give up trying to get appointments. Remember, for what it's worth it's your right to have the same access to health care as you would on road. In order to get a healthcare appointment, you normally have to fill in a special application form not a general one. As ever, keep your receipts.

While you are in jail you can have free access to dentists, physiotherapists and opticians. They may not be the best, and you may have to wait a *really* long time but it might be worth it if you don't have good access to these things outside. A word of warning on dentists though; they are notori-

---

1 Quoted in insidetime.org/dementia-in-prisons/

ously rubbish in jail. In one prison I was in it was common practice for people to come back with bits of tooth left in that got really infected, or have too many teeth removed. So, be warned, it's not without its risks!

In my limited experience of prison healthcare, I found that the jails using the National Health Service were OK(ish), however, many jails (private and state run) use Virgin healthcare and they are mainly *rubbish*. Because it's such a battle accessing healthcare, if you think you might have a specific condition, it's well worth getting people outside to research it and send you in information.

If you are unhappy with the healthcare you receive and you feel it's the result of discrimination, you should fill out a Discrimination Incident Reporting Form (DIRF). Seal it in an envelope marked 'confidential access'. For more information about discrimination you can also contact the Equality Advisory Support Service (EASS)[2], which provides information, advice and support on discrimination and human rights issues to individuals in England, Scotland and Wales.

It is a cliché, but prisons are dirty, dirty places. In one jail I was in, on one wing of 130 people, there were only four showers that were working, and the drain to one of them was blocked with blood. It was quite common for there to be no toilet roll or sanitary items available (you are normally able to collect these from the wing office), so people were having to use their socks. With so many people in such close proximity, with terrible diets and massive amounts of stress, no wonder people get ill.

## Meds and 'Sick in Cell'

As has been previously outlined, meds queues are long! If you aren't taking a restricted substance but regularly require drugs like painkillers or hay-fever meds, and you don't mind being risk assessed, it might be worth trying to get your meds 'in possession'.

It's quite a common occurrence for prison staff to mess with your script; especially if you are on expensive drugs, taking anti-depressants or anti-psychotics. It seems yet another way that they flex their institutional powers of control against those prisoners who are 'acting up' or on a manic hype. The prison system excels at turning individuals into docile individuals who shuffle along the corridors and do not question its authority. Prison psychologists wield a lot of power and routinely change the dosage and types of meds.

---

2 equalityadvisoryservice.com/

If you are ill (or want to skive off work) then you will have to go to the meds hatch first thing, and request an appointment with the nurse. Healthcare should keep a few appointments aside each day for this purpose. Some miserable screws will make you go to work until this appointment. The nurse will then write you a sick note for a certain number of days -normally only a couple at a time. You will then be written off as 'sick in cell'. All your meals will be brought to you, and you won't be allowed to leave your room.

## Hospital Appointments

Trying to get a hospital appointment in jail is a *nightmare.* Screws generally cannot be arsed to sort them out, and the combination of combining the precarity and length of NHS waiting times with the prison system means frustration, despair and a really long wait. If you need a hospital appointment you won't be told when it will be in case you try to plan an escape. You will be cuffed during the whole process, unless you've been re-categorised for open conditions.

Ambulances quite often come into jails; then everything goes into lock down. There will be a 'stand fast roll check' and everyone will be locked in until it leaves. If you require repeat appointments you may get 'shipped out' to a jail closer to the hospital.

There are currently massive delays in accessing hospital appointments and staff routinely lie to prisoners awaiting outside medical attention. Almost 75% of prisoners waiting urgent treatment for serious mental health problems were delayed in being transferred to NHS Hospitals[3]. I cannot emphasise enough how important it is to get someone outside to advocate for you in relation to your hospital logistics if possible when you are in jail. Get these systems set up as quickly as possible and keep all paperwork.

For long-term prisoners, hospital appointments can be quite traumatic as many have become totally institutionalised, and not been beyond the physical confines of the jail for many years. One Lifer friend of mine said how shocked they were by how much technology had changed and that they were actually relieved to get back inside. If you know someone has been out on an appointment, then take care of them when they return. Prison is obviously one of the most hostile environments to have serious health issues. I never had a hospital appointment when I was inside, but I did support mates when they came back from them. People in women's pris-

---

3 For support see insidetime.org/mental-healthcare-prison/

ons are generally solid in this respect, and will do all they can with the little resources available to help the person who has just been to hospital. If someone is in pain, try asking the screws for things like extra mattresses or chairs for them.

## Disabilities and Impairments

This is in no way an attempt to cover all aspects of physical disabilities in prison. There are so many different types of impairment this is obviously not possible. The examples included here are not because they are somehow more important than others, but just based on my limited experience.

PAS has some useful information for disabled prisoners[4]. They have documented many examples of people not having their basic needs met, for example: prisoners not being provided with auxiliary aids (like a working wheelchair) and inaccessible education classes.

The 'Equality Act' (EA) 2010 can help disabled prisoners access the services they need. It applies in both public and private prisons as they are acting as 'public bodies'. Prisons therefore have a legal duty to avoid practices that place disabled prisoners at a substantial disadvantage. Prisons have quite a wide margin of discretion (an old Victorian jail is not going to be forced to install lifts). However, prisons *must* take all reasonable steps to avoid putting disabled people at a substantial disadvantage. If they do not this could amount to unlawful disability discrimination.

The EA describes disability is as: "a physical or mental impairment and the impairment has a substantial and long-term adverse effect on his or her ability to carry out normal day to day activities."[5] This is a wide definition and can include a range of conditions from diabetes to dyslexia as long as the adverse effect is 'substantial' and lasting, or predicted to last for more than a year.

Section 20 of the EA sets out the duty to make reasonable adjustments, and this is very useful in the context of jails. PAS has stated:

> "Where a public body has in place a provision, criterion or practice that puts a disabled person at a substantial disadvantage in comparison with non-disabled persons, there is a legal duty to take such steps as are reasonable to avoid that disadvantage."[6]

4 PAS, *Information Sheet Disability Discrimination- The Equality Act 2010 (updated 2015)*
5 legislation.gov.uk/ukpga/2010/15/section/6
6 PAS, 2015

A disability liaison officer should exist in every jail. In theory, they organise auxiliary aids and oversee reasonable adjustments. Make sure you refer to section 20 in all your paperwork. The 'Care Quality Commission'[7] investigates all aspects of health care and can advocate for prisoners. If you have a long-term impairment it might well be worth adding the number to your PIN if security will allow.

As with all aspects of prison healthcare, those with ongoing impairments should expect a rough ride. In 2016 the 'Howard League for Penal Reform' published *Not Hearing Us: An Exploration of the Experience of Deaf Prisoners in English and Welsh prisons*. This extensive report found that 40% of health care appointments were missed due to lack of staff[8]. It is also a common occurrence for wheelchair users to be discriminated against through the visits process, often being the last people to be escorted into the visits hall, and the first ones out. In one jail, a wheelchair user was routinely told to leave 20 minutes early each visit due to 'health and safety issues'.

For people with visual impairments, some prisons now have a designated Braille unit. If you are in a jail which does not have one of these then you could request a ship out, or resources from there. At the time of writing, the Shannon Trust were also in the process of transcribing the books used in the 'Turning Pages' scheme into Braille.

If you have hearing impairments, prison life can be a constant battle. Users of hearing aids have repeatedly reported not hearing staff shouting on landings, and some people have been given negative IEPs and threatened with disciplinary action because they have not heard things. The prison environment -especially in Victorian jails-is very noisy and echoes can interfere with hearing aids immensely. It can also be very difficult to hear screws when they talk through the flap of locked cell doors. Very few prisons have people who are trained in sign language. If you are visually or hearing impaired it's a good idea to put a sign on your door indicating this so that staff have at least been made aware of this even if they do not change their actions.

## Diabetes

In 2017 the charity Diabetes UK updated their report *Having Diabetes in Prison*[9]. 'Type Two' diabetes massively affects the wider UK population,

7 cqc.org.uk/
8 Daniel McCulloch, *Not Hearing Us, Howard League for Penal Reform 2016*
9 diabetes.org.uk/How_we_help/Helpline/Your-rights/Advocacy-packs/Having-diabetes-in-prison/

and is very common in prisons. The report contains practical advice about managing your diet in jail to help minimise the impact of diabetes (and the chances of getting it in the first place.) It also contains advice on physical activity requirements, accessing health care inside with the condition, and issues relating to smoking and diabetes[10].

## Sexual Health

For obvious reasons, sexual health can be quite a big issue inside. The best thing to do is get screened for sexually transmitted infections (STIs) as soon as you get inside if you have any doubt at all. If you start having sex, don't be shy about asking your partner(s) to get tested. 'Bent Bars' has some excellent jail-specific sexual health resources on their website[11].

## Physical Exercise

My drug of choice in jail was endorphins. Many people use exercise as a coping strategy for anger release and general distraction inside. Even if you don't normally do much exercise, it's good to do your gym induction as quickly as possible, and take every opportunity to be in the fresh air. Even if you just go to the gym to socialise and play a bit of badminton, it's really important to stay mobile, and the gym is a good place to see people who aren't on your wing.

The 'Prison Phoenix Trust'[12] do weekly shows of yoga and meditation on National Prison Radio and they will also send in books and CDs on these activities if you request them. As with religion, many prisoners turn to meditation in jail. However, Thakrar has argued, this is quite problematic:

> "In an environment which is structurally oppressive coupled with the extreme discrimination present and brutal regime, any claim of a meditation class is totally ridiculous. Meditation is not the cure to being tortured, especially when it is being offered by those conducting the torture."[13]

10 If you know someone who is displaying any of the following symptoms then try to help them access healthcare for a test: passing urine more often than usual, especially at night, increased thirst, extreme tiredness, unexplained weight loss, genital itching or regular episodes of thrush, slow healing of cuts and wounds and blurred vision (Diabetes UK report, *Diabetes and Prison*)
11 bentbarsproject.org/resources?tid=8
12 theppt.org.uk/
13 Thakrar,*Why Allow it to Continue? 2016*

The PPT can sometimes also send in volunteer yoga teachers to your jail. Ask the gym to contact them. Our teacher was quite nice, though the relentless questions about prison life ("is it really like 'Orange is the New Black?'") during our precious 45-minute relaxation time got tiresome very quickly.

An ex-prisoner, L.J Flanders has published a book for doing your own exercise in jail; *Cell Workout*[14] uses body weight exercises and different training strategies. It's macho, but quite useful if you don't have access to the gym. The library normally has sections on physical exercise, however, in women's jails these often conform to depressing gendered stereotypes. I got frustrated by the amount of weight loss, calorie counting and pilates books there were, especially when I was studying anatomy and needed to practise a lot of techniques for doing weights. Ask mates outside to send in current ideas for training programmes, or get them to research titles of books you can request from library staff.

The gym should offer a wide range of activities, from hardcore high-intensity-training, through to group games like basketball. Aggressive team sports are popular inside and a good way to let off steam and work through any issues you might have with other prisoners. The gym should also have a variety of time slots available to help people with specific health/referral needs, and those detoxing. You should be able to access the gym at least a few times a week, regardless of your IEP status or work party. Gym orderlies can help devise training programmes for you, so don't be afraid if you aren't very confident. Having a gym buddy to go with the first few times can also help build up confidence.

Working in the gym kept me sane during my sentence and I did all the courses I could about fitness and health. If you like being active it's definitely worth trying to get a job in the gym, because extended bang-up and staff shortages means that access to it is invariably quite restricted.

---

14 cell-workout.com/

# AGEING POPULATION

In England and Wales there are currently 12,000 prisoners who are over 50[1]. The so-called 'ageing population' is rapidly expanding. There has been a 104% increase within this demographic over the two years, whilst the overall prison population has increased by 15%. In 2015 there were 2,177 over 50s serving life sentences, and 814 of these were 'IPP' (Imprisonment for Public Protection) prisoners. In 2014 there were 102 people over 80 in the UK prison estate. According to the PPO the average age of death in jail is 58[2].

The rise of the over 50s is mainly due to an increase in prosecution of historic abuse cases. 42% of men over 50 are inside because they have been convicted of sex offences. According to the MoJ, in 2015 there were 6,402 convictions for sex offences, an increase of 10% on previous 12 months. This is the highest for a decade, and has increased in the wake of 'Operation Yewtree'.

Older prisoners obviously have specific needs; such as dementia, Parkinson's, incontinence and mobility issues. However, these needs are unsurprisingly not met by the current system. The 'Care Act'[3] of 2014 has been applied since April 2015 onwards. It stated that local authorities *must* assess and meet the needs of adult prisoners. PSI2015-015 'Adult Social Care' (appendix 13) outlines services prisons can expect and the limitations of the prison estate[4].

---

1 prisonreformtrust.org.uk/ProjectsResearch/Olderpeopleinprison
2 bbc.co.uk/news/uk-34211681
3 socialworkhelper.com/2014/12/17/the-care-act-2014-and-what-it-means-for-prisoners-in-the-uk/
4 If you are seeking to challenge legislation connected to pensions it might be worth citing the Human Rights Act 1968 article 7 (I) "...nor shall a heavier penalty be imposed than the one that was applicable at the time the offence was committed." Article 17 (two) may

Due to the very limited range of accessible resources inside, conflict can easily arise. Someone I knew lived opposite a viscously racist old person because there were only two accessible cells in the whole prison.

> "I was forced to live opposite a racist woman (we are both disabled so have limited cell options). I used to help her out a lot, with everyday tasks and encourage her to leave her cell. But I had to put up with constant abuse from her, and her friends, calling me "dirty Paki". Some of her friends regularly "Sieg Heiled" at me and made really racist jokes. Officers ignored it."

Screws pay no attention to the increased support Disabled People and older prisoners might need, and it is normally down to other people on the wing to help with daily tasks. I interviewed someone who was 70:

> "In other prisons it was better, staff did help a bit. In one they had an older-persons section, which was quieter. You didn't pay for your TV if you were over a certain age, were given a more comfortable chair, and the IMB came to see you specifically. If you are over 50, you should be unlocked more, and be allowed to do laundry twice a week. Here they said that doesn't apply."

I am *not* advocating for specially designed jails; or more accessible rooms. In relation to the 'ageing population'; no one should spend the end of their life banged-up in jail.

Between 2004 and 2014 there was an 125% increase in prisoners over 60[5]. Prisoners from this age range are predicted to increase from 4,100 in 2015 to 5,500 in 2020[6]; again, due to prosecution for historic sex offences (and longer sentencing patterns).[7] In 2015 the 'all party penal affairs group'[8] advised a need to improve care for infirm prisoners, adjust accommodation needs for retired and immobile, better palliative care for those not allowed to die in 'community' and training for staff.

---

also be useful: "no one shall be arbitrarily deprived of *his* property (my italics, another example of how the subject in law is always assumed to be male.)
5 PPO, *Learning lessons bulletin Fatal incidents investigations Issue 11: Dementia, 2016*
6 PPO, 2016
7 A lot of older prisoners in the women's jails I was in were also in for fraud and this seems to be increasing.
8 prisonreformtrust.org.uk/PressPolicy/Parliament/AllPartyParliamentaryPenalAffairs-Group/December2015Olderpeopleinprison

## Healthcare and Older Prisoners

As has been outlined previously, *theoretically* prison health care should be equivalent to that outside in the community. This is unsurprisingly not the case and nowhere is this more obvious than in the provision (or lack of) for older prisoners. When the 'Care Act' (CA) came into place in April 2015 it was clear that incontinence, malnourishment, dirtiness and dehydration was common in older prisoners due to lack of access to facilities. The CA called for a "balance" between security and humanity[9]. I would argue that in prison this 'balance' can never be kept because prisons will always prioritise 'security' and that their very existence shows a lack of so-called 'humanity'.

A major issue highlighted by the CA was the need for an investigation into 886 deaths in custody[10]. This found that the use of physical restraint[11] had been found inappropriate in 51% of cases, and that the use of restraint (which was often kept on till point of death) was based on historical records not peoples current state of health. If you are terminally ill and have a life expectancy of less than three months then you can apply for 'Compassionate Release'[12] (though the reality is that by the time your claim has been processed its often too late).

In 2009 the mandatory minimum rate of pay for prisoners who are long-term sick or of retirement age was £3.25 per week[13]. Retired prisoners still have to pay £1 of this per week for their TV.

## Dementia

The Alzheimer's Society has been working with prisons in England on a pilot project aimed at understanding some of the challenges prisoners and staff face in dealing with dementia[14]. They found that symptoms are being

9 penalreform.org/wp-content/uploads/2013/11/security-dignity-v8-final_for-web.pdf
10 prisonreformtrust.org.uk/PressPolicy/News/vw/1/ItemID/245
11 For more information on the uses of restraint see bbc.co.uk/news/uk-30383191
12 Prison Service Order 6000, see also news.bbc.co.uk/1/hi/magazine/8201213.stm
13 Prison Service Order 4460 section 5.2.5 see also insidetime.org/pensions-for-prisoners/
14 There are many different types of dementia, but many share common symptoms, so if you become aware that someone inside is displaying the following it might be worth talking to them and trying to get medical advice: short-term memory loss, mood changes /changes in behaviour, difficulty reasoning or making decisions, withdrawal and loss of confidence, communication problems, loss of interest in others or in activities. The difficulty is that many of these symptoms are commonly experienced by prisoners (such as stress), and are also apparent in other conditions (such as depression). However, when a person has dementia the symptoms do not go away and gradually become worse. As the illness progresses, people need frequent reminders to do everyday activities such as eat-

missed, not recognised or confused for something else, which means a delay in diagnosis. Lack of knowledge about the condition means a lack of support. In addition, prisoners can be wrongly punished for behaviour that is actually a result of their dementia.

> "According to the Ministry of Justice, the over 60 population in prisons in England and Wales has increased eight-fold since 1990 and in the last decade, the number of sentenced prisoners aged sixty or above has risen by 74 per cent to almost 10,000. This, coupled with health-related problems, puts prisoners at a higher risk of getting dementia." *Alzheimer's Society[15]*

If you are supporting someone with dementia, contact the Alzheimer's Society, or ask someone outside to. Also ask about 'Dementia Friends'[16] sessions being held in your prison – and request them if there are none planned, and ask for the list of recommended books on dementia from the library.

### Emotional Impact on Older People

> "My advice to any older people would be escape before they get you! it's a hell of a shock., it will be for anyone. it's frightening, especially with all the young girls ("animals") up there on main block). Here no one cares." *70-year-old prisoner on my wing*

Both Disabled People and older prisoners can suffer from acute cases of what has been termed "entry shock" into jail; fear, withdrawal from other inmates and so on. Many prisoners experience this, but for obvious reasons, it can be much more acute in those with limited mobility or impairments. It is common for people with these health issues to be afraid (or unable) to access the shower, and other communal resources in jail. The routine transferring of people within jails and the wider prison estate also has a major physical impact. Older prisoners are not offered any assistance in carrying their prop when they have to move cells. One person I knew inside unable to climb the steps into the sweat box on a ship-out due to a recent hip replacement and was then threatened with disciplinary action.

---

ing, washing and dressing. They may become repetitive and struggle to recognise people, and become easily upset, angry or aggressive. People (especially in jail) may be reluctant to admit they are struggling with daily tasks, so may be adverse to admitting they need help.

15 Quoted in insidetime.org/dementia-in-prisons/
16 dementiafriends.org.uk/

Some prisons operate schemes such as 'Rubies' for older people in women's prisons, which is a weekly group. Prisoners over-60 are entitled to more association time, and Rubies normally happens when other prisoners are banged-up and focuses on knitting or crafts. One person I spoke to highlighted the issues of boredom among older prisoners:

> "If you are retired there should be relaxations on what your allowed. I'm lucky as I have my paints which I bought in with me but if you don't have that or a hobby you'd be very bored. Also we should be allowed to go to funerals. Well, everyone should, it's inhumane that we're not. Maybe we could have something like 'Rubies' we don't have that here."

The way older prisoners are treated in jail is symptomatic of a wider issue in the UK, where many are trapped in isolation behind closed doors. In one of the jails I was in older people were encouraged to live on the maximum-security wing (the "undead") along with all the sex offenders. Because the wing was so high security, they rarely got out, were forced to have all their meals on the wing, and weren't allowed to walk around the wider jail (even during so-called 'exercise').

## Pensions

The 1911 'National Insurance Act' ruled that sentenced prisoners over 65 cannot claim their state pension (apparently it is a 'benefit'). The government claims this is due to the cost of 'accommodation' and 'maintenance' in jail (on average £100 per day per prisoner). This is both arbitrary and discriminatory as prisoners *under* the age of 65 are *not* expected to financially contribute to their incarceration. As with the wider prison population, housing benefit can still be claimed for up to 12 weeks when remanded.

The lack of access to the state pension is obviously a major form a discrimination, as unlike most benefits, individuals who are eligible for it have contributed to it throughout their working lives. If individuals have their pension with a private firm they may be able to access it, depending on the type of scheme. This obviously adds a potential major financial stress to older people inside, many of whom do not have people outside who can send money in. The 1911 Act was challenged in 1997 in the cases of Szrabjer and Clarke[17]. However, despite the judge recognising the claims of discrimination, no changes were made.

---

17 swarb.co.uk/szrabjer-and-clarke-v-united-kingdom-echr-17-jun-1998/

# RELIGION

"Little by little my regrets and desires fade away. I let my soul float away into emptiness and my will soften. A dangerous but delicious numbness, leading surely, but insensibly, to the edge of nothingness." *Isabelle Eberhardt[1]*

Religion is unsurprisingly popular in jail. It is a sad truth that people's critical eye in relation to the regime and screws often overlooks those involved in the chapel. In response to a sense of the "edge of nothingness" many prisoners embrace religious doctrine, or become more devout than they were before being incarcerated.

"The church, the state, the school, the magazine, think they are liberal and free! It is the freedom of a prison-yard." *Henry David Thoreau[2]*

Every prison has a chapel, and most have a 'multi-faith' room as well. These buildings are normally used for a range of activities, mostly religious but also some 'entertainment'. It is also normally where non-residential programmes aimed at behaviour modification occur (for example 'Sycamore Tree' or 'Assertiveness' -see section on Psychology). The staff of the chapel will be on your case as soon as you get sent down. My advice would be steer well clear, and *never* show even a vague interest in religion.

Because space is limited, all the religions recognised by the prison have to share space and resources. Most world religions are represented in the

---

1 Eberhardt (1877-1904), *Criminal, 2011*
2 Thoreau, *I to Myself: An Annotated Selection from the Journal of Henry D. Thoreau* 1861

chapel. This means the chapel is also the site of a fair bit of tension. Mutual animosity can be quite high between different factions. As is often the case with religions outside prison, it's sad to see how quickly people become territorial and suspicious when they feel that their dogma isn't being respected.

If you are facing a custodial sentence and looking for information on the religious aspects of life inside, then this publication is not for you. No doubt there are numerous PSIs which relate to this area of prison life, but none will be quoted here.

THE CHAPEL AT BRIXTON.

# DRUGS

"Banged-up 23 hours a day in a large toilet with someone you have never met before – who wouldn't want a mind-altering substance?" *Former prison governor[1]*

Drugs are rife in prison. According to the house of commons, in 2013, 35% of prisoners were addicted to drugs[2] and this is now estimated to be closer to half the prison population[3]. In 2012 the cost of 'offending' in relation to these incidences was allegedly over £13 billion per annum in England and Wales alone[4].

Statistics like these have historically been used to justify a 'war on drugs.'[5] The state uses the guise of a moral campaign to invade and control people's private lives and personal choice. In the war on drugs, the fault is placed on the individual, not the substance. Women are especially impacted in this process, becoming "bodies to be dealt with"[6], not conforming to traditional models of femininity. In this model drug users (especially women) are 'infected' and 'polluted', and 'addicted'; and need to be cured/cleansed of their behaviours. The concept of the unruly as 'diseased' is a stereotype which also acts out on many levels in jail. For example, prisoners are not

1 Quoted in inews.co.uk/opinion/columnists/soaring-spice-use-inmates-shows-prohibi-tion-ineffective/
2 publications.parliament.uk/pa/cm201314/cmhansrd/cm130702/debtext/130702-0001.htm#13070275000006
3 aleretoxicology.co.uk/en/home/solutions/law-enforcement/drug-testing-in-prisons.html
4 ukdpc.org.uk/wp-content/uploads/Policy%20report%20-%20An%20analysis%20of%20UK%20drug%20policy%20(summary).pdf
5 For more information see Noam Chomsky, *Drug Policy as Social Control 1997*
"The so-called drug was was started in the 1980s and it was aimed directly at the black population. None of this has anything to do with drugs. It has to do with controlling and criminalising..."
6 Malloch, 2001

allowed to give blood, even if they pass the rigorous vetting procedure.

Drugs discourse places the blame with the individual user rather than the substance, or the social factors surrounding drug use. Drug enforcement legitimises the criminalisation of the marginalised through regulation and control. This is an important arm of state as drugs are perceived major threat to social stability. Allegedly half of all crime committed in the UK has a drug related element.

Women who engage with drugs are typically presented as being 'hyper sexual' and much is made in the media about the relationship between sex work and drug related crimes, and the fact that many drug users have been abused or in care. A further dichotomy exists between the tension of women either being 'misguided mules' or 'strong fighters' who supposedly deserve everything the judge throws at them. Malloch has highlighted how the category of 'drugs' doesn't have a scientific classification, and therefore includes a political/moral evaluation which is often overlooked[7]. Women's prisons also rely on a paradox; whereby people inside are condemned for drug use and dependency, whilst having a myriad of prescription drugs are forced upon them.

> "The ruling class shifts dope to
> you and me
> And don't get arrested, this is lunacy
> or is it pimp low magic in
> unity?
> Is it a war on drugs, or just my community?" *The Coup*[8]

## Anti-Social?

Nowhere is the arbitrary distinction of what is acceptable and what is 'antisocial' more apparent within the prison system than in relation to drugs. Prison life is a confusing mix of legal (i.e. substances controlled/enforced by the state) and illegal drugs. The most commonly used drugs in prison are spice (and other 'New Psychoactive Substances'), methadone, subutex ('subbies' or 'tex'; a heroin substitute), Pre-Gabalin ('gabs') and Mirtazipin (an antidepressant for sleeping). It is a grim irony that whilst the state and prison system are so quick to discipline drug use inside, people in women's prisons are routinely pumped full of prescribed drugs. Once you have been prescribed something in jail, you will face disciplinary proce-

---

7 Malloch, 2001
8 The Coup, *Drug Warz, 2005*

dures very quickly if you refuse to take it.

On one wing I was on, I was the only person out of 40 women who was not on meds. The use of prescription drugs in jail is big business, and it is also one of the many ways in which Virgin profit from the prison estate (they operate most healthcare units in women's prisons.) People who get prescribed meds in jail often end up with a heady cocktail to take, being given uppers to treat depression, then downers to help them sleep, then laxatives to help their insides function due to the shit prison food and the cocktail of drugs rattling around inside them.

Because so many people in women's prisons use drugs, it can be difficult to escape them. Many people have been sent down for 'economic crimes' to fund their habits and find themselves stuck in the so-called 'revolving door' of recidivism. Devlin has outlined the ways in which people, especially Lifers, self-medicate to get through their sentence[9]. Heroin has been known as "bird killer" because it helps pass the days in total oblivion. More recently, spice has replaced this as it is much cheaper (but still highly addictive).

In an attempt to further divide the prison population, punitive and repressive measures are employed for the 'hardcore' who refuse to quit, whilst others are selected for 'therapeutic rehabilitation'. The concepts of guilt and shame are perpetuated in this emphasis on individual failure in relation to drug use, and this model is very much encouraged by prison based treatment programmes such as the RAPT unit and CARATS ('Counselling, Assessment, Referral, Advice and Throughcare Service').

Sentencing around drugs is a further example of the way that patriarchy exerts itself within the CJS. Sentences are often longer for women than men, and Devlin and others have outlined how the discourse around drug use is used to criminalise and pathologise women. The rehab programmes inside are just another form of social control dressed up as 'healing'. Treatment and punishment have very conflicting aims, but this is conveniently overlooked by the prison regime.

## Technology

Prisons use an arsenal of technologies and programmes to deal with drug use inside. Some have designated detox wings, others provide programmes such as RAPT, CARATs or 'Drug Recover Communities' (DRCs), and self-help resources. These are combined with the disciplinary procedures such

---

9 Devlin, 1998

as Mandatory Drugs Tests (MDTs), searches, x-rays, surveillance (on visits; and the use of open or closed visits), drug dogs, prison staff and Body Orifice Scanning (BOSS) chairs.

The so-called 'war on drugs' legitimises invasive practices towards inmates, and the development of new oppressive forms of technology. Kilgore has argued that the war on drugs in America drives both the expansion of the prison population *and* a philosophical shift towards more punitive practices inside[10]. This can equally be applied to the UK prison estate. In 2016, Volteface, a think-tank which explores alternatives to current public policies relating to drugs published *High Stakes: An Inquiry into the Drugs Crisis in English Prisons*. This report has highlighted the farcical nature of these measures:

> "Current supply-reduction and security measures are not grounded in evidence. New proposed measures focus on drones and visitors when there is no evidence that these are the primary sources of supply. There is evidence suggesting corrupt staff may be a major source of supply."[11]

## Mandatory Drugs Tests (MDTs)

MDTs were introduced in 1994, as part of the 'war on drugs'. When MDTs were introduced a lot of prisoners stopped smoking weed (which stays in your system for 30 days) and instead switched to heroin. Doing an MDT sucks. You will get 'randomly' called out from your cell first thing in the morning where you will be escorted to a dirty cubicle with a bunch of other prisoners. You are not allowed to go to the toilet until your turn, and you will be kept there until you can piss in the specially designed toilet. Pissing in front of screws is one of the most humiliating things I have ever done, but if you are known for *not* using drugs then you better get used to it. No jail wants to be perceived as having a drugs problem so if staff know you are 'clean' you will get 'randomly' selected a lot more than girls who use. MDTs are meant to be conducted using 10% of prisoners per month, but I got called up way more than most of my mates.

MDTs are expensive. In 1996 they cost around £23,000 per month per jail and no doubt this is significantly higher today[12]. Each prison has to foot the bill for them individually, so there are many instances of the same girls

10 Kilgore, 2015
11 Volteface, 2016
12 thelancet.com/journals/lancet/article/PIIS0140-6736(96)06318-0/fulltext?version=prin terFriendly

getting tested repeatedly to give better results. Be warned, if you cannot piss on command or you get 'performance anxiety' about using the toilet then this is interpreted as an omission of guilt and you will face and adjudication and most likely extra time.

> "Avoid taking any drugs that you haven't been prescribed; a friend of mine borrowed cocodamol from his friend for his toothache, had an MDT a couple days later, tested positive for opiates and ended up having his television taken away and getting put on various compulsory drug treatment courses as punishment."[13]

Cattermole's point about getting busted for the use of non-prescribed drugs is important. Most legal meds will show up on results and this will be an automatic disciplinary procedure if you haven't been prescribed them, even if you have just blagged an ibuprofen off a mate lucky enough to have them 'in possession'. For determinate sentenced prisoners, this can be really annoying, but for those facing parole this could mean an automatic knockback.

It is worth noting also that if you fail an MDT you should expect a cellspin fairly quickly after, so make sure your yard is in order and remove any incriminating evidence! Also, be *very* careful who you are seen talking to about it, as staff may well try to find out where the supply came from. Like MDTs, cell spinning is never as random as staff make out, and just as you will be overlooked for MDTs if you are a known user, so you should expect many more cell-spins than someone who isn't.

In a detailed attack on the 2015 home office report into drug use in jail, Alice Gambell highlighted the absurdity of MDTs:

> "The annual report claims that positive drug tests are down as if this is an indication that drug use in prisons is decreasing. It is surprising that they have included MDT figures in such a recent report considering HMIP on several occasions argue that MDT figures are not an accurate reflection of drug use in prisons and the decline in positive tests does not mean a decline in drug use. As HMIP point out "they [MDT results] do not reliably measure drug availability in establishments – nor does testing necessarily deter prisoners' use of illicit drugs." It is a well-known fact that drug use in prison is high and that those who are deterred from taking drugs detected by MDTs

---

13 Cattermole, 2015

often resort to using undetectable legal highs that may prove more harmful..."[14]

Gambell highlighted an increase in deaths relating to drug use inside, and also post-release. She argued that this is a direct result of the government's drug policy, specifically the criminalisation of drugs, which only increases the use of new psychoactive substances: "Responding by further criminalisation of new psychoactive substances only exacerbates the harms that occur with risky drug taking. The rapid increase of the introduction of dangerous illegal highs is a direct response to the criminalisation of drugs."[15]

For more information about your rights surrounding MDTs see Prison Service Order (PSO) 3601 and PR 51(22)[16]. If you think you might fail an MDT, keep a record of all the events surrounding it and seek legal advice as soon as possible. Note that if you fail one, you may well be put onto basic/seg straight away or transferred onto a different wing whilst the prison 'investigates'.

## New Psychoactive Substances (NPS)

"Prisons are in crisis with record levels of suicides, violence and self-harm. Traditional drugs have been replaced by a family of drugs called synthetic cannabinoid receptor agonists, generically referred to as 'black mamba' or 'spice.' The Government has failed to recognise the important policy implications of these new drugs, and the lack of intelligent drug policy in the new white paper risks undermining the entirety of the proposed prison reforms." *Volteface*[17]

Between 2013 and 2015 there were 39 deaths related to new psychoactive substances in prison. Prison accounts for *half* the national number of deaths related to these substances, despite being a population of only 85,000. Spice has been blamed for an increase in bullying, debt and rising violence within the UK prison system[18]. Black mamba, spizzle, phish, spice, K2 and NPS (not to be confused with the National Probation Service which can also fry your brain!) are all examples and names of 'synthetic cannabinoids'. They mimic the effects of THC (the active compound in cannabis) but in a much

14 drinkanddrugsnews.com/uk-drug-policy/
15 drinkanddrugsnews.com/uk-drug-policy/
16 Also PAS *Information Sheet Mandatory Drug Testing (updated 2015) and insidetime. org/mdts-know-your-rights/*
17 Volteface, *High Stakes: An Inquiry into the Drugs Crisis in English Prisons 2016*
18 Volteface, 2016

more potent way. Spice is manufactured in labs rather than grown, and as such is odourless therefore much more difficult to detect.

In May 2016, a 'New Psychoactive Substances Act' made it an offence to produce, import/export and supply spice. In 'custodial institutions' possession is an offence carrying a sentence of up to two years inside. Users of 'spice' are allegedly more likely to suffer from depression, stress, anxiety and insomnia. The substance has been labelled potentially more damaging to health than heroin[19]. Side effects can also include paranoia, psychosis, heart attacks, high blood pressure, "behavioural disturbances", violence, convulsions, seizures and even death.

According to *IT*, in 2016 the UK spent £4 billion on drugs strategies (and £2.8 billion of this was in jails/probation services). The total value of the UK drug market is estimated to be around £4.6 billion[20]. In November 2015 there were 95 suicides in jail. This massive increase has been attributed to new psychoactive substances. The PPO has reported an increase in "NPS users acting violently and out of character, or getting into drug debts, resulting in bullying, intimidation and violence"[21].

It is unclear what the figures are specifically in relation to spice and women's prisons, but from personal observation I would say that it is easily available and many people in jail (and subsequently then also in bail hostels) are addicted to it. Because you get breathalysed routinely when you enter a bail hostel and can be subjected to drugs test and searches, a lot of people opt to use spice for the same reasons they do in jail: i.e. it doesn't show up on tests, and is easy to score.

The MoJ proposes to spend staggering amounts of funds on testing people when they enter and leave prison, and develop greater use of sniffer dogs to police the use of spice.

This text is *not* advocating for the increased criminalisation of drugs -in or outside the prison estate-nor is it a call for increased legislation around drugs, or state based interventions. I wanted to include practical information to give an insight into what to expect around drugs inside women's prisons.

> "Prisons house disproportionately high numbers of people in poor health, people with addictions and those with motivations to use drugs. Prohibition cannot work in prisons, but more than that, it is the most dangerous place in which to pur-

19 spiceaddictionsupport.org/side-effects-of-spice-use/amp/
20 insidetime.org/prison-drug-treatment-still-directionless/
21 PPO, *Homicides report, 2016*

sue absolute prohibition. Whilst wrong headed drug policy created a small but significant market for New Psychoactive Substances in broader society, in prisons it created the environment necessary for NPS to become the most widely used drugs, and a vicious industry built on unsustainable debt that further fuels criminality." *Volteface*[22]

## Detoxing Inside

As I have previously outlined, there are various rehabilitation programmes that will no doubt get slapped on your sentence plan if the CJS decides your 'crime' was the result of so-called substance misuse. These programmes are big business for jails as they are resource heavy. In acute cases; such as heroin addiction, you may get forced into residential units/detox wings if the jail has them, otherwise you may have to go to healthcare regularly or CARATs. It is worth noting here that as soon as any of these programmes gets put on your sentence plan it is highly likely that you will also be given restrictions and drugs tests as part of your licence conditions. Since the CJA of 1991, Magistrates and judges can issue probation/supervision orders for alcohol and drugs tests, and if you get sent to bail hostel they will routinely check. RAPT will also refer you to a 'secondary care' programme on release.

If you are addicted to heroin you will be placed straight on a detox wing when you enter a remand jail. These are *really* grim places, but the chances are you will be so wrapped up in your withdrawal process that you won't notice too much, and then hopefully you'll be moved on to another, slightly nicer unit. Detox wings can feel like oppressive psychiatric unit. The level of control by screws on them is *much* higher than most other wings, and the one in my jail had hardly any sunlight. Because it is high security chances for 'exercise' (i.e. a brief walk in the yard) are slim, although some gyms will run special sessions for people on detox wings.

## Meth

The prison system uses methadone as a daily way to control prisoners who rely on this substance. The 'National Institute for Health and Care Excellence' guidelines for over 16s are clear on the use of methadone: "it must be users informed choice, an expressed decision to be abstinent from the

---

22 Volteface, 2016

opiate your dependent on" (CG52 para 1.1.1.1)[23]. Having designated detox wings is costly, and resource heavy, so a lot of jails do not allow a total detox but rather promote dependency on methadone. As a user of opiates, if you are unhappy with the treatment programme your prison allows then it is an unlawful breach of CG52 para 1.1.1.1. Contact the Parliamentary and Health Service Ombudsman if the jail continues to enforce it.

One of my friends was keen to come off meth as quickly as possible, so that by the time her

HDC eligibility date arrived she could potentially go out to her children without any kind of drug dependency. Suffice to say, the prison did little to support her, and indeed, actively discouraged this. Another friend inside spoke of her frustrations and lack of control over her prescription:

> "Detox at my first jail was very inflexible -you have to come down in 5 ml doses. This makes a *big* difference especially when you get to a lower dose. This puts girls off detoxing because of physical and mental fear. I didn't want the jail to control my detox."

Methadone will be issued by healthcare and/or CARATs. Meth is normally given out mid-morning or afternoon; at a separate time from the main meds session. This can be quite disruptive if you have other appointments or work, and screws are often rubbish unlocking people to get their meth.

Some jails have been known to actually increase the methadone dose of individuals just before release in case people start withdrawing when they are out. This perpetuates a cycle of dependency and does not empower those who have been actively trying to remove drugs from their system. Increasing people's meth scripts prior to release is also problematic because prisoners are normally discharged first thing, missing their morning dose. Doctors in the community often do not prescribe meth, so people run the risk of going into withdrawal as soon as they are on road, and are therefore much more likely to turn back to heroin.

### Treatment Programmes

Once you've finished going cold turkey (or if drugs have been highlighted as a factor in any aspect of your 'offending behaviour'), you may well be have some kind of further 'treatment' slapped on your sentence plan. The 'Drug Recovery Community' (DRC) and the 'Rehabilitation for Addicted

23 nice.org.uk/guidance/cg52/documents/drug-misuse-detoxification-nice-guideline-draft-for-consultation2

Prisoners Unit' (RAPT) are residential programmes. Both require a fair amount of group work, using the 12-step programme popularised by Alcoholics/Narcotics Anonymous, and will involve *a lot* of engagement with prison staff. Both place the blame for substance misuse with the individual, and place them wholly responsible for their 'offending behaviour', and both perpetuate the 'disease' model of drug 'rehabilitation'.

In placing the emphasis and responsibility on the individual prisoner; both the DRC and RAPT units encourage a culture of snitching and bitching. People are forced to live very closely to each other (cells on both units are doubles) and you will have to engage with a lot of public sessions with your pad-mate. Because of this there is a sense of constant supervision/surveillance. If you use drugs as a distraction from trauma, then being forced into this very public process is highly problematic, especially as you have very little idea of the background of your pad-mate, apart from the fact that they also use drugs. People who do not "actively engage" with the programme or who are private are often labelled trouble makers, and their reluctance to disclose personal information is seen as proof of "minimising their actions" and failing to take responsibility for 'offending' and so-called 'destructive behaviours'. Autonomy is *not* encouraged. One of my mates who graduated from Rapt described the situation on the wing:

> "There is *a lot* of bitching and shit stirring. You are encouraged as part of your treatment to grass on each other ("being honest") this creates people exaggerating or entirely making up stuff-not just claiming people using but also "inappropriate behaviour" like being too loud, trying to use gym, associating with individuals off the unit. All behaviours/coping strategies get lumped together under the umbrella of "addictive behaviour", even if they are positive, like trying to do exercise. A lot of girls put on a lot of weight because they are not allowed off the unit, and constantly fed cake. The exercise that is offered to RAPT prisoners is really limited; for example, ten pin bowling, rounders or volleyball. Even this is all about working as a group, you can't do your own thing in the gym."

You are not allowed to talk to other prisoners outside the unit (and therefore also have significantly reduced time you are allowed outside). The first for weeks of life on the RAPT unit are called 'seeking safety' this establishes you on the wing and programme. Prisoners do not engage with group therapy during this time but do have to attend workshops, and 'emotional check-ins'. After four weeks, you then start your primary care; which consists of group 'meditation', and one and a half hours of group 'therapy' every morning, and workshops all together in the afternoon.

Prisoners 'graduate' from these programmes after completing the 12 steps. The DRC programme normally last three months, and RAPT takes about six. Both programmes encourage individuals completing them to view all prisoners outside their unit with suspicion; by further invoking the language and metaphor of 'diseased' individuals. The emphasis on addictive behaviour is so acute that many prisoners become obsessed with analysing it in other people. RAPT's 'Women's Substance Dependence Treatment Programme (WSDTP)' has had 450 'graduates' since 2000[24]. However, it will come as no surprise that rates of relapse are high. One participant told me that only about three out of 20 RAPT graduates stay clean.

The DRC is slightly less isolating than RAPT and you can still use the gym and library at the same time as other prisoners. Both RAPT and the DRC programmes contain a religious element once you do your step work and this permeates much of their discourse around 'recovery' (and creates some very self-righteous prisoners!). Gambell has critiqued this approach to rehabilitation:

> "Sticking to a purely abstinence based approach and continuing to ban new drugs will not make drug use disappear. It only puts people at danger, furthers stigmatisation, and places unrealistic and damaging conditions on those who would benefit from harm reduction practices rather than punitive measures that place an antiquated ideology upon people which is not based on any reality... The truth is that drug use is a reality for many people in this country whether the government likes it or not, and continuing on this path of denial will only continue to produce further harm."[25]

## Safety and Drugs Inside

I don't do drink or drugs, and so am probably not the best person to be giving advice on staying safe inside :-) but I wanted to include a few random points I observed during my sentence...

In terms of security, be aware how much people talk in jail if you start

24 rapt.org.uk/content/women%E2%80%99s-substance-dependence-treatment-programme-wsdtp
25 Gambell, drinkanddrugsnews.com/uk-drug-policy/

using. A sad reality is that women's prisons are full of grasses, and nowhere does this become more apparent than around drug use. Whether it's because people have just become so-called 'reformed characters' and are therefore keen to put others down, or because they are jealous (of your relationship, or popularity, or IEP status), if someone knows you are using, it is probably only a matter of time before the screws do. Be mindful of this when you are trying to source your drug of choice.

If you take drugs, and you are getting someone outside to sort out money for this, think *really carefully* about how this is managed. Obviously, it is in the user's best interests to make sure they don't get rumbled, but it can be easy, in a bout of desperation, to give out the personal details of someone outside. Only ever give out people's personal details *if* they have explicitly agreed, and to people you really trust, and don't refer too obviously to drugs, especially if you are a known user. People inside can get really mix-up about drugs and competition is fierce. I was amazed at times when someone knew a parcel was coming in that day, there would literally be a queue of girls outside the visits hall.

As with the use of drugs outside be aware of safety concerns around sharing needles (which are unsurprisingly in very short supply inside). It is also worth noting the Hepatitis B and C are real problems in women's prisons, and these viruses are often conflated with drug use.

If you are trying to score drugs which are legal/prescribed but are not on your 'script' (prescription) then there are various ways to go about this. Beware of obvious health and security risks in engaging in this practice. I'm sure the screws know what goes on, but just in case, I'll leave it up to people inside to go into details.

## Smoking

Please note that at the time of writing legislation surrounding smoking in jails is rapidly changing, so this section may be out of date fairly quickly.

Initially the much-publicised smoking ban in prisons was to be compulsory across the whole estate (136 prisons), but now the MoJ has allowed individual institutions to introduce changes "at their own pace"[26]. In private prisons, the ban is already enforced. In April 2016, a High Court Ruling overturned the compulsory, immediate ban on smoking in prisons (except in private prisons). Open prisons have been smoke free since October 2015. All closed jails now have a 'smoke free wing', though as the one in

---

26 gov.uk/government/speeches/smoking-in-prisons

my jail meant sharing with a load of people convicted of sex-offences on a high-security wing I decided to risk passive smoke but stay with my mates! Plans are in place to make Scottish prisons smoke free, but not Northern Ireland of Jersey. Guernsey since has been smoke-free since 2013, and the Isle of Man in 2008.

I'm not gonna lie; I hate smoking, and passive smoke in jail totally did my head in. Because so few cells have anything that could be interpreted as a window/air vent it can be really difficult for the smoke to dissipate. During my sentence, I shared a cell with someone who smoked and it was gross.[27]

Canteen baccy is expensive and nasty. When it gets close to canteen day, smokers get increasingly creative, making 'Frankenstein Fags' cutting precious dog ends with all kinds of shite: bible paper, prison issue teabags, dried fruit, even scraping nicotine off nicotine patches. I got reported to security for drying out nettle leaves (I used them to improve my prison issue noodles and make tea). One elderly woman on my wing who had serious mobility issues would suddenly start moving her zimmer frame at high speed and shouting abuse up and down the landing when her cravings kicked in, and she embarked on her weekly scrounge for dog-ends off people.

Screws who don't smoke routinely moan about their health, but as far as I'm concerned, whilst I'd love it if everyone *chose* to quit smoking tomorrow, if people inside want to spend their wages on burn to get through what is probably one of the most stressful experiences of their lives, then carry on. And if screws don't like it, then they shouldn't have chosen a job where their lives are so closely intertwined with those they seek to control.

I have massive respect for prisoners who give up smoking in jail; because everyone is at it. If you are trying to quit, keep yourself busy; go to the gym (even if you only manage a walk on the treadmill). Think about how much money you'll save on canteen, and how many more phone calls to loved ones you can make when you aren't spending all your hard earned spends. There are various support services inside you can access. Put an 'app' form into health care to go to the 'Smoking Cessation Clinic'. If you attend this clinic you may well be given nicotine patches. You may also be given a plastic twirly thing (not it's official name!) which the prison doles out to ex-smokers and self-harmers in a laughable attempt to distract them and keep their hands busy.

---

27 For what it's worth you could try quoting ukhumanrightsblog.com/2014/04/14/passive-smoking-in-prison-not-a-breach-of-human-rights-court-of-appeal/ to the screws

In anticipation of the smoking ban, NOMS and DHL introduced the 'E-burn' on the Canteen sheet in August 2015. This was a pilot project, as the 'E-burn' was specially designed for prisoners (who obviously couldn't access the components required for 'vaping'). The government claims that the E-burn is very popular in American jails, and launched a pilot project in Guernsey Prison which as apparently a great success[28]. However, my mates who tried it out were not impressed, as the E-burn hardly lasts for any time at all and is prohibitively expensive. Even people who were enhanced couldn't really afford it!

**Hooch**

A final note on hooch (home-brew), which is big business inside. PSI 68/2011, 'Cell, Area and Vehicle Searching', is used to do sporadic 'hooch runs' (searches of wings looking for hooch). On our wing screws often looked in people's sanitary bins which where the most commonly used vehicles for brewing. Historically it has been the toilet cistern. The quality of hooch varies hugely in jail. If you want to drink it, try to find out who is a reliable brewer. It will probably cost more, but is less likely to make you ill. If you are brewing hooch, be discrete. Staff have beady eyes when it comes to monitoring potential ingredients. They commented suspiciously several times on the number of green apples I kept in cell (many girls gave them to me because I was vegan and didn't like going to the dining hall). Many jails have restrictions on the amount of fruit you can have in your possession at any one time. In 2016 HMP Channings Wood even removed all fruit (including dried fruit) and sugar from the canteen sheet to try to stop people making hooch. HMP Dartmoor also implemented restrictions in order to stop people brewing 'pruno' ('prison wine').

If you want to drink alcohol there are also sometimes other ways to get drunk. Before staff got wise to it, the tipple of choice in my jail was the Avon perfume 'Little Black Dress' (which people could order a few times a year) and hair spray from the prison salon. Obviously consuming these products is potentially harmful as they weren't designed for human consumption...but whatever floats your boat!

28 insidetime.org/update-on-e-burn-and-electronic-cigarettes-in-prison/

# JAIL MAIL

## Letter Writing

> "You gotta do the time, you can't let the time do you. And without that connection to what's going on outside that wall, the time will end up doing you." *Miss Major[1]*

> "It is sweet but dangerous to wait for letters...to lay awake till the morning and stare at the ceiling... My advice to you would be: read and write as much as possible -and ignore the mirror" *Nazim Hikmet[2]*

When your inside one of the main highlights of the day is the lunch time mail distribution. People eagerly stand by their door, keen to get news from the world outside, putting off returning to work for as long as possible in order to savour the moment of opening a letter or reading an email. Mothers proudly show their friends the latest picture from or by their kid, those with lovers outside retreat to pour over precious heartfelt words and people awaiting sentencing anxiously anticipate the brown benefits envelope.

I don't know if the fact that there are so few anarchists inside is due to cunningly evading capture, or a sad sign of the times that not that many people are risking their 'liberty'. Either way, the result of this was that I got *a lot* of mail.

> "We see solidarity as a way of feeling oneself accomplice, of deriving reciprocal pleasure and in no way do we consider it a duty or sacrifice in the name of the 'good and sacred cause' be-

---

1 Miss Major, interviewed by Donahue, Jayden *Making it Happen, Mama: A Conversation with Miss Major, 2011*
2 Nazim Hikmet (Turkish Communist prisoner 1902-1963), *Letters from a Man in Solitary*

cause it is not of our cause, but of ourselves." *Pierleone Porcu[3]*

To me, letter writing is one of the simplest forms of solidarity, a beautiful exchange. Obviously, there are security implications for writing letters to prisoners. But you can always find ways around these if you really desire. On a practical level, I'd also say that even if you don't like writing letters, you can always send stamps, or stationary (and increasingly books now the laws have been a bit more relaxed). If you are posting stationary or stamps, check the jail will allow them, and it's better to send them a bit at a time, or security freak out and try to stop it all together. Whatever you are sending, make sure you list the contents in the letter or on the envelope so the prisoner can look out for it. Screws are known to have light fingers and mail in jail is notoriously unreliable.

I can only speak for myself, but I loved hearing about people's adventures and tales of the outside world. Some people feel afraid to go into details about this but for me what was more frustrating were the questions about my daily routine, and what I ate as a vegan prisoner. Poems and pictures were great (stuck up using prison issue toothpaste). Whenever I got stationary that was also exciting and a welcome break from the endless prison issue paper and scratchy pens.

## Security

When replying to letters, it is important to be constantly mindful of the security of your comrades, and yourself. This is especially important for the individual in prison before they put in their plea and are sentenced. It can be quite strange, and stressful writing with this constant pressure, but you do get used to it, and the pay back (receiving news from outside) is totally worth it.

The amount of 'NFI' I had ('Not for Issue') was staggering. NFI is a hilarious category, and shows the arbitrary nature of prison rules. For example, I wasn't allowed a postcard because it had a picture of a beer can on it, and could therefore be seen as encouraging alcohol. However, I was allowed anarchist publications including insurrectionist texts. CDs with 'explicit lyrics' or films rated 18 will not get past security. The irony is that you can watch most movies on normal TV, so it's a total farce. The same censorship occurs on NPR where any songs mentioning murder or drugs get bleeped out, to save prisoners delicate little ears. If you get sent post that is NFI they will try to make you send it straight out again on a visit as a 'hand-

3 Porcu, *Revolutionary Solidarity, 1993*

out'. Sometimes you can manage to access it if it stays in your 'stored prop' and a different screw is on shift.

It was also easy for me to access newsletters and pen-pals from groups like Bent Bars because I was 'out' and vocal in my involvement in LGBT-QIA issues. However, referring to an individual's sexuality is best avoided unless the prisoner discloses or discusses information on this issue first. Sometimes initial contact with someone inside can feel a little forced but it's better to tread lightly then build up an understanding of what feels OK. It is also worth noting that people's mental health fluctuates wildly in jail, so don't assume that just because someone was very open in one letter will mean they always want to talk about their politics or relationships. Likewise, don't be alarmed if sometimes people don't reply for a while. Prison life can sometimes feel uninspiring, and your pen-pal may not have much to say. It is also important to emphasise that if you write to someone inside and you don't get a reply, try to again after a couple of weeks. The prison mail system is notoriously unreliable. Unsurprisingly, screws rarely prioritise passing on mail from different wings/jails, so if you do get transferred, ask your mates to check for mail.

Writing to prisoners is great, but please do think about *what* you are sending, and the fact that by the time it reaches them, it will have been opened, and read by many other pairs of eyes! Here are some more examples of post I was sent but wasn't allowed: instructions on how to make a smoke bomb, a map of the surrounding area immediately around the perimeter fence (!?!), herbal tea bags and earrings. Security were even more on my case than normal when I received the map of the local area.

**Pen Pals**

If you are inside and you'd like a pen-pal, groups such as Bent Bars and the Anarchist Black Cross can help set you up with people[4]. Every prison should issue each prisoner with two O/L letters (second class letters paid for by the jail) and Foreign Nationals should get the same but for overseas mail. These are normally distributed late on Sunday night by the screws, but they are lazy so they often don't distribute them. Even if you don't write letters to mates, you may need them for legal stuff. Also, you can trade them with other prisoners. You are only meant to send two O/Ls a week you can get away with using more, as long as you don't put them all in the same batch of mail. There are various other ways to get around issues of postage, but for security reasons I'll leave that for people to find inside to provide more

4 See resources section for pen-pals

information.

> "The cage is society's coffin for him he has come to fear,
> where the only warmth comes in a letter,
> or falls in a bitter, shed tear.
> Time passes silently, like a thief in the night,
> creeps on by and leaves its etchings in the faces
> that long to stroll under the sky." *Harold H. Thompson*[5]

A lot of women in jail don't write letters for various reasons -literacy, language barriers, lack of confidence and resources are all common factors. One way I found to socialise without having to give too much away about myself was helping people write letters. I spent a lot of time during 'association' helping mates write legal letters, or maintaining their 'letter box' contact with their kids. Letter-box contact is the annual or bi-annual letter that mothers whose children have been taken by social services can write and it is an emotional roller-coaster and a minefield in terms of the language that can be used. For Foreign Nationals, especially mates with kids, having someone who can help them write letters home is a life saver. If you get a reputation as being trustworthy and discrete, you will have a lot of letter writing requests!

> "With midnight always in one's heart,
> And twilight in one's cell,
> We turn a crank, or tear the rope,
> Each in his separate hell,
> And the silence is more awful far,
> Than the sound of the brazen bell." *Wilde*[6]

Letter writing can be one of the best ways to uplift yourself in jail. Sometimes, however hard you try to avoid it, you will find yourself way too caught up in prison life. Sitting down and putting pen to paper can remind you of the world outside your "separate hell". I got a lot out of writing to other prisoners when I was inside, it was good to have pen-pals who could relate to the daily tedium of prison life.

## Emailaprisoner

Emailaprisoner is a brilliant service for those with access to a computer who don't mind the obvious security issues. Emails get distributed the day after

5 Harold H. Thompson (1942-2008) anarchist prisoner, *Caged* (in *They Will Never Get Us All!*) 1999
6 Wilde, 1904

they have been written (where as post can take quite a bit longer). It is easy to set up an Emailaprisoner account. Each email costs 40p, so cheaper than a stamp. In certain establishments, for an extra 25p the prisoner can even send a reply via email. These are listed on the Emailaprisoner website.

## Sending In Books

In 2013, Grayling instigated a book-ban as part of his crackdown on prisoners' "perks and privileges"[7]. However, in July 2015 this was revoked by Michael Gove[8]. It took a while for the prison system to accept this change, but people outside can now send in books from a wider range of suppliers, and for much less money. Also, the 12 book rule on books in possession has been relaxed. As long as all your belongings fit within the total volumetric control, the percentage of books is now unimportant. For more information on this see PSI 30/2013 5th Amendment August 2015, and PSI 30/2013 Annex 1.

If you want more political books to read, then 'Haven Books for Prisoners' is a good resource. They will send people inside two titles from their book list, which they can send in the post. Security around books is quite random. For example, I was allowed a book about Daesh, but not allowed a children's book. People outside should be able to send in books directly now, but acceptance of this is fairly inconsistent. If you are doing a course, you *should* be able to get books on an accepted reading list sent in. However, several people who have studied politics/criminology have been denied access to these titles due to supposed 'security' risks.

## Rule 39 and 'Confidential Access'

Legal mail is the one piece of mail that in theory the prison cannot open. Rule 39 (PSI 49/2011) clearly states that legal mail is confidential (see appendix 14). The PSI also extends the provisions to include correspondence with a range of other named bodies, including the PPO. This is called 'confidential access' correspondence, but the protections and the way the correspondence should be handled are the same as for the legal correspondence.

If you want to send a rule 39 letter, it's essential that you write 'Rule 39' clearly when you address the envelope. You will have to seal it in front of a screw in the wing office. They will then normally write their initial over the seal, and it should be sent out like that. Each wing should have a log book

---

7 politics.co.uk/comment-analysis/2014/03/24/comment-the-ban-on-sending-prisoners-books-is-part-of-my-reh
8 bbc.co.uk/news/uk-33497581

for legal mail sent out, so make sure they enter it in there. It's also worth making a note of the staff who signed it and the date for your records. When you get a reply, it *should* reach you unopened. However, as the PPO have highlighted this is often not the case. I'd say that of all my legal correspondence approximately two thirds had been ripped up; with the catch-all disclaimer "opened in error" scribbled across the front.

You have several legal numbers you can put on your PIN at any one time, separate to those of your social numbers. However, due to the irregular hours a lot of solicitors are in the office (many often at court, or on visits), and the limited time slots/credit prisoners have to use the phone, this can be tricky. Every jail should have a designated screw who oversees legal issues. If they are OK, they sometimes allow people to use the wing phone for legal calls, as long as they put the call through. Even though the Home Office claim legal calls are monitored, it's best to assume all calls are.

## Unwanted Admirers

A lot of individuals in men's jails will watch the local news, and Crimewatch, and once they hear someone has been sentenced, they will write to the local jail they have been sent to. Whilst post gets processed quicker if you have someone's prison number, you don't necessarily need it. As has been already outlined, as most courts will always discharge to the same prison, so you don't need to be Sherlock Holmes to work out where a new prisoner will get sent. I had an unexpectedly high volume of post from male prisoners after I had been sentenced.

Because I am a perfectionist, and I don't like seeming to be rude, I set myself the challenge of replying to all the mail I received in jail (if you did not get my reply, you can blame HMP!) However, after long reflection I did not reply to these letters. Some were pages and pages long, and sexually graphic, and I decided that even writing a brief "thanks but no thanks" letter would probably be seen as encouragement.

It is worth noting though that some people in women's prisons, especially 'straight' women, do enjoy having a male pen-pal to flirt with, especially on a long stretch. Having a fellow prisoner to write to can be cathartic as I said, as they can genuinely empathise with your situation. If you are inside, and you think this would help, then it may be preferable to get someone you know well in your jail to hook you up with a pen-pal. The sad reality is that there will always be someone in women's prisons with a partner in a men's jail so they can sort this out.

# VISITS

"Visits are a strange airlock between prison and the real world. It's definitely not an ordinary form of interaction. Even if you want to hold a normal conversation it's pretty impossible... watched over by CCTV cameras and over-zealous screws all the prisoners are sat there wearing hi-vis tabards like some kind of cycle proficiency training trying to not spill the emotional beans, light-headed from overindulging on sweets and fizzy drinks that you can rarely get on the wing...People are crying their eyes out, arguing, joking around and sick of the fifth year of this, others are desperately trying to pass drugs to their partner and everyone's ever-conscious that the clock is ticking towards boot-out time." Cattermole[1]

Prison visits are a minefield. Every prisoner is allowed visits no matter what their IEP status (though if your 'enhanced' you get more.) Each prison has a different visit duration, between an hour and 90 minutes per visit (and normally three a month, four if enhanced). You can normally have up to three adults and three young people (under 16) on a visit. Each prison also has a different booking system. You will normally have to issue a 'VO' (visiting order) for the first time someone comes to see you, with their name, address and date of birth. Once they have been accepted they can then book directly themselves. Some jails also issue 'PVOs ('privileged' visiting orders). This means that if you get put on basic, or face any kind of disciplinary proceeding they can take this visit away from you.

---

1 Cattermole, 2015

## Security

Once the visitor has shown ID and queued up they will be given a 'rub-down-search', sent through a metal detector and have their photograph taken. They may well also have to provide fingerprints. So-called 'passive drugs dogs' are used routinely in jail. They will sniff at you before you go in. If they 'indicate' it may well mean closed visits.

There are many PSIs which are relevant to security and visits:

- PSI 2011-016 emphasises the importance of "maintaining family ties" (the prison service loves this phrase) through visits as a way to stop re-offending (according to the MoJ prisoners with these links are 39% less likely to 're-offend').

- PSI 2011-015 covers the management and security at visits. It replaced PSO 3610 which dealt with smuggling drugs and visits. It states that "staff must act reasonably and proportionally and visitors cannot be banned on an indication by a drugs dog although it might be proportionate, on that occasion, to order a closed visit".

Once you are have made it through the minefield of security barriers, it is important to be mindful of security at all times during visits. Assume everything you said can be heard by the staff, even if you are lucky enough to get a table quite far away from them. The seating layout of visits is well-planned; in my limited experience, they seemed to put any one they had an interest in very close to the screws, then families, then prisoners who they weren't that interested in, and people convicted of sex offences at the very back.

Even if the screws aren't obviously earwigging, they will still be looking at who is visiting and how you are interacting. Lip readers are also sometimes used in visits so if you're on remand or waiting for news of an appeal/parole be really aware of this. Also, be aware that other prisoners may well be listening in to your conversations (people inside always commented on my "interesting" looking mates on visits!). It is also worth noting that the *duration* of the visit will also be observed by the screws. Some of mates who were receiving parcels would clearly be uncomfortable in their visit and request to leave after a very short amount of time, or go to the toilet. As most prisoners savour every precious moment they get with their visitors this looks suspicious and will most likely mean you get a more thorough search.

## Searches

PSI 67/2011: 'Searching the person': was updated in August 2016, in connection with the 'National Security Framework' (see appendix 15). There are various issues that relate to specifically to women's prisons.

A few notes on gender and searches. The much feared 'squat and cough' searches and searches on return from ROTLs now *only* apply to people in men's jails. I'm not sure why this is, and I am *not* advocating that these practices should be reinstated for those in women's prisons, but it's a further example of how the prison system is rife with inconsistencies based on gender. Also, whilst prisoners in women's jails can *only* be searched by female staff members, prisoners in men's jails can be searched by staff of *any* gender.

If you think any search has been carried out which contravenes instructions in this PSI you should study the relevant parts carefully before submitting a formal complaint listing the sections and/or paragraphs which you believe have been contravened. You should also ask to see a copy of the search report.

After the visit, prisoners are given a fairly thorough pat down search, and normally asked to remove shoes and socks. Screws will also 'wand you' with a metal detector, and often check you mouth, and ears.

## Closed Visits

> "Closed visits are an administrative measure, not a punishment…Administrative measures may be applied using evidence which equates to a balance of probabilities rather than the "beyond reasonable doubt"…Any period of Closed Visits or bans will follow a prisoner if he/she is transferred."[2]

Closed visits mean that the prisoner and their visitor cannot touch. According to PSI 2011-15, closed visits (and visitor bans) could be against 'ECHR Article 8' ('Right to Family Life') and must be considered individually, be proportionate (to alleged risk), and be reviewed regularly. Any continuing closed visits must be based on a time frame and *not* the number of visits. Visitors and prisoners must be informed of any sanction put in place (in writing) because of "suspected or proven inappropriate behaviour during visits"[3].

The most common reason cited for closed visits is because the visitor

2 PSI 2011-15
3 PSI 2011-15

has been 'indicated' on. However, this is not an exact science. As *IT* has highlighted: "There are lots stories about false indications and why this may be and these vary from the dog handler making a signal for the dog to sit, the dog mistaking petrol (from a car), to sitting on a bus after a drug user has sat in the seat. If the visitor is a user but has no substances on them it is likely that the dog will still be able to smell it on the clothing."[4]

PSI 2011-15 is a classic example of the way that violence and repression are encoded within prison legislation. Closed visits can be extremely upsetting for both the prisoner and the visitor. To claim that this practice is an "administrative measure, not a punishment" is a farce. The PSI then goes on to specify that Legal Aid is *not* available for assistance in relation to closed visits.

### Remand and Basic Prisoners

If you are remanded but not yet sentenced you can have as many visits as you like, so make the most of that while it lasts! Especially as at this point you are most likely to be in a jail relatively close to your home town (or as close as it's gonna get). Once you've been sentenced, you could be 'shipped out' anywhere so unless you have the luxury of a good support crew and family who can afford to travel, you will probably get less visits. Also, be aware that many jails restrict visits if you end up on 'basic'. Whether on seg or basic, you are still entitled to some visits. But it will be reduced and you may get significantly more grief from staff during and after them, or even be put on 'closed visits'. So, make the most of your time on remand!

### For the Visitor

Here are a few practical tips for the visitor:

- Don't forget your ID, and proof of address. In order to get on a visit, you will have to bring various forms of identity. Prison staff do not make exceptions for this and they will gladly turn you away. You can normally put all your valuables in a locker.

- Take money. Make sure you find out the specifics of the prison you are going to in terms of money being taken in. Some will only let you take in notes, others pound coins, so it's all quite confusing. Personally, I normally found that seeing my visitor was far more exciting than the gack they could buy me from the visits hall tuck shop. However, for many people,

4 insidetime.org/the-problem-with-closed-visits-and-banned-visitors/

this is the highlight of the visit/day/week and people will fantasise about what they will consume on a visit, then dissect it afterwards on the wing as part of their post-match analysis.

- Allow plenty of time to get there. Security will take ages. Also, if you are really keen, it's good to get to the prison early because then you will be processed quicker, and can get into your visit faster. The screws have no interest in how far you have come, or how emotional you are, they won't rush, and it is very common for people to get let in really late to a visit because they've had to wait to get searched. On a couple of my visits I was sat in what my mates called "cunts corner" (waiting for your visitor to arrive) for up to 45 minutes. All visits also have a cut off time when they will let visitors in, so be aware of this. Also, if someone in front of you in the queue gets 'indicated' on by the drugs dog then this can slow everything down massively.

- Ask at the jail about the Assisted Visits Scheme or any financial support that might exist. Prisons are often in difficult to reach places (many have a bus that takes people from the nearest town centre), and expensive to travel to, so take what you can if money is available! Some visiting groups also can provide financial support, though many of these are religious.

- If you are bringing children; bring plenty of toys to occupy them during the long processing procedure. Staff should not have any physical contact with children on visits, though there are searches. Be aware that people in women's jails often get really excited to see kids charging around the visits hall; it cheers everyone up. But it might also mean random people start talking to you!

- Always check with the prisoner before you book a visit. Having lots of potential visitors is great, but can also be quite difficult to manage. Don't be offended if someone inside doesn't prioritise you for a visit.

- Think before you speak. As with letters, don't be afraid to talk about life outside. I much preferred hearing about this on my visits than fielding a million questions about the tedium of daily life in jail. However, also don't moan on about yourself the whole time. Never, ever say "it sounds a bit like a hotel" as one of my visitors did, or make judgements/assumptions about what life must be like for the prisoner. If they seem like they are doing OK, they may well be putting on a brave face or sugar coating the grim realities of prison life so as not to upset/stress you. Unless you've been inside you will *never* know what jail is really like so *don't* make suggestions or assumptions unless invited to by the prisoner.

"I often hear people talking about how prisoners have it easy inside: they have televisions and live in 'luxury'. The thing people don't realise is that it is not appliances and simple comforts that give people their freedom, but the ability to exercise options...Your freedom to make decisions based on what you want is the only thing that sets you apart from an animal in a zoo." *Fellows* [5]

"If you haven't been there, you don't know. Listening is helpful, reassurance is helpful, talking shit about things you have no frame of reference for is harmful." *Halliday*[6]

For more information and support services available for friends and families of someone in prison please see resources section at the back.

## 'Prison Visitors'

If you don't get regular visitors, and you would like some, then ask in the library or chapel about having a 'Prison Visitor'. The 'National Association of Official Prison Visitors' started in 1901. Volunteers come into jails and you can see the same person regularly. Some people who didn't get any visits got a lot out of this (especially the opportunity for free munch!). However, as with a lot of charitable organizations it's worth noting that many of the volunteers are from quite a specific background (i.e. white, middle-class and middle-aged women). The rhetoric NAPOV uses on their website shows the slightly patronising/benevolent tone that the organisation adopts:

"Prison Visitors want to extend to those imprisoned something of the emotional and intellectual enrichment experienced through friends. They particularly try to encourage the development of a constructive use of a prison sentence whereby inmates gain both a sense of belonging to the community and the realisation that they themselves have the ability to contribute to society's well being. The contact between the 'outside' and the 'inside' enables both to understand each other better."[7]

5 Fellows, 2000
6 Halliday, *2014*
7 naopv.com/

## Official Visits

Official visits can be highly stressful. You will most likely get put into a small sealed cubicle for them, and all the usual security considerations should apply. Official visits normally happen on different days to normal visits, and do not come out of your monthly allowance of VOs.

Official visits normally mean legal visits. Be warned, even if your solicitor seems ok, they are notoriously slack at turning up for these visits. If you have a duty-solicitor (one working directly with the state) you should assume they won't turn up. They have a terrible track record.

It's worth making notes in preparation for your visit. Don't write too much (screws have beady eyes) but if you are nervous; especially if you have just been remanded, you'll no doubt have a lot of questions; and so having a memory jogger can help.

Other types of official visit can be social services or immigration. When I was inside I got a visit from the Metropolitan Police Counter Terrorism Unit. As this interview took place at a prison, I was "interviewed as a volunteer", which means no solicitor. Sometimes police arrest prisoners and will then take them to local cop shop. If the police say you are being interviewed as a volunteer you don't have to consent, and if they insist on interviewing you, then do this as a "no comment" interview.

> "When you are interviewed by police in relation to potential new matters, wherever that interview takes place, you are entitled to the same rights. i.e. ongoing and free representation. Generally, the police will do this when evidence comes to light in relation to further offences. What you need to be aware of is the police sometimes speak to people in prison with a view to getting them to admit to offences, so that they can "clear up their statistics."[8]

My old solicitor contacted the Counter Terrorism Unit on my behalf after I was told I had a visit from them coming up. The police said:

> "This is a routine visit in which the police will not be speaking to you about any past or present offences. This is nothing to do with any police investigations and police officers (apparently) visit prisons to reduce offending. You will not be interviewed under caution as this is a general chat about the

---

8 Notes for my old solicitor, 2015

prison system.""[9]

The police presented the interview as an 'opportunity' for me to talk about my experiences in prison. During the visit I was asked a bizarre range of questions to which I answered no comment in increasingly hostile ways. Topics included were: "How can the police force be improved? What protests have I engaged with? What is the structure the organisations I am involved with? What are their protocol's and guidelines? What are my views on violence? What do I think about 'proportionate policing'? Did I agree with my pre-sentence report? Why did I think people didn't like the police? What types of anarchist projects were there in the South West? Did I think that "Greek style tactics" would spread to London in light of all the cuts? What was my experience of prison like as an 'extremist'?"[10]

No one else that I knew had a visit like this when they were inside. The legal advice I was given was: "if they do talk about anything other than the prison system, this will be to see if you can provide information or have the potential of becoming a future informant (in exchange for early release?) It can be the only reason why someone from counter terrorism would come to speak to you about your welfare and experiences within the system."[11]

9 Counter-Terrorism Unit, 2015
10 Notes from my interview, 2015
11 Notes from my old solicitor, 2015

# CANTEEN

Prisoners face a double whammy of exploitation inside, where they are expected to work for peanuts, and then forced to pay massively inflated costs on their 'canteen sheets'. Canteen sheets are the way in which prisoners do their weekly shopping, and so national contracts are big business. DHL and Bookers make a hefty profit by supplying basic goods at luxury prices across the prison estate. British Telecom have the monopoly on prison phones and charge way over the odds. No wonder so many prisoners are risking mobile phones inside.

Canteen orders are processed by people in men's prisons. Many of my friends who smoked used to have a weekly whine about the light-fingered inmates of them who would routinely skim baccy off their orders. Fags available on canteen are rank. Turner's is basically pipe tobacco, and when I was padded up with someone who smoked it the stench hung in the air all the time. Prisoners have to pay way over the odds for this (often one pouch costs half a week's wages) so when someone takes the piss and nicks a bunch of it, it's very noticeable. There are some clear rules in relation to canteen and 'prison retail'. PSI 2013/023 is valid until 10/07/17:

> "This instruction enacts and supports the Prisoner Retail Specification in order to provide a retail ordering service, catalogue items, and newspapers/periodicals to prisoners which meet the diverse needs of the local population, has transparent prices, does not compromise control or security, and has standardised products, prices, and operational procedures."[1]

It is worth noting here the inclusion of the phrase "diverse needs". Trying to get stuff changed on canteen is a tedious process, but if you feel that

---

[1] PSI 2013/023

the specific daily demands of your lifestyle are not being met and it is an equalities issue, then try to speak to your Canteen Rep. Most prisons will have a designated member of staff, and also an inmate who liaise on these issues. I tried to get vegan omega supplements on the canteen as there was only cod liver oil. A lot of people from Jamaica campaigned to get a range of hair care products that reflected the diversity of styles and types among the prison population. However, the reality is that change is slow, and did not happen during my time inside. The 'National Products List' contains 1,000 products at any one time, and any changes must be authorised by the head of One3One Solutions[2].

The arrival of canteen is one of the highlights of the week. When you eventually get your weekly shop, it will be in sealed bags. Check it in the presence of DHL staff and the screws. If you think any items are missing you must challenge it there and then. It is always worth checking your fruit (it is often mouldy). If anything is missing or unsatisfactory get DHL distributors to give you a complaint or credit note. Your account should either be credited, or you should get more the following week. Receivers of canteen are literally a captive audience and you should assume you are getting fleeced at every opportunity.

If you have a mate on basic, or 'loss of', it can be really helpful to order a few items for them, especially if they smoke, as they will probably prioritise using their limited 'spends' on burn. Beware that if you are getting a vegan pack from the jail, they *will* check your canteen sheet. For me, this wasn't a problem because I am a vegan, but some girls who claimed to be but then ordered a bulk load of mackerel got busted.

If you are ordering stuff on canteen for someone else as payment for some kind of contraband be *really* careful, and discrete. The prison system keeps a beady eye on any kind of procedures that may be construed as bullying, and so will take disciplinary action against people giving items away. Never forget that everything from the library books you request to the items you order from DHL get analysed by staff.

We had some good (brief) parties using items off canteen. It takes a bit of planning, but people get very creative out of the meagre options on canteen and a few perks from the dining hall. Frantic Friday meals of dumplings, fish curry, elaborate noodle dishes and cakes made from evaporated milk and prison issue biscuits were regularly rustled up in the association room microwave before early bang-up.

---

2 One3one Solutions is the front of HMPPS used for organising labour in prisons. It runs over 100 'locations' in England and Wales (one3one.justice.gov.uk/index.html)

# LEGAL

"The government's Legal Aid and Punishment Act 2012 which came into effect in April 2013 represents one of the Tories most serious and vicious attacks on the poorest and most disadvantaged groups in terms of their relationship with an increasingly more repressive state, removing as it does the right to publicly funded legal redress for the already most powerless in society." *Bowden*[1]

Obviously, a lot of legal issues have been previously outlined in this publication, but this section will look at a few (fairly randomly selected) specifics that commonly come up inside. The legal system in the UK broadly falls into two sections: criminal law (everything up to sentencing) and prison law (post-sentencing). If you are on remand, or staging an appeal, this will still use the criminal law process. If you are challenging conditions, adjudications or licence conditions this is all within the remit of a prison law firm. If you are lucky enough to have found a criminal law solicitor that you rate (or at least tolerate) then it can be worth asking them for advice on any prison law firms they'd recommend, in case you need one at short notice. Note that in May 2017, the cuts to legal aid for prisoners that were instigated by Grayling during his time as justice secretary were ruled unlawful by the court of appeal.[2]

## Governing Structures

The secretary of state for justice (currently Liz Truss) controls the ministry

---

1 Bowden, 2010

2 This case was bough by PAS and the Howard League for Penal Reform, and began in 2013 howardleague.org/news/courtofappealrulingonlegalaid/

of justice; including NOMS, HMP, NPS, One3one solutions and the parole board. Traditionally, NOMS has been responsible for budgets, security and ensuring prisons adhere to the PSIs. However, as of April 2017 NOMS was replaced by 'Her Majesty's Prison and Probation Service' (HMPPS)[3].

HMPPS is now responsible for the "operational management of people custody and in the community". This will include strengthening security and intelligence, tackling 'extremism', rolling out the government's reform programme and a new 'leadership programme' for staff. There will also be the new role of Director with specific responsibility for women across the whole system. The MoJ will take over all aspects of prison policy, perform-ance and commissioning, and will have increased powers over policy and implementation. Liz Truss has stated that "creating HMPPS will bring clar-ity to managing our prisons and probation services while further profes-sionalising staff and building pride in their work". Apparently, "prison and probation officers do a vital job and they deserve to work in a world-class organisation which supports them in reforming offenders and keeping the public safe." [4]

The creation of HMPPS is another example of how the PIC is depend-ent on not just on *expansion*, but also *reinvention*. The system is endlessly remodelling itself, using the same tired phrases, reorganising its maze of departments, initiatives and governing bodies. This keeps a whole army of high ranking 'civil servants' in work, and is a big economic driving force behind the PIC in the UK. For example, there are various 'parliamentary under secretaries' who support the justice secretary, such as the secretary for prisons and probation, for victims, youth and family court justice and so on. There is a minister of state for Courts and Justice. The justice commit-tee is just one of 19 select committees. Its role is to examine the MoJ and other public bodies, and oversee the policies of the MoJ and justice minis-ter. The reality is that all these changes and organisations rarely mean much for the prisoner, other than even more grief, bang-up and discipline.

## Prison and Courts Bill 2017

In March 2017 Liz Truss published a new 'Prisons and Courts Bill'. This apparently is going to be the "biggest overhaul of prisons in a generation"[5]. Truss has talked of creating "safe and sustainable" prisons, and once again

---

3 insidetime.org/no-more-noms/
4 Truss, quoted in insidetime.org/no-more-noms/
5 gov.uk/government/news/justice-secretary-elizabeth-truss-unveils-landmark-prisons-and-courts-bill

this bill harks on about improving conditions for prisoners. According to IT "the Bill will enshrine into law, for the first time, that a key purpose of prisons is to reform and rehabilitate prisoners and takes forward measures announced in last year's Prison Safety and Reform White Paper."[6] Governors will be given control of education budgets, and there will be a league table system. 2,000 new senior staff positions will be created. All this will no doubt result in yet more compulsory courses and 'therapeutic' interventions.

## Inspections and Complaints

In terms of monitoring the prisons daily operations, 'Her Majesty's Inspectorate of Prisons' (HMIP) also informs the work of these minsters. HMIP does unannounced prison visits. Each establishment will get a visit every four to five years. The 'Prison and Courts Bill' gives increased powers to the HMIP and PPO (though as they are still run by the state this is highly unlikely to lead to much change). The Independent Monitoring Board also work routinely in jails, and publish their findings annually. The IMB relies on volunteers, so you can expect to see a lot of well-meaning middle class people wearing their badges. A lot of prisoners also write to their MPs if they have concerns. Personally, I see no point in this, but I guess if it makes you feel better and passes a bit of bang-up then good luck to you!

## Pre-Sentence Report

If you have been remanded and put in a guilty plea, you have the option to give a 'pre-sentence report'. This is a fairly daunting process (see appendix 16). A major motivating factor for me was that I wanted to be clear that I stood by my action, and was not sorry or remorseful in any way, and to provide some context for my actions, not for the media but for comrades and other people. Be warned: unsurprisingly, the cops will delight in selectively editing what you say to sound totally irrational (and in my case legitimise their claims of 'extremism') and waste no time in press-releasing your report in an attempt to discredit you and legitimise their legal proceedings against you. A note here to people outside: remember that the main stream press are total parasites and you cannot trust what they report! This sounds fairly self-evident but I was saddened -and enraged-by how quickly quite a lot of people forgot that in relation to my case and took their articles on face value.

---

6 insidetime.org/prison-not-for-punishment/

In order to save money, most pre-sentence reports now take place via video-link with the courts from jail. You may well be unlocked late (deliberately forgotten?) You don't have a solicitor present. Pre-sentence reports are conducted by a probation officer, and as in police interviews, they ask you the same questions repeatedly but in slightly different ways in order to try to trip you up. Take your time. You don't have to answer every question. It's worth thinking ahead about what main points you'd like to cover, as you will probably be overcome with rage, and also you obviously want to minimise the chances of messing up your security (and others).

If you are an anarchist, don't be surprised if they use the hate crime label against you in an attempt to enforce 'extremism' related work. In my case they said "your offence entailed physical damage to property and was targeted at direct victims due to 'hatred of an identifiable group'."

Here are some further examples of the nonsense from my pre-sentence report:

- "She accepts responsibility for the offence....however, she attempted to minimise her actions by contextualising/comparing them to violent tactics used by state"
- "Negative attitudes that will remain unchanged as a result of this conviction" (Note: they did change, they got more intense!)
- "Due to the nature of the offence and the amount of pre-planning involved he [probation officer conducting the report] suspects that you would have been involved with others engaged in this type of activity."

The prison system is obsessed by the concept of risk. This is returned to repeatedly in the pre-sentence report process, and they will use this as a way to legitimise licence conditions. For example, they decided in my case that risk was highest "when she is involved with others who hold similar views and decide to take direct action" and when I had any "association with anarchist organisations".[7]

Your solicitor will get sent a copy of your pre-sentence report and they should send you a summary. The pre-sentence report is obviously very one-

---

7 In the 'Offender Assessment' they will ask you lots of questions to try to ascertain if any of the following areas are issues or 'risks' for you: accommodation, education/training/employment, financial management and income, alcohol misuse, drug misuse, mental health, thinking and behaviour, additional behaviour. Note that if you answer *yes* to any of these aspects of assessment they will probably slap something on your sentence plan to 'help' you 'address' these issues. Don't expect support, it's just yet another way for them to try to demoralise the prisoner and inflict their poxy courses and 'treatments' on you.

sided. Any attempts you make to give context *will* be written off as being an example of you not taking responsibility for yourself. They call it "minimising your actions", and you'd better get used to hearing this phrase. It is also worth noting that if your alleged 'offence' required any amount of "pre-planning" they will use that as evidence of how 'high risk' you are. This assessment of risk has a gendered aspect: the CJS often takes an especially dim view of people they perceive to be women who have thought about their alleged crime before executing it. It is often the case for the legal system and the media to make very hysterical claims about female murderers in cases which were "pre-meditated", but comment much less on their male accomplices.

A word of caution, do *not* listen to the probation officers 'recommendations' arising from your report. It is really common for them to advise "consider a 12-month community order with requirements" (for example a curfew, or unpaid work/community service). However, this is normally totally ignored by the judge so don't think you've got a get out of jail free card if you see this on your report.

**OASys Offender Assessment System**

An OASys file is the detailed 'risk assessment' which will be used to justify your licence conditions. It is the document that prison staff use in an attempt to threaten those who do not comply with the regime. According to NOMS (now HMPPS), the OASys assessment consists of the following areas[8]:

- Needs: current offence, offending behaviour, social factors (accommodation, education, employment, financial management, life style, family links), personal factors (emotional well-being, thinking, attitudes)
- Risks: of harm to others, self-harm, escape and control risks, public protection issues
- Targets: plans to address risks and needs, motivation, offending behaviour programmes, interventions needed to reduce livelihood of re-offending.

OASys has been operating in all prisons (including private) since 2004, for all prisoners of 12 months or more. It is used by internal and external offender managers/Supervisors and the National Probation Service. See PS02205 for more information.

Your OASys report will include: your pre-sentence report, licence, ac-

8 westmerciaprobation.org.uk/page.php?Plv=3&P1=5&P2=20&P3=10

tivities, personal officer allocation, education, hours done at work, work party reports, evaluations on your 'performance' ('acceptable', 'standard'), visiting orders (and adjustments/issues), IEP status, disciplinary actions/ adjudications, and spends. It will also include 'contact logs' which are random comments from staff.

## Proceeds Of Crime Act (POCA)

Custodial sentences in relation to fraud/money laundering have massively increased over the last few years. The main reasons for this are the 'Criminal Finances Bill' (October 2016) and amendments under this bill to the 'Proceeds of Crime Act' (POCA, 2002). Also the 'Terrorism Act' of 2000 was amended to introduce 'unexplained wealth orders'. Suspects of fraud *have* to explain assets. Disclosure orders are normally used in relation to financial assets.

A POCA hearing is part of a civil regime. There is no jury. POCA hearings are now being extended to include the Financial Services Authority and HMRC (tax), POCA hearings are also affected by changes to the Policing and Crime Bill of February 2016. My experience of supporting mates waiting a POCA hearing, was that it can be extremely stressful. You have to provide evidence of, and account for, all of your finances and 'assets'. On a practical level, this is obviously quite difficult if you are inside. Emotionally, it is even more so if you are a Foreign National Prisoner, and/or you have dependants such as children. Many of the mothers I was inside with were properly pushed to their limits in this process as they feared their children would lose their home. If you know someone facing a POCA hearing, they may well appreciate support going through all their finances if they trust you. In 2015 the use of restraint orders increased in relation to POCA so that 'suspicion' replaced the concept of 'belief'. These restraint orders meant that the state could freeze assets that may be ceased at a later date[9].

In 2017 a new 28-day pre-charge bail-time limit was invoked for the POCA act. However, it's worth noting that this limit *can* be extended by a superintendent officer or higher. Prison law firms can help with POCA hearings and advertise on NPR, and in jail based publications. It's also worth speaking to PAS, or St Giles (if the POCA relates to your home)[10].

## Joint Enterprise (JE)

"Joint enterprise is a doctrine of common law dating back

9 accountingevidence.com/blog/2013/02/restraint-orders-under-poca-2002/
10 See resources section

several centuries that has been developed by the courts to allow for more than one person to be charged and convicted of the same crime. If it can be proved that the participants were working together in some way, then they are all guilty of all the crimes committed during the course of their joint enterprise, regardless of the role they played. Unlike the crime of conspiracy, in which the offence consists of merely agreeing to commit a crime, in joint enterprise all parties are convicted of the actual offence, for example: murder." The Bureau of Investigative Journalism[11]

The doctrine of common purpose, common design, JE, or joint criminal enterprise relies on the concept of *liability*. It was commonly applied in public order situations and 'violent crimes'; where knowledge of the intentions of someone associated with you was equated with executing the act that they were convicted of. As with many aspects of the PIC/CJS, the common purpose doctrine was established in England and Wales and later adopted in countries that were colonised by England, such as Scotland, Australia, Trinidad and Tobago.

In February 2016, the Supreme Court and the 'Judicial Committee of the Privy Council' found that the law had been incorrectly applied. The case of R v Jogee (2016)[12] highlighted that foresight and intention are equated but *not* synonymous. Because of the 2016 case, JE cases *should* be revisited investigating not just what the alleged accessory saw, but also their state of mind. The high court ruling found that the law been misapplied for 30 years: and that foresight *doesn't* prove guilt, and that knowledge was *not* the same as assistance[13].

Between 2005-2013 there were 500 convictions of murder under JE. Following the logic of the UK legal system, these convictions should have actually been for man slaughter. However, as with most IPP cases, many JE prisoners have not had their cases reviewed despite the legal changes, and so are still in prison.

For more information also see the informative pamphlet *Miscarriages of Justice (and How to Avoid Them)*[14] and the JENGbA website[15]. This campaign was launched in 2010 by families of those found guilty under the

11 The Bureau of Investigative Journalism, *Joint Enterprise 2014*
12 supremecourt.uk/cases/docs/uksc-2015-0015-judgment.pdf
13 supremecourt.uk/cases/docs/uksc-2015-0015-judgment.pdf
14 Inside Justice, *Miscarriages of Justice (and How to Avoid Them)* 2014
15 jointenterprise.co/

# BIGGER CAGES, LONGER CHAINS?
# TAG, OPEN AND ROTL

If you want to play their games and 'progress' through the prison system then these are some of the main options presented to people in women's prisons. Please note that I don't have any direct experience of any of them so apologies if the information is inaccurate.

## Home Detention Curfew (HDC) 'Tag'

If your sentence is between three months and four years long you can apply for early release (HDC or 'tag'). This is an electronic tracking device that enables the authorities to check where you are. In order to get a tag you have to prepare a report proving you are a repentant and reformed character, and present it to a board consisting of prison staff. As with the parole board and court of appeal, there is often a huge back log of peo-

Chris
Stain,
*Chains*

191

ple waiting to sit these boards, and so don't pin your hopes on the date they put on your sentencing sheet. The HDC board will look through all your contact logs, work party reports and IEPs, and ask you a bunch of questions. If you haven't completed your sentence plan, and you aren't 'enhanced' it is unlikely (though not impossible) that you will get tag.

A lot of people, especially those with children, get really excited about tag. To be eligible you *must* have a home address probation can check. This is a luxury many people inside do not have. If you don't have an address you can go to, you can apply for tag and be in a bail hostel. Your solicitor can help with this. Various organisations advertise on NPR and St Giles may also be able to provide some help[1]. Individuals on tag are subject to it until their release date when the next phase of 'supervision' begins.

The HDC suitability assessment takes place approximately ten weeks prior to your eligibility date. The usual assessment is a standard test and is carried out by probation. Information about you will be gathered from not only yourself (or via your solicitor's representations) but also a member of prison staff who has daily contact with you. Internal probation will also contact the probation office of the area into which you wish to be released, in order for a home visit to be undertaken and to consider if you are suitable for release on HDC[2].

If you have been convicted of a violent or sex offence, or are currently serving an extended sentence under the 'Crime and Disorder Act' (1998) you will *not* be eligible for tag. You will also be excluded if you are serving an extended sentence, or have previously absconded (for example from open-prison), have previously breached a curfew order or were recalled for breaching the HDC scheme, or have any issues specified by the Mental Health Act. If you have been out on tag previously but not complied with your curfew before you *may* get refused (though one of my mates successfully got HDC despite absconding on a different sentence so worth a try). If you have a history of substance misuse or violence you will not be considered.

If a prisoner is on HDC they must sign a licence which has curfew times, normally 19:00 -07:00. An electronic tag is fitted at the address agreed by probation, and to the prisoner. Monitoring equipment is installed at the address by a private contractor.

"If the prisoner breaks their curfew, the electronic tag will

1 See resources
2 For more information see firsttimeinprison.co.uk/release/ and insidetime.org/hdc-and-the-presumption-of-unsuitability/

alert the contractors and the prisoner may be recalled to prison where they will stay until their automatic release date. If they are recalled for breaching the HDC curfew conditions, they will not be released again on HDC either for the rest of their sentence or on any future custodial sentences they may receive."[3]

One of my probation officers tried to encourage me to opt for a so-called 'buddy tag' system once I had been released, in order to demonstrate that I was compliant enough to leave the bail hostel and could be trusted at a home address. The 'buddy tag' is used for 'prolific or high profile' individuals who have completed the custodial part of their sentence. Unlike HDC, it is not linked to a box, but rather uses GPS satellite software. You don't have a curfew, but it does mean the state can track your every move, the rationale being that then *if* a crime occurs in your area there is proof that you were elsewhere. Unsurprisingly, I turned down this 'opportunity' to prove my 'innocence'.

## Open Prisons

As I have outlined earlier, if you are in a women's prisons everyone is mixed together inside. However, you may decide to apply for 'open conditions' if you have two years or less left to serve on your sentence. Again, eligibility is all dependent on your on-going risk assessment, i.e. your OASys report and other input from staff.

In theory, unless you have a sentence of three years or longer, have been category A whilst on remand, are a MAPPA level two or three, or identified as a PPO (Priority or Prolific Offender) or are convicted of a terrorism related offence you *should* be entitled to go to open. If you have any outstanding charges, or are subject to a Confiscation Order you will be refused.

If NOMS/HMPPS have decided you are likely to escape or abscond, risk or harm the public or demonstrate any so-called 'control issues' that impact on the security of the open prison then you will not be eligible to have your conditions reviewed.

Some reformist organisations have demanded that *all* women in custody be sent to open prisons, arguing that women have specific needs, and these are much better met within this less restrictive environment. They also cite the fact that most people who abscond after being transferred

---

3 justice.gov.uk/offenders/before-after-release/home-detention-curfew

to 'open conditions' are those from men's prisons. *No* prisons -open or closed-can *ever* meet the 'needs' of their inmates and that *no one* regardless of gender should be kept behind their doors. Fences are not just what makes a jail and it must all be destroyed.

It is not my place to tell you how to ride your sentence, and certainly I would say that Lifers or those with a long sentence may well want to work towards open-conditions, as they will have to show 'progression' to be eligible for parole. However, going through the process to get a transfer is like applying to be enhanced. I have never been to an open prison, but have seen the process people had to go through to get there, and it seemed to involve a fair bit of interaction with staff and playing their games. I'd also be aware of people trying to get to open-conditions, as they may well be more likely than most to try to get the approval of prison staff.

Some of my mates seemed to really buzz of being in open once they got there. However, everyone I know who went there said that bitchiness, back stabbing and grassing are all fairly common, as people are so desperate to get parole, or not lose their place in open. As with being 'enhanced', those who have climbed the ladder to get to open conditions are expected by staff to comply. Superiority and snitching seem to go hand in hand with this.

## Release on Temporary Licence (ROTL)

As I have previously outlined, the main use of ROTLs is for working outside the gate. For more information see PSO 6300. You can also apply for a ROTL if a partner or close family member is terminally ill, or you want to attend a funeral. However, *do not* be surprised if your request gets rejected outright, or if they deliberately long out the administrative process so that the chance to do this is no longer relevant.

If you haven't been risk assessed for open conditions then you won't be eligible for ROTLs, and you will be handcuffed whenever you are escorted outside the gate (for example hospital or court appearances).

Because of lack of staff, and general staff laziness, in 2015 ROTLs fell by 23% from the previous year (Lifers being accepted for ROTL were hit particularly hard, with a 40% decrease)[4]. Prisons often use an alleged fear of absconding to deny people ROTLs, yet the failure rate is only actually 0.5%, and this was mainly by individuals from men's prisons. For more information see PSI 13-2015 'The Use of ROTL'.

If you are prepared to jump through the hoops and get ROTLs, you can

4 PRT, *Inside Out: Release on Temporary Licence and its Role in Promoting Effective Resettlement and Rehabilitation, 2015*

work outside. 'Working out' means majorly sucking up to prison staff as you have to prove you are not at risk of absconding. Normally you will have to do a stretch gardening just outside the prison gates, or working in the staff mess (canteen). Then you might get the 'privilege' of cooking pasties at Greggs, or driving the screws and governor around. As has been previously outlined, be careful around inmates looking to work their way up this labour ladder, as they will be engaging with prison staff on a daily basis. However, if you can find someone who is playing the game but also up for taking risks it does have its advantages.

To those considering selling their soul to get jobs outside the gate, it's worth noting that you should not expect to get national minimum wage. The prison will fleece you of your earnings. Outworkers pay a 40% levy on wages. Under the 'Prisoners Earning Act' (1996)[5], prisoners working outside the gate can get up to £20 and the rest goes to the jail. So even if you are doing the old 9-5 you won't be able to save much.

Despite claims of their help in rehabilitation, number of prisoners on ROTLs has been steadily decreasing over years. Timpson's and Sue Ryder have reported a major drop off in numbers since 2013. Restrictions on ROTLs were increased in March 2015 under Grayling, after many individuals from men's jails absconded[6].

ROTLs are perfect for big business because they get cheap labour *and* can dress it up in some philanthropic nonsense. Richard Branson has bigged-up Virgin Trains as benevolently "giving people the dignity of work"; by recruiting 25 candidates who had recently left the prison system. Branson has also publicised Virgin trains use of prison labour: "The more productive you can make people while they are in prison the more they can learn and the better their chances of succeeding once they are let out"[7].

James Timpson, Managing Director of Timpson's has stated "I find the staff we've recruited from prisons are among the best colleagues we've got...We see this as a great way of not only helping people but of getting people to work for us."[8] Timpson's currently employ 89 ex-prisoners, who began working for them in their prison workshops. Timpson's pays an annual fee of £37,000 to the prison estate to employ inmates, so it's obviously big business for all parties (except the prisoner!).

5 legislation.gov.uk/ukpga/1996/33
6 prisonreformtrust.org.uk/PressPolicy/News/ItemId/285/vw/1
7 insidetime.org/people-with-convictions-need-the-dignity-of-work/
8 gov.uk/government/news/timpson-works-with-prisons-to-turn-around-lives

# PROTECTION?

"Prison is never going to be 'safe' or 'protective'. It is an institution designed to repress, punish and control people."[1]

"Prison, a social protection? What monstrous mind ever conceived such an idea? Just as well say that health can be promoted by a widespread contagion". *Emma Goldman*[2]

The prison estate claims to have a benevolent and well as disciplinary function, and this is especially true in relation to women's prisons. This rhetoric is a diversion from the grim realities of everyday life. With the blame laid at the feet of the prisoner, the state becomes a protective force, supposedly supervising the individual for their own benefit. As the quotes above show; the prison estate is a clear manifestation of the systemic violence inherent in institutional control. I do not want protection from the state. It is incapable of protecting me. The examples included here show this. Please note this is a tiny fraction of people locked up, at a specific moment.

- My father died in police custody when I was 18. No one was held accountable. When I was 14 I was handcuffed and 'de-crutched' (having an officer remove drugs from my vagina). I have been in and out of custody ever since. I have had all of my children taken away from me.

- She has severe epilepsy. On one day, she had six fits. When fitting, she often knocked her head. Fellow prisoners helped hold her and look after her. But then she was banged-up in a cell on her own, and left overnight. She saw the prison nurse but was never taken to hospital and staff ignored her cell bell several times.

- She has a history of mental health issues and has been on suicide watch.

---

1 *Lockdown, 2008*
2 Goldman,*Prisons: A Social Crime and Failure,* 1911

She is on an ACCT, and repeatedly told prison staff she wasn't coping and needed help. She is being bullied and on a noisy landing. She was ignored until she threw a cup at a screw, and is now being done for assault, so she is banged-up on "basic" on the wing, which was the cause of all her problems initially.

- I tried to kill myself after years of being blackmailed. I took an overdose and cut my wrists. The police found me five minutes before I would have died. I was unconscious. When I came to, I was handcuffed tightly over my cut wrists. I was arrested straight away. I wasn't offered any mental health support.

- She is a Lifer. She has been inside for many years. One day she ended up in hospital. As soon as she returned to jail, she got put on basic for having items that the hospital    had given her for her treatment, and that reception had allowed.

# LAST FEW WEEKS

As your release date looms, you will spend an increasing amount of time being called up to the all powerful 'OMU' ('Offender Management Unit'). The 'OM' you have in jail works closely with probation outside. They are proper scum. Do not trust them. I saw a lot of prisoners who had a healthy mistrust/dislike of screws be lured in by their offender managers patronising promises of 'rehabilitation' and what life could be like outside if they complied with their licence conditions.

## Offender Supervisors (OS)

> "You are obliged to pretend to respect people and institutions that you consider irrational. You live by fashion in a cowardly era, attached to ethical and social conventions you despise, that you condemn and you know the lack of any background... In this unbearable struggle, you lose every dance for life, all sense of your personality as every moment they oppress, they limit and control the freedom of your strength." *Octave Mirbeau*[1]

By this time you are close to your release date you will most probably have had several video-link or telephone conferences with your outside probation officer (now officially called 'offender supervisors' for some reason). External offender supervisors have a track record like that of duty solicitors in terms of actually turning up for appointments or doing any of their work. It is worth putting their number on your PIN (though they rarely answer the phone).

---

1 Mirbeau quoted in CCF, *Chaotic Variables, 2016)*

Probation wield a huge amount of power (it is them, not the police who will have the ultimate say over your case) but they always make it seem like they are trying to help you. Your OS 'in the community' should specifically help with parole, resettlement, HDC (tag), ROTL, and external organisations. They will use officious and patronising language to disguise the fact that they are making your life hell and enjoying every minute of it. NOMS claims that "all prisons are working to deliver a safe, decent, rehabilitative culture which promotes desistance. For all staff, this means that every contact with an offender should be seen as an opportunity to engage; to motivate, to act as a positive role model."[2] Every "contact" I had with my offender supervisor just made me want to scream in his face.

Do not believe *anything* *t*hat your offender supervisor says *before* you sign your licence. For example, about five months prior to release mine told me I could return to my home town and my old work. Then, two weeks before release I got hit by an epic four-page licence, plus supplementary pages (such as exclusion zones) which meant that none of this was possible[3]. You won't sign your licence until you are released, but it is valid whether or not you sign it.

## Local Release

If you have been serving a long sentence and have left your local remand jail behind, you may get shipped back there for so-called 'local release'. This is in theory meant to prepare you for joining the world outside. In reality, it's still a cage, and many people don't want to go through with this. The end of your sentence can really drag, and it's nicer to spend it with your mates inside than return to the high-drama and mix up that exists in most remand jails. A positive of local release is that you'll be closer to your loved ones, so you may well get more visitors, but otherwise it's just another way for them to unsettle you. If you get news that they are considering shipping you out for local release, or it seems like a common procedure in your jail, then you can resist it. If you have any outstanding education or work party commitments this can help (though in reality if the governor has decided you're going there is very little you can do).

## Saying Goodbye

Never have I had such a bitter-sweet experience of saying goodbye as leav-

---

2 PSI 04/2015 and PI 01/2015
3 See appendix 18 for the standard licence and additional restrictions

ing jail. A lot of my mates were long-term prisoners and due to my licence, it was going to be difficult to stay in touch with them whilst I was complying with it. A lot of people get 'gate fever' several weeks (or even months) before they are released; they cannot stop talking about that glorious life that awaits them on the other side of the fence. Whilst it's obviously nice for people to have stuff to look forward to in jail (good news is a rare occurrence and worth celebrating!) this can get tired fairly quickly. Even if you are super excited, it's worth being aware of all the people you are leaving behind, many of whom do not have the luxury of a release date at all.

Most people give away most of their belongings just before they leave. Competition for this can be fierce and don't be surprised if some people you never really spoken to before get pally when your release date nears. There are definite codes of conduct on this in women's prisons; it is frowned upon to ever use or take anything you had with you inside once you've been released. Some jails will let you officially put items from your prop onto someone else's card; but most don't, because they say it encourages bullying, so it's best to keep it discrete.

> "Before your cell-bye-date distribute your belongings among your friends. It's a weird vibe when you're walking down the corridor towards the gates with all your stuff in big HMP bags, there's an understandable longing and jealousy from all the people who you've made friends with. Don't forget these people – it's easy to do when there's so much to do in the outside world but you've got to make a conscious effort to keep in touch." *Cattermole*[4]

A final word of warning; be a bit careful about who you give your contact details to. It can be easy to think that someone you are close to inside will be a friend for life, but you might feel differently when you reflect on your relationships after release. Also, don't make promises you can't keep; like saying you'll visit loads of people if you think you'll be too busy or this will be too traumatic for you.

---

4 Cattermole, 2015

# SOLIDARITY

"And, if I know anything at all,
it's that a wall is just a wall
and nothing more at all.
It can be broken down."[1]

The much quoted poem above by Assata Shakur encapsulates a beautiful combination of hope and aggression, both of which are sustained when you are in prison by the concept of solidarity. From a coded message, to a noise demo, from a banner drop to a bunch of flowers, the actions of others those

1 Shakur, *I Believe in Living* printed in *Assata: An Autobiography Second Edition* 2014

outside can give the person inside strength, courage and resolve.

> "A rebel and insurgent is a serene spirit, a spirit without time because it lives in a continuous present made of solidarity. Solidarity which by definition unites generations, unites efforts, unites action, unites our lives, unites our hearts, as differently and physically distant as they may be, they have lived, live, and will live!"[2]

As this quote from former prisoner Marco Camenisch outlines, solidarity is a great unifier: across walls, bars, continents, and even time. It means that the prisoner is never alone. Solidarity gives strength and courage. Solidarity means attack.

> "I will not deny it, in every action that someone salutes us as anarchist prisoners, both in Italy and the rest of the world, my heart fills with joy. This is my life today. The war continues, never give up, never give in. Long live FAI-FRI. Long live CCF. Long live the black international."[3]

---

2 Camenish, a long-term anarchist prisoner was released in March 2017. Quoted in *Mapping the Fire: International Words of Solidarity with the Conspiracy of Cells of Fire – Black International Editions, 2012*
3 Cospito, 2017

# PART TWO: ON ROAD

## RELEASE

"Bang. The door is shut. This time however, you are one the outside...Your prison survival strategies helped you deal with an environment that is not really suitable for human life. Now all the strategies you internalised get in your way. The prison experience teaches you to keep what is important to yourself, not to reveal anything, not to make yourself vulnerable... Not wanting to be dependent on anything complicates possible bonds. The ability to be alone turns into a desire to be so...It is difficult to switch off the control over your emotions that you have worked so hard to attain." *Viehmann* [1]

Everyone in jail says "don't look back". People are very superstitious about not taking a glance over your shoulder as you take that much anticipated walk through the prison gates.

There are good reasons why people are so superstitious on release, as the chances of recall are high. Much has been written about the minefield of problems women face when they go back out on road. Being given a custodial sentence can be deemed to be making oneself 'intentionally homeless' and therefore many people are unable to access benefits or get kids out of care. Citizenship issues, destitution, poverty, health and addiction are just some of many reasons why being released can be stressful. However, these issues are just as likely to affect *all* recently released prisoners, *not* just women.

---

1 Viehmann, 2009

"Prison wasn't 'the best days of my life'. But, when a number of very particular human beings who are forced to cohabit against their will make it to come together on the basis of this common denominator, and simply be themselves for a moment with their exquisite idiosyncrasies, a strange alchemy occurs that transcends all walls and becomes the moment of freedom, and a threat to the status quo of the prison." *Weir*[2]

When my release date came, I had highly mixed emotions. My licence meant that once I left the confines of the prison I couldn't communicate with most of my close mates, both inside the jail and out. The person I was most upset about leaving was my girlfriend and I will never forget seeing her silhouette gazing out of her cell as she watched me being escorted through the grey dawn.

"We all tell ourselves a story to get through prison... The reality is that it never comes true... The excitement is amazing and I don't mean to downplay that at all, but there's always an element of disappointment". *Jeff Luers*[3]

Once I'd been processed and given my release money (you get issued with £46, to last you till your first instalment of the dole), and my two black prison issue holdalls, I was then ushered into a police car. My licence stated that I had to have a police escort to the bail hostel that I'd be forced to live in for the next three-six months. So, walking through the gates never happened.

When people get released they have a whole range of responses. Many are met by family or friends. Some get high at the first available opportunity. A lot of dealers loiter at train stations near prisons, keen to hit up recently released people for their travel/release grant for drugs. One of my mates went to the off licence near our jail, got drunk waiting for the bus, fell asleep and then ended up straight back inside within 24 hours.

"I woke up this morning, you know?
And the sun was shining and everything was nice
and I thought...this is going to be one terrific day, so you better live it up, boy...
Because tomorrow, maybe, you'll be gone." *James Dean*[4]

---

2 Weir, 2010
3 In Halliday, 2014
4 Dean, *Rebel Without A Cause, 1955*

# PRACTICAL INFORMATION

"We believe you are the best person to find solutions to your problems, but we will help you find them. You can be crime free and we will support your efforts to get there."[1]

"Homelessness, unemployment, drug addiction, mental illness, and illiteracy are only a few of the problems that disappear from public view when the human beings contending with them are relegated to cages. Prisons thus perform a feat of magic...But prisons do not disappear problems – they disappear human beings."[2]

There are an overwhelming amount of supposed support services for prisoners when they are released, though in my experience, as with all aspects of 'rehabilitation' they often fail to deliver even the most basic level. As Davis has clearly argued: prisons do *not* solve the many reasons people end up incarcerated, and individuals are normally in a worse position when they are released than when they got sent down.

It's depressing seeing people excited about the possibility of some new initiative or funding, only to be crushed weeks later by the inevitable realisation that very little has changed and these glimmers of hope have come to nothing. Also, as with most charitable or reformist organisations, the emphasis is very much on *individual* not *social* change. The resources section at the back of this publication has lots of contact details, but I wanted to highlight some of the most commonly used.

Note that the organisations below are all national[3], but there are most

1 Kent, Surrey and Sussex Community Rehabilitation Company (KSSCRC) and Seetec Justice, 2015
2 Davis, 2012
3 See resources section for contact details

likely a whole bunch of groups/resources in your local area as well. There may well also be small grants you can access. Yes it feels degrading asking for these poxy crumbs but every penny counts when you've been released and haven't had your first instalment of the dole!

Organisations like 'Women in Prison', 'Unlock' and 'Nacro' can help you access different services, training and funding when you are released. Nacro is a charity that has been going for 50 years and helps people access health, education and housing. Unlock also provide similar information, but are aimed more at anyone with a criminal record not just ex-prisoners. Women in Prison (mentioned earlier in this text) also provide a lot of support for ex-prisoners. Like St Giles, they operate a 'Through the Gate' service that can organised for your release. They also have various support initiatives and centres 'in the community'. Ask your probation officer about these, or if you are in a bail hostel staff (or the other people inside) might be able to make some suggestions. PAS is also still useful even if you've been released for practical information on licences.

## The First Few Days

The first few days of release can feel confusing. You better grit your teeth and prepare for either unspoken judgements and cold indifference, or patronising excitement and inappropriate, invasive intrigue, as you try to make sense of the minefield that awaits the newly released prisoner. It can be really daunting, especially if you have a restrictive licence. If you are over 18 you'll get a discharge grant from the jail of £46. If you don't have a home to go to might get an extra £50 which will be paid directly to the accommodation provider. The 'Resettlement Officer' will apply for this on your behalf in jail. You can also ask probation for a travel warrant if you have far to go to get to your approved address (but they are extremely reluctant to give these out).

If claiming benefits, you will need your National Insurance number and a bank account. If you don't have proof of identity, use your licence. It's really easy to end up trapped in a Kafkaesque nightmare of bureaucracy: you need ID to apply for benefits, but then you don't have proof of address to get ID. Some local councils will give you £50 for clothing if you present them with your licence and proof of address in that area. Other small grants may be available.

## Housing

St Giles is good for housing advice. They train prisoners up to give advice, and can also organise for ex-prisoners to support you when you are released. Their 'Through the Gate' service is re-assuring for a lot of prisoners.

If you have concerns about housing; speak to your personal officer, or Shelter before you are released. Remember, everything in jail moves *really* slowly and so allow plenty of time to address your concerns and make a plan. Housing benefits are available for up to 13 weeks when you are on remand. However, be warned, some judges deliberately give sentences of 14 weeks in some areas to ensure that the defendant will lose their home if claiming benefits.

If you are getting housing benefits and they stop, you will be in danger of losing *all* your stuff. This can obviously be extremely upsetting, so if you think you will be in danger of becoming homeless due to a custodial sentence try to make sure someone can clear your stuff out.

You may well be considered a 'priority need' by council, but if you are not then consider asking friends and family, or looking into council run B&B's, night shelters, refuges, hostels, approved premises or supported housing. If you are hoping to rent privately make sure you search for landlords that take will accept 'DSS' (people on benefits), and consider applying for a Discretionary Housing Payment (DHP) for help with your deposit. If you are in a bail hostel and trying to leave, ask for help from the housing officer (but beware, they are sometimes very nosy/unhelpful).

## Benefits advice

The Citizens Advice Bureau (CAB) is the most reliable source of benefits advice. They can also advise on housing and other areas. If you are in a bail hostel, a member of the local CAB team might come in. Or try to find out when they are open. In these dark times, the CAB is often used by a lot of people trying to get information, so you may have to wait a while to get an appointment.

CAB provides free, confidential advice across the UK. They can help with all aspects of the benefits system, and also help with legal advice and prepare for tribunals and debt. They publish loads of useful resources on their website.

## Signing on and careers advice

Unlock gives practical advice on things such as disclosure of your convictions, trying to get insurance, and other aspects of life post-jail. According to Unlock there are over 10.5 million people in the UK with a criminal record[4]. The main aim of this charity is to provide advice and support issues connected to seeking work. They can advise on the best process of disclosure (for CRB/DBS checks and job interviews) and other aspects of employment with a criminal record. They can also provide information on when a conviction is 'spent' (expired).

Most people go on 'Job Seekers Allowance' (JSA) when they are released. If you are applying for jobs that you actually want, then it's worth following Unlock's advice. You *must* disclose your criminal record if asked (unless your conviction is spent), however, you can just say on the application form that you have a criminal record, and provide more information at interview. This way you don't have to go into details. You might also want to use a 'disclosure statement'. If you are unsure how/what to disclose and how much context to give, then there are some organisations that can help. They do work with probation, but if it's just to draft a statement it won't mean selling your soul.

All my licence conditions made me the least attractive employment prospect ever. Be warned, if you are signing on these days you will get *a lot* of grief from the Job Centre and they expect a high number of job applications per week (this is difficult if you are living in a bail hostel and not allowed to use a computer!)

### Older Ex-Prisoners

The Restore Support Network mentors and befriends older prisoners. It uses the requirements of the 'Care Act' and provides a focus on person centred care and care planning. This includes the provision of advice and information as well as signposting to local services. It aims to enable people with criminal convictions to have control over decisions about their care and live independently[5].

The Restore Support Network has addressed the problem of social isolation amongst older ex-prisoners (and older people in general). This is a *huge* problem which risks becoming an epidemic. *IT* has compared it to obesity in terms of being a future time-bomb/death trap if left unchecked: "both are potential killers with the only difference between the two being that older ex-prisoners are more likely to be victims of social isolation."[6]

---

4 unlock.org.uk/policy-issues/key-facts/
5 restoresupportnetwork.org.uk/
6 insidetime.org/age-related-loneliness-is-a-ticking-time-bomb-waiting-to-explode/

## Drugs and Alcohol

There are various support groups for people with addictions. If you have the misfortune to be in a bail hostel or council B&B then you will probably be around a lot of people who are either using or recovering from addiction. This can be really tough. Also note that if you are in this situation and you decide to go to your local Alcoholics or Narcotics Anonymous then you may well see people from where you are staying, which can be quite a difficult experience if you are trying to deal with a lot of emotional stuff.

If probation have an inkling that your crime was the result of 'substance misuse' they will be very fast (and assertive) in trying to get you to attend support groups for people with addictions. You will most probably have licence conditions which reflect this supposed benevolent concern for your welfare. But remember, apart from subjecting you to routine drugs test (and breathalysing you if in hostel) they cannot make you go to any support organisations. Nacro can provide some alternatives to the AA/NA model in your area.

## Structure of the National Probation Service (NPS)

Getting your head round probation is stressful. Remember how confusing all the procedures in jail seemed when you first got sent down? Well it's ten times worse, because this time if you mess up, you won't just get a negative IEP, you might well end up back inside. Probation use a whole heap of rules and regulations. As well as your licence, they will expect you to comply with the many rules of the bail hostel (if you have the misfortune to end up in one) and also 'Probation Instructions' (PIs). These are similar to Prison Service Instructions and follow the same format. Many PSIs are also published as PIs.

The language around all this stuff is constantly changing, but it is currently the case that what was called a 'probation officer' is now referred to as an 'offender manager' or 'offender supervisor' (OM or OS). They will be allocated based on the location of your alleged offence. If you are sent to a bail hostel/AP and are therefore quite far away from them you may well end up with two supervisors. They will conduct any psychological/behavioural interventions or programmes on your licence.

As with many aspects of the CJS and PIC, probation has been massively privatised, and now operates a 50/50 split. This means that if you are a 'low risk offender' you will go to a private 'Community Rehabilitation Company' (CRC)[7]. If you are high risk, or a 'MAPPA' ('Multi Agency Public Protection') case, you will be assigned to the National Probation Service (NPS). Please note that, as outlined earlier, at the time of writing, NOMS was being replaced with HMPPS, and so this will no doubt impact on NPS. Bored of all the acronyms yet? :-) See glossary if it's all getting confusing!

## The Offender Rehabilitation Act 2014 (ORA)

Under the 'Offender Rehabilitation Act' (ORA) 2014, a process of mandatory community supervision was introduced for short sentenced prisoners. The ORA states that "the purpose of the supervision period is the rehabilitation of the offender"[8], and should allegedly focus on reintegration into community. The ORA means that all determinate prisoners will be released at the half way point of their sentence, and then be under licence. It applies for all sentences over one day or more (i.e. all custodial sentences). Any one over 18 is now subject to at least 12-month's probation supervision. The 'post-sentence supervision period' can be used to top up supervision for up to 12 months. If you are recalled for the duration of your licence you may still have a 'post-sentence supervision period'. It has led to some confusion. For more information see Probation Instruction 27/2014 and PSI 31/2014.

The ORA was combined with various other policies in 2015 when the government launched a *Transforming Rehabilitation Agenda*[9]. As with the parole board, the probation service is massively unequipped to deal with the number of cases it is meant to process. This makes life highly frustrating for the individual 'under supervision' and is yet another example of why these claims for 'rehabilitation' are both insulting and dangerous.

## Community Rehabilitation Companies (CRCs)

In 2014 the government made significant changes to the way in which the National Probation Service (NPS) would be run and effectively the service was divided into two. Community Rehabilitation Companies (CRCs) were set up to supervise 'low and medium-risk offenders' and are run by private companies. Probation deals with so-called 'high-risk' offenders.

In 2015 there were six companies involved in the CRCs. Not all of these

---

7 Note that many of these are run by the usual suspects (Sodexo and MTCnovo being obvious examples) for more information on the structures see *Transforming Rehabilitation, MoJ 2014*

8 legislation.gov.uk/ukpga/2014/11/contents

9 gov.uk/government/publications/2010-to-2015-government-policy-reoffending-and-re-habilitation/2010-to-2015-government-policy-reoffending-and-rehabilitation

companies had any previous experience of dealing with prisoners (Guildford CRC is owned by a computer company) CRCs are big money-making exercises for the government and those companies who decide to deal in human misery. They do not meet the needs of ex-prisoners and have a high turnover of staff. It is common for women under CRC supervision to have four or five offender supervisors in two months. Privatisation has meant little personal contact, and longer custodial sentences mean longer licences. The 'National Audit Office' has raised concerns that the CRCs are not achieving their targets and that there is no consistency between them.[10]

## Foreign National Prisoners (FNPs) on Licence

FNPs should check PSI29/2014 and PI26/2014 for information regarding their licence conditions.[11] FNPs who meet the Home Office eligibility criteria for deportation are mostly managed by the National Probation, but a few will be under CRC supervision due to immigration law.

> "The Criminal Justice Act 2003 introduced the Early Removal Scheme (ERS) for FNPs. Guidance regarding the early removal of FNPs is covered in section six of PSI 04/2013 'The Early Removal Scheme and Release of Foreign National Prisoners'[12]. This instruction covers the processes in place when a Foreign National Prisoner who is pending deportation is released within the jurisdiction of England and Wales rather than being returned overseas."[13]

FNPs with a determinant sentence *should* be released under licence at the same point as UK 'citizens'. FNPs will then be given a 'Single Point of Contact' ('SPOC'), which will combine probation with 'Home Office Immigration Enforcement' (HOIE).

Please note that licences, deportation issues and FNPs are a total minefield, especially as legal aid is so difficult to get for this area. Please seek professional advice if possible, speak to PAS, or get people outside to research for you before release. They may also be a 'governor for FNPs' within your jail so ask them for information.

10 Comptroller and Auditor General, National Audit Office, *Ministry of Justice: Transforming Rehabilitation, 2016*

11 These are interim 'instructions' and officially expired in April 2016, however, they have not yet been replaced.

12 For more information see prisonreformtrust.org.uk/Portals/0/Documents/PIB-Foreign %20national%20prisoners.pdf

13 justice.gov.uk, see also PSI 38/2012

## Psychological aspects of release

"You go into prison fast. You come out slowly"[14]

"I'd spent *so* much time locked up inside my own head that I had to learn everything again, including how to be myself. I felt warped and self-conscious, raw but dulled, aggressive and cold-hearted but at the same time vulnerable."[15]

The mix of emotions Cattermole outlined is exhausting and exactly what I experienced release from jail. I was much happier inside than when I was on my licence (and specifically, in the bail hostel). When you are in jail you potentially have good support, and you are psychologically prepared to battle every day. When you are on licence, it's much more confusing (especially if your conditions mean you can't access most of your support network).

"In prison I felt safe from the outside world. Women surrounded me and I wasn't judged. Little did I realise my sentence would begin when I went home".[16]

I can't emphasise enough how grim being on licence is. I accepted my conditions for my family. I don't regret it because it helped me build bridges with them and prove that whilst I maintained my political beliefs, I was still their daughter/sister. However, I will *never* accept licence conditions again. If I end up back behind enemy lines, I'm doing my whole sentence inside. Every day I was on my licence felt like a disgusting compromise, one of Libertad's "partial suicides"[17].

"Well I don't care how long I live. Over this I have no control, but I do care about what kind of life I live, and I can control this. I may not live but for another five minutes, but it will be five minutes definitely on my terms." *George Jackson*[18]

---

14 Unknown, Bangladesh
15 Cattermole, 2015
16 Sue Thomas, ex-prisoner in *Ready, Steady Go! 2015* (magazine of 'Women In Prison')
17 Libertad, *We Go On*
18 Jackson, *Soledad Brother: The Prison Letters of George Jackson, 1994*

# LICENCE

"Are we persecuted? Well, it's logical that we are persecuted because we are a constant threat for those who represent the system. In order not to be persecuted we would have to adapt to their laws, comply with them, integrate into the system, let bureaucracy penetrate our spinal cord and become perfect traitors... Our strength is our ability to resist. We can fail but we must never bow down to anyone." *Buenaventura Durruti[1]*

## Context

"Licence conditions are designed for risk management and public protection purposes. Licence conditions must be necessary and proportionate. The restriction to the person's liberty must be the absolute minimum required to manage their risk. According to the guidance, necessary means that the condition is necessary to enable the supervising officer to manage the risks identified and no other less onerous condition will suffice."[2]

I am using my case as an example of what you should expect from probation if you are an anarchist prisoner (or they have decided you are an 'extremist')[3]. Please note that I am using *their* language deliberately. It is

1 Durruti, quoted in *Hallucination, Intimidation and Control: Letter from Francisco Solar on 'Operation Pandora' (Spain) 2015*
2 Legal advice, 2015
3 Prisoners charged with terrorism offences may be subject to a different set of additional licence conditions. Annex B of PSI 12/2015 states that additional licence conditions must be both *necessary* and *proportionate* to manage individual *risk*. Under the Criminal Justice Act (CJA) 1991, governors are responsible for drafting any licence conditions in

highly problematic (for example "vulnerable adults", "terrorism"), but you better get used to hearing it if you have the misfortune to be on licence.

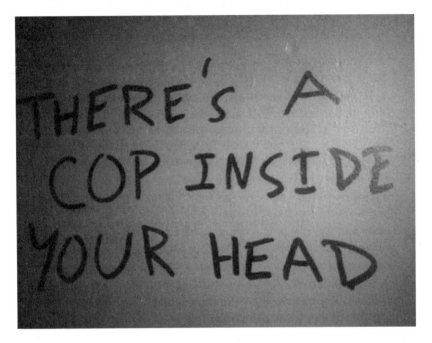

## Licence Conditions

My licence conditions involved the 'standard six', but also a whole army of restrictions (see appendix 18)[4]. For more information on these see PSO 6000. Licence conditions are designed to control, and can relate nearly every

addition to standard licence conditions. However, following the CJA of 2003, if you are serving an 'Extended Determinate Sentence', the parole board must be consulted about any additional licence conditions, and the final decision as to such conditions lies with the secretary of state.

4 The licence is prepared by the governor in conjunction with the 'custody/discipline office' and should be explained to you *at least* one week before release. A 'Pre-Discharge Form 1' (PD1) must be given to the supervising officer 13 weeks prior to their release. If they are *requesting* any licence conditions in addition to 'the standard six' they must provide a full explanation as to why additional conditions are deemed necessary and proportionate. The extra conditions must come from a list agreed by probation and this drafting must be done no later than 28 days before the person's release. The governor is then responsible for *imposing* additional conditions if necessary and these must come from a list approved by probation. If the governor or probation wish to impose a licence condition that is *not* on the approved list then advice must be sought from the 'Public Protection Casework Section'.

aspect of your life. Both the 'standard six' and my additional conditions contained a combination of very specific restrictions (for example, supposedly having to provide the make and model of any vehicle I travelled in regularly) to more general ones (such as "to be of good behaviour"). As they say, the devil is often in the detail. However, in the case of licences, if they can't get you on specifics they'll just claim you aren't complying with the broader conditions which are harder to challenge.

Note that if you are a Lifer or IPP prisoner it is the parole board, not the governor, who will have final say over your conditions. For IPP prisoners these restrictions could apply *for the rest of your life*. If you are a Lifer it's up to ten years. Because of this, recall can have a big impact for either group. I am *not* trying to dissuade any one from breaching their licence. Rules are there to be broken, right? ;-) and I fully support anyone resisting the army of professionals who will try to make your life hell while under 'supervision'.

## Multi Agency Public Protection Arrangements (MAPPA)

> "Multi Agency Public Protection Arrangements or MAPPA is the process through which the police, probation and prison services work together with other agencies to assess and manage violent and sexual offenders in order to protect the public from harm. It is a system of sharing information and combining resources to maximise the risk management in place for each individual offender."[5]

If you are an alleged 'high risk offender' then you will most probably be a 'MAPPA' case. In 2003 the Criminal Justice Act introduced the use of 'Lay Advisors' as part of 'Strategic Management Boards' (SMBs)[6]. Lay Advisors are 'professionals' who are external from the police/probation but are from an institutional background, such as education and social services.

5 westmerciaprobation.org.uk/page.php?Plv=3&P1=5&P2=20&P3=7
6 Lay Advisors have oversight of the MAPPA programme (supposedly their involvement will boost public confidence in arrangements and credibility in the scheme). In England and Wales, each SMB has two Lay Advisors, and there 84 nationally. The MAPPA board makes recommendations, and it meets once a month with everyone involved in your case (from police, to the Key Worker you have if living at an AP). However, it is your probation officer *not* the MAPPA board who make final decisions. The individual on licence is not allowed to attend these meetings. However, you can make written representations (I did this a couple of times when I was fed up of my probation officer and didn't trust them to represent me or report back from the meetings). Also, you should be able to find out when the meetings will occur, and request a bit of feedback from your Key Worker.

To quote my old solicitor they are "responsible authorities" tasked with managing those deemed a high risk to public.

> "Under the European Convention on Human Rights, we can interfere with those rights where it is for the prevention of unrest, violence and crime."[7]

There are three categories of MAPPA:
- Category One: Registered sex offenders
- Category Two: All offenders who have received a custodial sentence of 12 months or more in prison for a sexual or violent offence and whilst they remain under probation supervision.
- Category Three: Anyone who poses a "risk of serious harm to the public" who has received a conviction and whose risk would be better managed in a multi-agency setting).

I was a category three MAPPA for the first six months of my licence, but I then went down to category two[8].

MAPPA convicts will have a "management plan", and all information relating to their case will be stored on the 'ViSOR' database[9]. This will mean more licence restrictions than the standard six, and will include: accommodation at AP, Civil Orders (for example, if convicted of a sex-offence the individual will be bound by a 'Sex Offender Prevention Order'), increased reporting to an offender manager (as well as your probation officer) every week, to undertake "offending reduction counselling and work" and the use of covert monitoring "to protect the public"[10].

## Extremism, Terrorism and Language

> "Unless you can define what extremism is very clearly then

7 National MAPPA Team, National Offender Management Service, Offender Management and Public Protection Group, *MAPPA Guidance 2012 Version Four*
8 Note that as with most aspects of your licence, probation will *not* be forthcoming with information. I only found out I was a MAPPA when I got read my licence, a couple of weeks before my release (most people know throughout their sentence). Because I couldn't use a computer, I was unable to do research. I asked probation repeatedly for information on the MAPPA guidelines but was told several times that all their copies were "in storage". It's worth getting someone to print them out for you, as they are very detailed. For more information see MAPPA Guidance 2012 Part One. They were updated in February 2015, but read the same.
9 mappa.justice.gov.uk/connect.ti/MAPPA/view?objectId=263059&exp=e2
10 This is legally allowed under 'Schedule 15' of the 'Anti-Terrorism Act' and relates to individuals who are 'high interest/risk'. For more information see also MAPPA Guidance 2012

it's going to be really difficult to enforce. We absolutely don't want to be the thought police."[11]

Simon Cole took the police lead on the government's controversial 'Prevent' Strategy. This aimed to promote 'anti-radicalisation'[12]. The 'Counter-Extremism Bill' of May 2016 included those labelled "extremist but who do not advocate terrorism"[13]. The bill gave increased powers to authorities to ban organisations deemed extremist, gag individuals and allow councils to shut down premises assessed as being "used to promote hatred". It is clearly an example of the so-called 'thought police', and is also a further, brutal example of the racist application of the legal system in this country. The Counter-Extremism Bill has been used indiscriminately and excessively against the Muslim community, people of colour, and young people. From stop and searches, to incarceration, the 'Prevent' strategy works in conjunction with this bill to censor and criminalise.

Probation use the catch all "to be of good behaviour"[14] to cover all possible deviations from your licence if they can't get you on the other more specific restrictions. As with 'extremism' the concept of 'good behaviour' is left conveniently vague so they can threaten you with it indiscriminately. My supposed 'extremism' was used as a rationale for refusing contact with my girlfriend ("dragging her into my web of extremist ideologies and views"), stopping me from volunteering and possible employment. It was because of this label that I got a visit from the Counter-Terrorism Unit in jail. I was advised against trying to find out what the legal definition of 'an extremist' is:

> "Pressing the Governor for a definition of extremism may lead to a more restrictive interpretation of the phrase than that currently adopted by your probation officer. In addition, as set out in the guidance, your ability to identify which groups and ideologies fall within the definition of extremism is viewed as a key part of your rehabilitation. There is a fall-back licence condition to 'be of good behaviour' which probation can rely upon where a licensee is behaving in a way which is generally

---

11 SimonCole, *theguardian.com/uk-news/2016/may/24/anti-radicalisation-chief-says-ministers-plans-risk-creating-thought-police 2016*
12 secretary of state for the home department, *Prevent Strategy 2011*
13 gov.uk/government/uploads/system/uploads/attachment_data/file/524040/Queen_s_Speech_2016_background_notes_.pdf
14 See appendix 18, 'the standard six licence conditions'

felt to be inappropriate"[15].

Probation gets away with a lot by being vague, and this tactic works well for them as it means minimal disclosure, and maximum potential to install a 'cop-in-your-head'. People on licence used to be able to present probation with specific names of organisations or individuals they wanted to interact with, in order to ascertain whether or not this would constitute a licence breach. However, now trying to get disclosure from them these days is really hard as they don't want to reveal their mechanisms of control.

> "Supervision officers should be aware that in some cases, offenders will attempt to use this condition to ascertain whether permitted members of certain organisations are either of interest to, or under investigation by the police. Supervising officers should avoid being drawn into discussing individuals if the offender provides a name of list of names. The condition places the onus on the offender to determine whether or not a named individual has been charged with or convicted of a relevant offence."[16]

The condition prohibiting computer usage should only be used where past offending is linked to use of internet, or if there is sufficient risk that the 'offender' may in future use the internet to re-offend. However, 'extremism' is one of the categories of offences for which the policy states that this condition is usable. The same is true on the restrictions on mobile phones. The condition is applied to stop the individual on licence "concealing offending behaviour", so you better be careful on this front, especially if you are living in a bail hostel, as staff check people's phones sporadically. It also states in the MAPPA guidelines that the use of "external monitoring devices" and covert surveillance is permitted.

**Fire Arms Licence**

All prisoners are also required to sign a 'Firearms Licence' when they leave jail[17]. If you have a sentence of four years or less this applies for five years from release. If it is over four years then in theory this licence is valid for the rest of your life. The firearms licence prohibits the use of guns and gun powder (including automatic weapons, air rifles and down to BB guns). It

15 Notes from my old solicitor, 2015
16 MAPPA Guidance, 2012
17 You don't get issued with a copy of this when you leave jail, and I can't find an example of it online.

also includes matches, party poppers, sparklers, fireworks. I'm not making this up. I asked the screw if I would be allowed to use a lighter and he said that was fine, but emphasised to me that they can do DNA/forensics tests so I'd better watch out if I was thinking about using party poppers!

## Challenging licence conditions

The only way to get legal aid for challenging licence conditions is via the process of a Judicial Review (JR). Your case will go before a High Court judge who will decide whether the condition(s) are so unreasonable that *no other governor would have made them.* Using a JR means representation has to be framed in a very specific way, and this makes it difficult to challenge most restrictions.

If you are unable to secure funding for challenging licence conditions and do not have a parole or recall matter then you can challenge licence conditions without representation. This can be done by applying to your supervising officer. Reasons will need to be provided as to why an additional licence condition may need removing. As a last resort, a complaint about the necessity or proportionality of additional licence conditions imposed could be sent to the PPO for their consideration.

If you are on licence and the decisions of probation or the MAPPA affect your employment, potential employees *can* lodge a formal complaint against them. For example, in my case, I was not allowed to work with so-called 'vulnerable people'. Using this licence condition, probation routinely make assumptions about who are 'vulnerable' people without getting input from the individuals they are allegedly protecting.

# RECALL

> "Recall is the process by which someone subject to licence in the community is returned to custody. It is instigated by the Probation Service (offender manager) when it's felt that their risk is no longer manageable in the community."[1]

There are two types of recall: fixed term (28 days; or 14 days if serving a sentence of less than 12 months, available for determinate prisoners only) and standard recall (unspecified time; potentially until sentence expires, or *indefinitely* if you are IPP/Lifer). If you are subject to a standard recall, and have a sentence of two years or more, release can only be granted by the parole board. As with ISPs you will have to create a dossier and then have annual reviews if you are recalled on a long sentence. If faced with recall, it is important to ensure that the parole board are appropriately appraised of the circumstances of the alleged breach. Legal aid is available for recall and related court proceedings, so if summoned contact a *criminal* law firm (not prison solicitor) as soon as possible.

> "Back into a box not because of a new crime, but because of rules that are designed to be impossible to fulfill."[2]

According to the Howard League for Penal Reform, over the last 20 years, the number of prisoners recalled has increased by 4,300%[3]. Between September 2015-2016, 22,094 people were recalled, including 7,798 for "failing to keep in touch". Recall is used indiscriminately and excessively. It

1 Darryl Foster and Laura Collins Solicitors, 2017 www..insidetime.org/recall-when-do-i-get-another-chance/
2 Imarisha, 2016
3 Howard League, *Call to Stop Revolving Door to Prison as Numbers Recalled to Custody Soar, 2016*

is one of them main reasons for massive overcrowding in jail, and a key example of why the whole system is rotten to the core. As Bowden has argued in *Neo-Liberalism and Prisons*:

> "Now a close equivalent to the American parole officer, probation officers and criminal justice system social workers in the UK now see their roles as policing parolees or 'offenders' on supervision orders and returning them to jail for the slightest technical breach of their licence conditions. The massive increase in the use of community supervision orders as a form of social control has created a veritable ghetto of marginalised people in poorer communities who exist constantly in the shadows of imprisonment and the omnipotent power of their supervising officers."[4]

If you are perceived to have broken supervision you will be returned to jail and/or court. You may well be recalled straight back to jail. A Magistrate can return you to prison for 14 days, issue a fine or Supervision Default Order (SDO). An SDO can be unpaid work or electronic curfew.

Prior to 2014, the NPS would not have been able to recall prisoners who were serving a sentence of less than 12 months. They would also not have been involved in the supervision of those prisoners after release.

## Relationships and Recall

> "All relationships are challenging when you get out of prison to a degree...it's tricky to navigate the world of love and sex and friendship, and trying to do it when everything around you is so overwhelmingly intense and absorbing. It's a bad comparison, but it's like going to the big city for the first time and seeing shiny lights everywhere, and you just want to take it all in and be part of it because you haven't for so long."[5]

PSI 12/2015 relates to the issues/conditions around risk and prisoners in relationships. It states that the Probation Service should consider imposing a condition *if* the prisoner poses a specific risk in this area. This condition is used inside jails before release as well as similar rulings on licences. It is used in cases where the 'index offence' was committed against a partner, or in the context of a relationship, or if the prisoner has previous convic-

---

4 Bowden, *Neo-Liberalism and Prisons, 2013*
5 Luers, in Halliday, 2014

tions against a partner or there are "behavioural concerns". As with many aspects of legislation, this PSI is an example of the procedure often used where the prison system will slap on lots of specific applications/conditions, then add one final more general one in case they others don't apply when they want it to. This is also true of the phrase "intimate relationship" which is deliberately vague within law.

Probation and the prison system hate seeing prisoners happy and doing things autonomously or behind their backs, as it upsets their feeling of omnipotence. Both me and my girlfriend had complex issues relating to the prying eyes of the state. She had a condition on her sentence that she had to disclose any 'intimate relationships' she had on order to get parole, and my licence conditions meant that communicating with her would have been instant recall.

> "The supervising officer will want to assess that there has been no increase in an offender's level of risk and look at whether any new relationship is healthy, pro social and offence free...It is advisable for an offender to discuss any relationship that they think may be a developing intimate relationship with their supervising officer. In any such discussion an offender should ask what is expected of them in terms of further disclosure so they are clear where they stand...It is vital for offenders to ensure that their and their supervising officer's understanding / interpretation of what a developing intimate relationship is the same."[6]

The onus is on the prisoner or licencee to disclose the relationship. Probation and the parole board may well decide that failure to disclose a relationship was a deliberate act in order to conceal 'risky' or 'criminal' behaviour. Probation like to think that they know *everything* and like screws they hate it when you aren't cowering in a corner seeking approval or bowing down to their authority.

I wasn't sure whether or not to include legal information here in case it was too personal, but decided that it might be a useful case study for others in relation to women's prisons. My legal challenge was to the condition below on my licence, which meant I could not communicate with my partner as they were still inside:

6 Emma Davies and Nicola Blackburn, *Love Actually… When Relationships Lead to Recall (IT, 2016)*

"XVII Not to contact directly or indirectly any person who is a serving or remanded prisoner or detained in state custody without the prior approval of your supervising officer."[7]

My legal challenge was based on 'Article 8 of the European Convention on Human Rights': "the right to family and private life"; as my licence condition incompatible with my relationship. Challenging licence conditions *must* happen within three months of signing your licence. Your solicitor will give the prison a pre-action letter, threatening court proceedings. They will write to the governor of your old jail. The prison then had 14 days to respond, before then invoking the so-called 'pre-action protocol'. The governor then has three weeks to amend the relevant condition or potentially face a court appearance.

If your case goes to court you will then have to apply for a 'Public Funding Certificate'. The Legal Aid Agency (LAA) will consider whether you meet both the financial means test and merits test (you need to prove matter is of "overwhelming importance" if not for financial compensation.)[8] If your challenge to the licence condition is successful you are entitled to an award of damages.

In order to stand the best chance of success, your legal challenge must have really specific demand. For example, I wanted to be able to communicate with my best mates inside as well as my girlfriend, but this would have been too vague. Be prepared that you will have to give quite a lot of personal information, and this can be traumatic after an extended period of the state trying to get into your head.

In my case, I had to outline the background to my offence, the amendment sought to my licence, personal details about my relationship (duration, understanding of the other persons offence, and reason for challenging said condition). To me I felt really conflicted because I have no faith in the legal system and did not want to ask for the crumbs of the state. On the other hand, I was deeply in love with my girlfriend and desperate to communicate with her.

A word of warning. Your probation officer will get *very* defensive with you if you get a solicitor involved in your case. They do not like being made to look a fool in front of their seniors. Probation will try to derail you by claiming you are inconsistent, and trying to distract them from your 'offending behaviour'. I kept a log of all the claims they made about my

7 From licence 2015

8 gov.uk/government/organisations/legal-aid-agency

relationship:
- It was inherently negative.
- I didn't have the emotional capacity to handle a relationship.
- I was a 'domestic extremist' and therefore the restrictive conditions were proportionate.
-The ban on communication was my own fault because I did not disclose my relationship, or tell the authorities when they issued me with my licence[9].

My probation officer asked a series of invasive and prying questions about my relationship, then, in a logic typical of the police and the state, interpreted my refusal to cooperate and share information as an admission of guilt. He claimed it was "more than I can handle". He also said that I needed to take responsibility for starting a relationship, and then deal with the consequences when things "don't work out my way". They will do all they can to present you as some naughty adolescent, and dismiss your relationship as some non-event or teenage crush. I think that homophobia may also play a part in this, because they do not recognise relationships that do not conform to a heterosexual model as being of equal seriousness[10].

As with all attempts to over-ride decisions made by the prison system, quoting their own nonsense at them can provide some leverage. So make sure you look up the relevant PSIs. In my case, PSI 12/2015 ('Licence Conditions, Licences and Supervision Notices') was helpful:

> "A blanket ban on contact with prisoners can be made where an offender is associating with other criminals and there is reason to believe that the association will lead to re-offending. The guidance is clear that blanket bans on communicating with groups of people should only be used in extreme cases."[11]

My legal challenge stated that as I was not a co-defendant of my girlfriend, and we met after my conviction, we should be allowed to communicate. The solicitor also pointed out to the jail that as all mail, and phone calls are routinely monitored, the governor could keep tabs on our interactions, and so-called "inappropriate communications". In the face of a potential legal case, the onus is on the prison to demonstrate the queried condition

---

9 Arguments with probation, 2015
10 My legal challenge cited the incidences where probation disrespected me. "We consider the attitude of XXX in respect to this issue to be inappropriate, overly restrictive and unlawful."
11 PSI 12/2015

is *proportionate,* and why it is necessary to protect the wider society from the licencee.

Predictably, despite much painful disclosure and legal wrangling, my challenge failed:

> "I can confirm I have reviewed your request and have spoken with our Counter Terrorism Lead Senior probation officer who has sought the advice from the Extremism Unit in NOMS. Having reviewed your request the decision is as follows: The licence condition was deemed necessary and proportionate prior to release to ensure no vulnerable person was at risk of becoming radicalised or drawn into XXX offending behaviour or domestic extremist ideology and views. Therefore we would need evidence of a significant reduction in the risk to vary the said licence condition. At this point there is no evidence to support a reduction in the said risk."[12]

As a final note, it is interesting that as soon as my girlfriend disclosed our relationship to her offender manager in jail, she was then interviewed by external probation officers and the 'Domestic Extremist/Counter Terrorism Unit' about me and our relationship. As with all the aspects of social control and surveillance during my sentence, this has only made me hate the authorities more.

---

12 governor of my old jail, 2015

# APPROVED PREMISES (AP) 'BAIL HOSTELS'

"The main purpose of Approved Premises (APs) is to provide intensive supervision for offenders or defendants who present a high or very high risk of serious harm. Most will have been released from prison on licence. Some will be serving community sentences or be subject to a suspended sentence, while others be on bail pending trial...APs do not just conduct monitoring and surveillance. They are also obliged to provide key workers who form an integral part of the offender management process, and each resident will have a programme of purposeful activity that is intended to help with reducing re-offending and reintegration into society."[1]

So, you've been released, you're feeling fairly positive, or at least, definitely ready for a change from prison life...you've heard a lot of horror stories inside about bail hostels from folks inside, but they can't be that bad, right? It's gotta be better than jail? Think again, grit your teeth, and prepare for a rough ride...

"That place, the horrors that occurred and the loss it delivered me is buried in my heart forever. And from that, I'm afraid, I can't ever be free"[2]

## Context

There are 101 'approved premises' (AP) or bail hostels in the whole of England and Wales (four in Wales). Out of this 101, only six are for wom-

---

1 *The Approved Premises Manual and Specification*, PI 04/2011.
2 Fellows, 2000

en[3]. The total capacity is around 2,200 beds (of which 112 are for women). They are managed under section 13 of the Offender Management Act 2007. Most APs are directly run by the NPS. There are 11 that are run independently, for example, Elizabeth ('Lizzie') Fry in Reading, which was established in 1925 and is funded by the MoJ as an 'Independently Managed Approved Premises'. Elizabeth Fry is the only AP in the south of England. If you have the misfortune to be sent to an AP you will stay there between three and six months.

APs are mostly used for supposedly high-risk offenders (mainly MAPPA)[4], so they are mainly used by the NPS, but CRCs can refer individuals to them as well. Because of the increasing numbers of women being given custodial sentences (and licence restrictions including "residing at an AP") there is great pressure on beds, and in some cases a waiting list.

> "Offenders should be placed in APs only where it is clear that this level of monitoring and intensive activity is needed. APs should not be treated as the default option for all high-risk offenders; given the limited spaces available, the need for a placement should be determined, and the placement designed, as an integral part of the offender management process."[5]

In May 2017, the 'supreme court' ruled that people released from women's prisons were discriminated against in the current provision of APs. Because there are only six APs for those labelled 'women' inhabitants are much more likely to live further away from their families than those in an AP for 'men'. According to the 'Howard League for Penal Reform', "the issue in this appeal was whether the current distribution of APs constitutes unlawful sex discrimination against women"[6] The judge of the case, lady Hale, ruled that:

> "Being required to live in an AP a long way away from home is a detriment. A woman is much more likely to suffer this detriment than is a man, because of the geographical distribution of the small number of APs available for women. This is treat-

---

3 Bedford, Birmingham, Leeds, Liverpool, Preston and Reading. There are none in London or in Wales.
4 Because most people there are MAPPA cases (more on this later) there are a very high number of people convicted of sex-offences in bail hostels.
5 PI 04/2011
6 Howard League, *Supreme Court Rules the Provision of Approved Premises for Women is Discriminatory, 2017*

ing her less favourably than a man because of her sex."[7]

Let me be really clear: bail hostels are *part* of the problem, not the solution. They are grim, dysfunctional and damaging places. A lot of reformist organisations often talk of having houses 'in the community' for women prisoners to be sent to rather than being given a custodial sentence. If they are to be anything like the AP I was at, I'd rather be in jail, and I nearly opted for recall several times. These institutions are part of the PIC and calls to build more are dangerous, and legitimise their existence.

It is interesting to note that even though there are less APs for women than men, the "reside at an AP" licence condition is used a lot more against those released from women's prisons than men's. This is a further example of how the state views women as out of control and in need of extra guidance.

A quick note on language. I am using the term 'residents' to refer to people who are forced to live at an AP. This is a problematic term as to me it minimises the coercion involved in this arrangement, and also because it is the language of probation. However, I couldn't think of another way to refer to individuals who are legally bound to stay in bail hostels that wasn't confusing, so it will have to do for now…

**Activities**

The range of enforced activities available in women's bail hostels today continues an oppressive gendered tradition. Art therapy, baking and beauty sessions are commonplace. Courses also exist on certain aspects of behaviour, for example 'assertiveness'. As with jail, acceptable behaviour has a gendered element. Lack of assertiveness at the time of an alleged offence is used as a stick to beat residents with, and analysed in oppressive group sessions, but those who are deemed too confident are disciplined and aggressively patronised. Physical exercise is permitted as long as it doesn't perpetuate aggression. Swearing is prohibited and will often result in a verbal warning. Language is policed rigorously using the justification of 'non-violent communication'. As far as I'm concerned, *any* methods of communication where one party has the power to incarcerate the other is inherently violent, the individual words used are unimportant.

---

7 Quoted in Howard League report, 2017

## Risk Management

> "They open wide the door
> "you've done your time, you're free"
> But I still feel locked and chained
> deep down inside of me"[8]

Being in an AP, and being on licence feels like a protracted form of suffocation. You have the double whammy of licence conditions plus the petty, but oppressive rules of the bail hostel (see appendix 19). This is a toxic mix, all delivered under the pretence of 'risk management'.

> "It is essential to bear in mind that AP residents are in the community. This means they are free to leave and to move around the surrounding area, although this is always subject to the constraints of their licence conditions. In particular, conditions such as programme requirements that oblige offenders to be in a specific place (including the AP) can legitimately restrict their freedom of movement without counting as custody, provided their primary purpose is not to replicate custody but to manage risk".[9]

Don't get too excited about your new 'freedom'. My restrictions meant that due to my various exclusion zones, signing times and the group therapy sessions, the longest I could be away from the hostel at any one time was four hours (and it was mostly significantly less than this). The individual under supervision is an object to be contained and managed. The authorities do all they can to obscure the reality that is extreme control and surveillance behind this rhetoric. In the hostel I was in, there were 68 cameras, but only 22 residents. Using this system, the friendly faces of oppression smile sweetly as they threaten you with recall or a licence warning, implying it is for your own protection.

> "We provide an environment where residents' behaviour and any additional restrictions included as part of their licence or bail conditions can be monitored. This is achieved through 24-hour staffing, CCTV monitoring, room searches, random drug and alcohol testing, curfews and monitoring of additional licence conditions. Staff from Elizabeth Fry Approved Premises work closely with the National Probation Service

8 Anonymous, *Canada's Prison for Women*
9 PI 04/2011

(NPS), Community Rehabilitation Companies (CRC) and Thames Valley Police and make a significant contribution to the assessment and management of risk and the MAPPA process."[10]

The physical confines of the prison are replaced with a whole heap of rules in an AP. Each one is slightly different, but the MoJ dictates a lot of the procedures for them all (see appendix 19).

## Courses/activity

"We aim to provide residents with the opportunity to examine their lives, reflect on past attitudes and behaviours and assist each individual in their efforts to avoid re-offending. To provide a safe living environment for women, which is sensitive to issues of discrimination and disadvantage. To minimize the institutional effects of Approved Premises life, whilst maximising resident's personal strengths, with a view to reintegration within the community."[11]

This is really offensive nonsense and does not in any way reflect my experience of life in a bail hostel. Discrimination is rife, and staff *love* the institutional power they have over you (and the fact that one phone call to the cops will get you recalled.) In your new 'residence' you aren't locked in at night. But if you step out of your door during curfew time you'll get a warning and ultimately get recalled, and the jangle of keys will still permeate your psyche and put you on constant alert. Yes, there are some positives to be outside of jail, but it also feels like they come at a heavy price; mainly installing a cop-in-your-head (and they are a nightmare to evict).

You quickly learn how to work the system and my advice to anyone who has the misfortune to end up in an AP would be find a way to get the hell out of there as much as possible. Voluntary work (once agreed by your probation officer) might be a way out. Also try to get staff to accept that you need to do lots of exercise (the threat of obstructive behaviour if you don't get to do this sometimes worked for me). Once you've been at the AP a few weeks, these activities can be counted as 'constructive activity' if you play your cards right and means you can escape the horrendous group therapy sessions. There are other ways to avoid these nightmarish psychological invasions but for obvious reasons I won't go into detail here, other

10 Elizabeth Fry website (elizabethfry.co.uk/Approved-Premises/Support)
11 elizabethfry.co.uk

residents can bring you up to speed with how to get out of them!

As well as the enforced group sessions which occur five times per week and last for about two and a half hours, you will also have to meet once a week with your 'Key Worker' (who works closely with probation). Your 'progress' is monitored and analysed by staff fortnightly and fed back to probation. This is on top of the external sessions you will have to have with probation. You can see why, by the time you've added in Job Centre appointments and the courses they inevitably force upon you, the 'freedom' you've been looking forward to is limited.

The staff at the AP have a whole arsenal of 'interventions' that they used:

- Group-work: "Structured daily programme throughout the week, from 10:00-13:15. Topics include anger management, self-esteem, substance misuse, housing, financial management and life skills. All residents who are not employed or involved in a purposeful day time activity are expected to attend this programme."

- Activities: "The staff team deliver evening and weekend activities in order to assist residents in making constructive use of this time. The activities include arts and crafts, baking, bingo, karaoke, Pictionary and yoga."

- Life Coach: individual sessions for counsellor. In collaboration with the mental health team.[12]

NPS has identified 'Nine Pathways to Re-Offending'[13], and these get shoved down your throat at every opportunity. The pathways are: accommodation, employment and education, health, drugs and alcohol, finance/benefits and debt, families, attitudes and behaviours, abuse and violence and sex work. The AP staff will use all these different aspects as ways to try to worm their way into your head and grind you down. In keeping with the Victorian concept of appropriate ways of behaving for women, residents are expected to show willing, and be grateful for, the "opportunities" that they are given in these educational programmes. You will be forced to complete an 'Outcome Star' which analyses any potential problems that might stop you from becoming a reformed citizen. This is especially offensive if you are awaiting trial (the AP is used a fair bit to remove individuals from the area where their alleged crime was committed), or if you are maintaining your innocence. If you have an appeal in process *do not* talk to

---

12 Information Leaflet for Elizabeth Fry AP, 2015
13 As outlined in *Wales Reducing Reoffending Strategy 2014 – 2016, gov.uk*

anyone -staff or residents-about it, and be aware of prying eyes.

As part of your weekly 'service charge' all residents feed into an 'activity fund' which then gets used in your free time. Because there are so many restrictions on the types of behaviour that are 'acceptable', and also as hostel staff do little to challenge gender stereotypes, the activities that occur are unsurprisingly often tedious and discriminatory. During my time at the AP nail art, beauty, painting and baking were fairly regular occurrences. Your participation (or lack of) gets fed back to probation on a daily basis, and as with jail, if the individual isn't seen to cooperate, then it is assumed that the fault lies with them not the session/course/institution. One of the most stressful group session I endured was about stress management!

As with psychological programmes in jail, the concept of 'therapy' within the setting of the bail hostel is *extremely* problematic. Due to a very high concentration of MAPPA cases, there is a staggering number of individuals who have been convicted of sex-offences. As with women's prisons, there is no categorisation and in the group sessions everyone is expected to talk openly, regardless of their histories. It is also true that as with sex-offenders in prison, hostel staff are much more likely to allow them to miss sessions, and to believe whatever they say against other residents. I do not want to make generalisations *but* in my limited experience a lot of the people who were in for sex offences were way to pally with hostel staff, and *very* quick to accuse other residents of bullying. It is true that if you have been convicted of a sex offence that most other people will not talk to you. But there is no excuse in my book for going to staff to solve your problems.

It is also an unfortunate truth that some people in the nearby area capitalise on the location of the bail hostel and use it as a way to groom younger or more vulnerable residents for sex-work (some of which is definitely not consensual) or sell drugs. I am *not* trying to add to the tired rhetoric surrounding the concept of the vulnerable female offender, and I fully advocate an individual who is informed and empowered opting for drug use or sex work. But there were definitely some highly sketchy practices going on at the AP I was in, and as with lots of aspects of hostel life, this gets played out in the public arena of the 'therapy' sessions.

### Staff and Discipline

Staffing in an AP follows similar class lines to jail. A lot of the lower level managers are from around the immediate area the hostel is in, and have working-class back grounds. At the hostel I was in, there was a whole army of extremely irritating do-gooder types who were posh university students seeking to cut their teeth in social services by making our lives miserable. Simultaneously vicious and patronising, they are particularly officious and nosy because they haven't been in the job long and are trying to impress their seniors. As with prison, everyone in the AP -staff and residents-can get caught up in the dramas of daily life. All the group interventions that make up the routine of the hostel mean that people have a constant, captive audience for their rants/allegations/fights whatever. Some people really thrive on this, and members of staff are no exception, especially the younger ones who haven't yet seen the full range of dramas that life in an AP brings.

The rulers of the AP are the managers who work within probation but who also manage the hostel. Most hostels will have a couple of senior staff members ('CEOs' or 'operations managers') who are also normally senior probation officers. They have *a lot* of power. They organise recalls. and can also evict you (which amounts to recall). As I highlighted earlier, beds (or lack of) are an ongoing issue for APs and so these managers can make snap decisions about allocations and so on.

There are a whole range of patronising volunteers who come into work with the residents of the hostel. Being around these people is exhausting. They will ask you a lot of questions about prison, your 'crime' and so on. If you are too obviously rude you'll most likely get given a warning (hostel staff hate it when they don't look good in front of other people), so the best way is to be polite but really distant and disappear as much as possible!

The AP runs on a system of discipline that they expect people to bow down to. The staff work closely with probation to implement this.[14] 'Licence Warnings' stay on your record for the duration of your licence. If you get more than one licence warning you are highly likely to get recalled. However, it is also possible to bypass this system and get recalled straight away if staff decide you have done something that warrants immediate return to jail (for example, missing curfew).

### Drugs/Alcohol

As has been outlined earlier, if your alleged crime was connected with drugs in any way, then expect to get a whole heap of restrictions slapped

---

14 The warnings system goes like this: informal warning > verbal warnings > contract warning > formal written warning (a licence warning).

on your licence. Staff in the AP will also watch you very closely, and there is a designated substance misuse worker who you will be expected to see on a regular basis.

The use of drugs in APs shows what an inconsistent nonsense legislation around 'controlled substances' is. When I was in one, spice and other highs like it were still legal, and at least a third of residents were off their heads most of the time. I bet it makes the interminable horror of morning meeting more bearable!

The AP will use substance misuse as a way to rationalise all sorts of invasive procedures and surveillance. If you are getting or using drugs, be discrete! In their spice-fuelled highs a lot of people forget any concept of security. If staff suspect you are using they may well force a drugs test upon you, or ask other residents for information.

If you drink alcohol, also expect the possibility of regular room spins. You will also get breathalysed on a regular basis. If you blow at all on the scale you will get sent straight to your room. Get a mate to come to your door if you need support, but be discrete because you are not allowed in each other's rooms or wings, and staff will no doubt be watching on the cameras. Any instances of using alcohol or drugs will get reported straight to probation.

Be aware that staff have the legal power to seize and check your mobile phone if they want, and if they suspect you of using, they quite often do this so think carefully about your messages, and *never* leave your phone lying around no matter how wasted you are!

You can't even keep a sticking-plaster in your room if you haven't been risk assessed by the hostel staff, and they will do regular room searches (and 'checks' several times a day) so be careful if you have any drink or drugs in your room. If you get prescribed meds then you will have to endure the grimness of asking staff for them. In the hostel I was in, this was used as a way to interrogate you, as they kept you waiting for ages in an overly bright room with very strange pictures on the wall, whilst they asked you all kind of personal questions before eventually giving you a poxy tablet.

Note also that if you are prescribed meds, the healthcare centre will fax this straight to hostel staff and they will collect them, not you. They will also closely monitor if you have been coming to take the medication, especially if you are on Employment Support Allowance (ESA) and will report to your GP.

Everyone in the AP has different coping strategies. If you are using/

drinking then it's good to be aware of other people around you who may be in recovery and struggling. Bail hostels will push you to your limit and make you want to reach for whatever coping strategies you have.

## Practical information

Most of the general tips I had for surviving prison life can equally be applied to bail hostels, so see part one on reception/induction for more info. Throughout my sentence (and after) I have been conscious of my privilege, compared to many of my mates, and my time in the AP was no exception to this. Most of my mates there did not have a move-on address, or folk supporting them.

To add insult to injury, residents have to pay for the privilege of living in a bail hostel. Annoyingly, because it is counted as a 'maintenance charge' (£30.90 in 2016 per week) you cannot claim housing benefit (it's not 'rent'). According to the MoJ when you are at an AP you are a *resident* not a *tenant*. £30.90 is a big chunk of your dole money! They expect full payment, in cash, the day you get your benefits. As you have to open any brown envelopes in front of staff, and they normally photocopy the contents, they will know exactly when this is.

You will get used to all the restrictions and internalise them eventually (not that this is healthy!) at the beginning it can seem like you are constantly rattling off lists in your head, unsure as to whether or not you are breaking any conditions (this is exhausting, especially in the hostel where you are under surveillance the whole time). Your routine will settle down. Mine looked something like this: curfew ends 07:00 (and that was my first 'signing' time in the office), morning meeting 09:15, 'groups' till 13:15 (with a signing time in the middle at 11:00), 1315-14:45 'free time' :-), 15:00 sign, 15:00-18:45 free time, 19:00 sign, 21:00 curfew begins.

Generally, I'd say keep your head down, avoid staff at all costs and get the hell out of there as quickly as possible. If they see you aren't too much of a problem they should support you in your requests to have signings dropped. Because probation decided I was such a high-risk case this took weeks of negotiation even when the hostel staff were supporting my claim. Never, ever let staff feel like they are doing you a favour. It's not a big ask to have your signings reduced, it is common practice, and meant to happen once you've been around for a few weeks. They are just doing their poxy job, and anyway it's in their interest to help you "move on" and "progress" because they need to bed for some other poor individual...

Be assertive. Keep everyone at arm's length. Find balance between kicking off and getting out. This can be really difficult, especially as where I was got very nasty between those convicted of sex offences and all the other residents. Also with some of the older residents who clearly needed a lot more support -physically and mentally- than they were getting.

The minimum you can stay is three months but probation will try to keep you there longer if they think you are 'high risk' (or you don't have a move-on address). The maximum any one can stay is six months.

Lots of young people are proper mix-up when first released, and will talk far too much to hostel staff as they are desperate for attention. Be aware that staff will try to talk to you when you are feeling vulnerable. They are like patronising vultures and can smell misery a mile off. If, like I did, you have the misfortune to have several 'signing' times as well as a curfew, then you will feel like you can never escape them as they have to authorise your signature several times a day. They will then also come and do 'checks' on you three or more times a day. They do not care if you are asleep or clearly don't want to be disturbed, they always have some comment or judgement on the level of 'constructive' or 'purposeful' activity you may or may not be engaging with.

## Hygiene/Conditions

This next bit will make me sound like a total snob, but I'm not! Just a word on hygiene. The hostel I was in was *really* dirty and this was difficult for my OCD. I'm not super precious, but there were a lot of big rats and all the communal areas were disgusting. The kitchen was a total health hazard. One time on one of my angry shower scrubbing sessions I found a massive lump of human shit in it. The glare of the blue light is everywhere (it is used to stop people 'pinning up' -injecting heroin). You better get used to the constant invasion of fluorescent lights (if you weren't already after jail!).

Because I'm vegan I managed to get the 'housekeeper' to order me some special food, and it also meant that I didn't have to engage in the nightmare of the cooking rota. Everyone is meant to take it in turns to cook for the others, as part of their 'rehabilitation'. Peoples standards vary hugely. Even my mates who weren't vegan would do all they could to avoid these meal times, especially if certain people were cooking. The hostel has a (very small) food budget which comes out of everyone's service charge, so they are super strict on what food is available when, but if you are a bit crafty you can find ways to avoid the hell of the group meals, which often turn into a total soap opera, especially because a couple of staff members will *always* come and eat with the group (gross!) this means once again that there is an audience for all kinds of emotionally charged exchanges and outbursts.

## Strategies for Resilience

"One must live, one must desire to live still more abundantly. Let us not accept even the partial suicides. Let us be eager to know all our experiences, all happiness, all sensations. Let us not be resigned to any diminution of our "me". Let us by the champion of life, so that desires may arise out of our turpitude and weakness... Let us love life!" *Libertad*[15]

Living in an AP will test you to your limits and whatever your Achilles heel: drugs, booze, food, exercise, self-harming, they will find it and trigger it. The combination of having to monitor yourself constantly, the dirty feeling that comes from complying with their regime (way worse than any rat or shit!) and the feeling of separation from your comrades and friends will eat away at you.

"You hold onto what you have;
you do not give it up easily,
even when you know it is
poisoning you." *Poppy Z Brite*[16]

Being angry in prison felt gloriously straight forward and simple. I could communicate with people who related to my politics and could find inspiration from hearing about resistance, attack and anarchist projects from around the world. In the bail hostel, it's much more mix up, as you inevitably turn a lot of that anger towards yourself, and once you start doing this it's hard to turn back. But never give up! They are the problem, not you!

Even if you've got no money and no place much to go, if you can get out, go out! I spent a lot of time sitting on a park bench watching people walk their dogs, silently fuming to myself but enjoying the glimpses of freedom and the sunlight on my face. Find a secluded spot and scream and shout. Experiment with how far you can get from the hostel within your restrictions (I loved my slightly stressful high speed bike rides and long runs

---

15 Libertad, *We Go On*
16 Brite, *Wormwood: A Collection of Short Stories, 1994*

to put as much mental and physical distance between me and the AP as possible). Join a gym (if you can afford it) and work the punch bag. I tried to get some of our 'activity fund' to be spent on one of these but was told I was trying to encourage aggressive behaviour.

A final note on the use of computers in the AP. If you have restrictions like me, you will find looking for work extremely difficult. I wasn't even allowed to use the computers at the Job Centre, in case I managed to hack into them. When I was job hunting I was allowed to use the hostel computers but only in the office, with a member of staff watching me the *entire* time. They then checked my browser history (pointless as they had been watching me but when did logic ever matter in this situation?!). As someone who tried to avoid interacting with staff as much as possible, this was really frustrating.

## 'Constructive Activity'

As time goes on you will be allowed to miss groups if you can demonstrate you are engaging with "constructive activity". So, I would recommend either lining up lots of 'appointments' (they will sporadically check these so be a bit careful), going to the library, or organising a voluntary job. A lot of people volunteered in charity shops, especially Sue Ryder (they also take people who are 'working out' on ROTLs so are used to dealing with prisoners). If you think you might want to volunteer, get the process started as soon as possible. Probation have to authorise everything (jobs or voluntary) and this takes weeks or even months.

## Visits

No visitors are allowed in the hostel (not that you'd want them in that dump anyway!). People cannot even use the car park. In the winter this can be a bit tough, because you don't have many places to go without spending lots of money. My advice would be, if you have access to a vehicle and you are coming to visit someone, whisk them away for a couple of hours. If they have restrictive signing times they will most probably have exhausted all their local options for entertainment. I will never forget the moment I made it to my first patch of pine trees once I'd been released. The visit will always feel slightly pressured because you'll be clock watching; but it's so nice to escape for an hour or two! If you are visiting someone who can't use a computer do a bit of research into the local area for them.

So much emphasis is placed on how amazing it must be to get out of jail, that it can be hard to admit that you are not having a good time. I felt really conscious of all those I couldn't communicate with (especially mates still inside), and felt massive guilt about this, even though I knew rationally that it wasn't my fault.

If you are visiting someone in an AP think carefully about what they are allowed before bringing them gifts. For example, I got a delivery of my bike tools which had to go back straight away. Staff do bag searches nearly every time you enter the building (especially if you've been out for a few hours). Room searches mean that having lots of photos of people you aren't meant to be in contact with may not be the best idea.

By now you will be really used to the highs and lows of having a visit. One thing I would definitely say is that just because in theory you *can* see more people (licence conditions dependent) you don't *have* to. When I was in the AP I felt so angry and messed up from not sleeping I didn't really want to see anyone. If people are solid, they will understand that they just need to wait a bit longer to see you. Remind yourself that you are lucky to have people who want to visit you (many don't) but also don't feel pressured to accept all invitations!

If you are going to visit someone living in an AP be aware their mood may fluctuate hugely. Sometimes they might need to rant for ages about life in the AP. Other times they might not want to discuss it at all. For me, I wanted as much information as possible from my visitors about people I cared about, politics and generally all the areas of my life which I couldn't access due to my restrictions. When I was inside I got sent loads of anarchist publications from across the world and could publish texts and put up pictures on my walls etc. Now I was starved of all the things that had given me strength, and I was desperate to hear what was going on outside the grim confines of the AP.

If you are expecting visitors, my advice would be to challenge your pride. Ask for help. Don't be ashamed. I *hate* asking for help and one of the things I was most looking forward to about life on road after jail was making up for all the support I had been given inside. My licence conditions rendered me fairly useless on this front. But don't despair. Be honest on visits.

The regularity of your signing times can make visits quite hard work, especially initially if you haven't seen people for ages. They are deliberately designed to distract and disrupt. Also, as you are constantly out in public, you may be concerned about covert surveillance (MAPPA guidelines clearly state that surveillance of this nature is commonly used)[17]. This is especially likely on your first home leave(s) so be careful.

It's exhausting having to 'police' yourself constantly and not let on that they are really affecting you. Recall often seems like positive option (especially when you're not sleeping) because then you can be yourself. But if you can reach the point where you are discharged from the hostel, it will get easier...

## Home Leaves

Once you have been in the hostel for a month you can apply for your first 'home leave'. Probation will have to check the address and contact the people who live there. If it is cleared, your first home leave is meant to be of one night, but can increase over time up to four nights in any two-week period. Because probation gave me so much grief, and the physical distance between the hostel and my 'move on' address, I only went a couple of times, but many people go as much as possible towards the end of their time in the AP. Home-leave is normally granted to see family members, but if you stand the interrogation, some of my mates successfully applied to stay with their partners. In order to do this, you will be repeatedly asked to demonstrate that your relationship is 'healthy' and not contributing to any of your supposed 'offending behaviours'.

The restrictions of the hostel (for example, physically signing in) will not apply when you are on home leave. Though for some maddening reason, they still made me do 'telephone signings' at my allotted times. No one else had to do this and all my mates in the AP thought it was farcical how I was singled out for special treatment. You will have to ask the hostel for a home leave form (they won't offer it up), the staff (your Key Worker and someone more senior) will have to authorise it, and then it gets passed on to probation. As with all these things, it takes a while, so get it in as quickly as possible. As long as the date of your proposed home leave is after your induction period, you can submit it before you have been in the AP for a month to get the process started. If you want to be allowed to 'move on' then applying for home leave is the best way, to show some supposed 'progress'.

---

17 "Cases qualifying for level 3 tend to be more demanding on resources and require the involvement of senior people from the agencies, who can authorise the use of extra resources. For example, surveillance on an offender or emergency accommodation." (mappa.justice.gov.uk/connect.ti/MAPPA/view?objectId=262963&exp=e2)

Some people who had probation in different areas from me successfully blagged them for a travel warrant to cover their transport home. Probation are much more likely to accept your application for home leave, and front travel money if you state that you are using it for 'resettlement' (job research, maintaining family ties and so on).

A couple of points on the emotional aspects of home leave. It can be quite a roller coaster. Make sure you factor in a bit of time for yourself as well as seeing people at your 'home'. This will be the first time you've slept somewhere that feels safe since you went to jail (or were in the cop shop). It will be both energising and exhausting at the same time. Little things like the train ride, and being able to see family in a private environment felt amazing.

**Curfew checks**

These don't seem to be common practice (no one else who was at the hostel same time as me was subject to them) but I had one every night I was on home leave the first few times. The curfew checks involve one or two coppers coming to your house. They will do this at different points throughout your licence (not just while you are at the AP). They will try to ask you questions. All they need to see is that you are physically there. So, open the door then shut it again. They will *normally* be coppers from the local area who know very little about you, so they may be intrigued and start trying to ask you questions. Do *not* engage with them.

I found the issue of curfew checks extremely frustrating. You are constantly (certainly initially) half expecting the door to go as soon as your curfew time commences. The people you are staying with will also probably be feeling this pressure. It does eventually become normalised but it also means that the good nights kip you were looking forward to often doesn't happen because part of you is waiting for a knock at the door. They aren't subtle either. My family live in a small village and so the sight of the cop car late at night (or sometimes a van) was very noticeable! Luckily, I had been open and honest about being in jail but this could be quite traumatic if you were trying to be discrete.

Curfew checks also mean that any one who is in the house will know potentially that you are under police surveillance, or that something is up. One home leave I had coincided with a visit from some younger family members who didn't know I'd been inside. I was concerned that they would be confused (and maybe upset) by the fact that the police were at the door. Another time *eight months* into my licence (I am including this because by this time probation should be in theory be more hands-off), the police went and interviewed members of my family before an event, then turned up and did three curfew checks. Also, I got made to have a police escort back from the train station, and they watched me get on the train. This was the last time I applied for a home leave, because I was so angry at their constant grief.

## Legal

A final note on legal issues. As I said earlier, avoid chatting any of your business about legal stuff to residents or staff and if they try to open your legal mail, don't let em! It's worth getting clued up on your rights, so read through the 'Approved Premises Manual' (annex A of Probation Instruction 32/2014). This PI expired in 2015 but it has not yet been replaced. It contains useful information about the introduction of CRCs, and searching resident's rooms in APs. Also see PSI 'Licence Conditions, Licences and Licence Supervision Notices'.

Once you are released, if you wish to challenge any aspect of your licence/AP conditions you will need to get guidance from a prison law firm. In order to be able to access them you may have to negotiate with probation. My solicitor was based in London, so I had to ask permission to miss a signing time and get written confirmation from the solicitor as to my intentions of the appointment, and also a letter confirming I had attended, and have him call my offender supervisor when I was in his office.

## Conclusions

APs claim to help their residents but the reality is that they just make everything worse. As PI 04/2011 states, it costs a phenomenal amount to keep someone in a hostel. The hostel is massively restrictive and does nothing to encourage independence. Residents are controlled and patronised at every turn. As most residents are 'high risk' they may well have already served long jail sentences, and the AP just contributes to a general feeling of institutionalisation and a dependency on authority.

If you can ride it out, leaving the AP behind is pure joy. One of the best bike rides I've ever had was cycling away from that poxy place. But even the process of being 'released' can be stressful. I only found out less than 24 hours before I was being evicted that I could go to my 'move on address'. I think in my case they were concerned because the police force that arrested me did not want to relinquish their power over me. When I 'moved on' I got a new probation officer and MAPPA board because it was in a different area and this irked them I think.

At the end of their time, people are spat out into the wider world, often with no resources, and feeling de-motivated. I was lucky to have an address, many just get put into a homeless shelter, ready for the 'revolving door' of the CJS to start turning again... The hopes that filled people before they were released invariably crushed by the grim realisation that life on licence means very little support, and a whole heap of restrictions.

# PROBATION NOTES

"The process of liberation is a violent one." *Frantz Fanon[1]*

You've probably realised that probation is a malevolent, seemingly omnipotent force when you are on licence. This section outlines some further ways they legitimise their control, using the violence of administration and bureaucracy, again, drawing on my own experiences as context.

## Inaccuracies and Reports

IT has reported how many prisoners have been let down by their probation officers[2], common grievances cited include: inaccuracies within OASys reports, recommendations that do not support progression and licence conditions that do not necessarily reflect risk factors. These conditions, combined with the daily frustrations that arise from repeatedly attempting to contact, clarify or challenge the individual's probation officer can be extremely stressful. Often, due to the distance required to travel to prisons and the lack of resources, probation officers conduct meetings by video link, or miss the appointment entirely. I was summoned repeatedly to the 'OMU' when I was inside to have video-link or telephone-conferences with my probation officer, only to find I was invariably disconnected after a few minutes.

> "Its front-line managers face increasing pressure, including dealing with higher than expected workloads, now of high-risk offenders, while assimilating a heavy influx of trainees, who will take time to become fully effective professionals."[3]

1 Fanon, The Wretched of the Earth, 1963
2 insidetime.org/insidetime-report-failing-london-probation/
3 National Audit Office, Transforming Rehabilitation, 2016

Because of the issues around the work load of probation, reports which hold great weight for the prisoner (particularly in relation to recall and parole cases) are often produced by an individual who doesn't know them. It is also a common occurrence for prisoners to be issued with many different probation officers within a short time frame, have really long waiting times for any changes, and for probation to use draconian applications of conditions in order to indiscriminately control people. Reformists sometimes frame these practical issues in terms of a sense of sympathy for the individuals who make up the National Probation Service. In my view, they signed up to a career which is based entirely on making people's lives as miserable as possible and they deserve whatever stress they get. There can be *no* reform of the NPS. Their administration will *always* be violent, the current 'crisis' just reveals the inherent ugliness of the system taken to its logical conclusion.

## Police Tactics

Contrary to what they say, probation do *not* like it when you are -if not triumphing-surviving in the face of adversity. During my licence, I had several run ins with the police that revealed to me the desperation with which they wanted me to trip up and rile me. Here are a few examples.

- Police escort from prison to the AP. What was unusual was that my 'escort' was two coppers from the area I was arrested in (which was far away from where I was incarcerated and the hostel I was sent to). They wasted no time trying to 'chat' as soon as I was put in the vehicle. I asked them to turn up the radio.

- Before I got released from the bail hostel I was given an official licence warning for "refusing entry to the police" when they did a curfew check on my first home leave. Neither me, nor my parents, heard the knock. How can you refuse entry to someone if you do not know they are there? The police had my parents phone number, they could have easily called to check if I was inside. Apparently, this instance is an example of how I was not "doing my part". One of my offender managers told me that in their own report, the police admitted in their report that they knocked "exceptionally quietly". Therefore, by their own admission would've been easy for me/us not to hear. Having this licence warning stopped me getting home leave for a while, and if I received another one I would have been recalled. No mention of this incident was made to me directly, either the following night when the police returned again, or when I returned to the AP. It was over a week after 'the incident' that I found out I had allegedly "refused entry". Even my key worker at the hostel wasn't told, which implies some kind of attempt to sneakily slap a licence warning on me.

- Once I left the AP I had *regular* visits from probation *and* the police officer who covered all the MAPPA cases for the surrounding area. I had a lot of phone calls and visits from them at various points and this was *really* challenging. The MAPPA copper in charge of my case also turned up and did an unannounced checked my parents browser history on their computer.

- Despite the police force involved in my case having kittens at the thought of me returning to the area and authorising a lot of curfew checks, attempting to interview all members of my immediate family because they were so concerned about my "welfare", and issuing me with a lot of exclusion zones, 11 months into my licence I got repeated invitations to visit my home town, despite my being really clear that I had *no* intention of doing this. My probation officer compared me to someone addicted to smack, saying that I hadn't tested myself, and that while I had been supposedly "clean" during my licence, I hadn't exposed myself to any possible situations where I may want to "use" (or in my case, cause trouble). The MAPPA copper also encouraged me to return to the place of my arrest and conviction.

**Random Suggestions for Dealing with Probation**

Firstly, pick your battles. Don't try to challenge too much at once. Work out what you absolutely want to challenge. *Never ask permission* for your own sanity and sense of self-worth, frame it in the context of being confrontational and not accepting their demands.

Avoid communicating with probation as much as possible. I found writing statements and letters (obviously not on the computer!) was helpful for this because I could be really clear without getting drawn into their nonsense and refer to relevant legislation/legal precedents.

Get whatever information you can out of them. It will be redacted to fuck, and most likely incomplete (especially if you are subject to the anti-terrorism laws) but it might provide some useful information, and if nothing else shows that you are exerting power against them. Get a copy of your

OASys report, as this will help to make sense of the alleged 'risk' in your offending behaviour. This may help you challenge their justification for your licence conditions. My probation officer said the following:

> "XXX has outwardly complied with her licence conditions. However, supervision gains will have been modest as she still strongly identifies with anarchist beliefs and so in the cycle of change models is in pre-contemplation...until anarchist principles lose clarity or meaning for her then I think the end result will be the same."[4]

**Subject Access Requests (SAR) and the Disclosure and Barring Service (DBS)**

Towards the end of your sentence you might want to ask a solicitor to conduct a Subject Access Request on your behalf. This will mean you can get a print out of all your OASys reports. The police used to request a £10 fee for this, but now it's free. Guidance and a template cover letter is on the 'Netpol' website[5]. Be as specific as possible, and cite relevant police operations. If it's vague they'll use that as an excuse not to process it.

The 'Data Protection Act' (DPA) 1998 means any individual can submit a SAR, and the MoJ 'Despatch Team and Data and Compliance Unit' (DACU) should get a copy to you following your request. Unsurprisingly, much of the data about you will no doubt be withheld because some information is exempt from disclosure under section seven of the DPA, and the 'Terrorism Act', especially in cases relating to alleged extremism. You will need to send a copy of your passport or drivers licence for proof of ID and bank statement/utility bill from last six months to show address.

Once your licence expires, it's worth contacting DBS (Disclosure and Barring Service) to check if you have been flagged or barred. Challenging any DBS stuff while on licence is difficult as you have the double whammy of licence conditions (i.e. maybe not working with vulnerable people), plus DBS (which may be more long-term)[6].

---

4 OASyS report 2016
5 See resources
6 If you are a MAPPA case this will most likely affect your DBS checks. If you have a so-called 'Indexed Offence' listed by the DBS you can get barred from working with so-called vulnerable adults. Unfortunately for the filth mine was not one of these offences. Unfortunately for me, they found a bit of a way around this by putting a 'flag' on my DBS record which says something to the effect of "we cannot bar her but we would like to."

# PSYCHOLOGICAL

"I shall not die
A thousand deaths of compromise...I shall not die
A million times
I shall not die
you will only get my corpse."[1]

"Every second an anarchist spends in prison his [or her] spirit
strengthens, expands beyond the walls and nourishes the
solidarity that he or she inspires."[2]

This is a brief overview of some of the key psychological issues that can
occur when an individual is released from prison and/or on licence.

## Post-Traumatic Stress Disorder (PTSD)

"Post-traumatic stress disorder is characterised by traumatic
memories and flashbacks, depression, difficulties managing
mood and behaviour, and problems with normal daily activities
such as eating and sleeping."[3]

'PTSD' was highlighted in the 1980s and is *really* high in prisoners. PTSD
can be isolating and disorientating, and normally occurs after a specific
traumatic incident or event. Symptoms may include disturbing thoughts,
feelings, or dreams related to the events, mental or physical distress,

---

1 Poem sent to me in jail written by a comrade from Hambach Forest, hambachforest.
blogspot.de
2 Weir, Revolutionary Struggle Trial: Statement to the Terror Court of Korydallos, 2012
3 Nicole O'Driscoll, PTSD Nurse (peopleof.oureverydaylife.com/problems-after-prison-
5898.html)

alterations in how a person thinks and feels, and an increase in the fight or flight response. These symptoms can last for a long time.

Much has been written about PTSD (see resources section). Obviously, if you are suffering from PTSD, are skint and living in a bail hostel with lots of restrictions your choices and funds are somewhat limited in terms of accessing resources. Friends or family may be able to do research for you. It can be hard to ask for help when you have spent a lot of energy building mental barricades and have a healthy distrust for all those in authority.

I am really resistant to counselling, and words I associate with it instantly rile me. This is not necessarily healthy, but an outcome of my

Josh McPhee, *Bars 2*

experiences. If you do decide to get counselling, be warned that trying to get NHS appointments can be a long process, and quite triggering if you have issues around authority and surveillance. If you are in an AP they will know if you have been prescribed medication. What you say to the doctor *should* be kept confidential (unless they perceive you to be a big risk), but it's always worth specifying that you do not want information shared, and try to give as little away as possible when presenting your case.

A good mate told me about the concept of 'Post-Traumatic Growth' (PTG). This is a positive way of surviving and learning from PTSD. According to the Post Traumatic Growth Research Group, PTG "is positive change experienced as a result of the struggle with a major life crisis or a traumatic event."[4]

The research group has outlined five key ways PTG manifests itself: new opportunities that have emerged from the struggle, a change in relationships (closer relationships, and/or an increased sense of connection to others who suffer), an increased sense of one's own strength and a greater appreciation for life in general. They also cite a spiritual element, but that's not for me!

> "Post-traumatic growth refers to how adversity can often be a springboard to a new and more meaningful life in which people re-evaluate their priorities, deepen their relationships, and find new understandings of who they are. Post-traumatic growth is not simply about coping; it refers to changes that cut to the very core of our way of being in the world."[5]

## Post-Incarceration Syndrome

> "If you can do prison, you can do not being in prison. Sometimes we have to remind ourselves of that…It might suck, I might not like it, but if I'm strong enough to survive the worst that my enemies can throw at me, I'm strong enough to survive life."[6]

'Post-Incarceration Syndrome' is a common occurrence in those serving, or recently released from, long sentences. Symptoms include: distressing dreams, institutionalisation, emotional numbing, complex PTSD and feeling overwhelmed by choice. This is quite common in those serving

---

4 ptgi.uncc.edu/
5 Stephen Joseph What Doesn't Kill Us: The New Psychology of Post-Traumatic Growth, 2013
6 Luers, in Halliday, 2014

an indeterminate sentence. People can get institutionalised very quickly in jail. A lot of Lifers report stress and anxiety when going on hospital trips, to funerals, or out on ROTL. Even after my relatively short spell inside I felt dazzled by how much technology had moved on, and the amount of choice available so I can't imagine how it must feel for long-term prisoners upon release.

## Loneliness

"You have to figure out what you really believe in and then find other people who feel the same way. The only thing you have to do alone is to decide what's important to you."[7]

When you are in jail you have no privacy, often sharing a cell, and are constantly around people, or at least near people. Staff routinely come and annoy you at your hatch with their various checks and demands. To suddenly go from the noisy hecticness of this regime to totally isolation can be quite a culture shock, especially for older prisoners.

"There is no questioning the extent to which ex-prisoners in particular suffer from social isolation upon release. Recent research reveals that loneliness is twice as damaging as obesity when it comes to older people's health and is almost as significant as a cause of death as poverty. In young people, loneliness has been found to contribute to stress, anxiety, paranoia and addiction. The Mental Health Foundation has called it a growing problem of "huge concern".[8]

If you feel lonely and are frustrated at trying to access resources it might be useful to quote the 'Care Act' (2015). However, this relates more to basic physical requirements such as accommodation than meeting mental health issues.

## My Solution Rehabilitation Programme (MSRP):

As with jail, psychology is big business in connection with licences and those under 'supervision'. Because of this, the state is constantly re-inventing the wheel. One example of this is MSRP. The catch phrase for this is: "my problem, my solution": "It is designed to challenge attitudes, develop

7 Feinberg, 1993
8 insidetime.org/ex-prisoners-face-loneliness-epidemic/

improved behaviour and skills needed for a crime-free life."[9]

As with the structure outlined at the AP, MSRP uses the probation model of "the nine aspects of re-offending" to try to change the person on licence. Once again, the emphasis is on the *individual* to engage and change:

"You'll need to take responsibility for your own rehabilitation and understand only you can make the changes needed to stay clear of crime. You need to do the following: follow through with actions agreed, tell us if there are problems, be honest with us and yourself. Doing this will give you the best chance to turn your life around. If you don't, enforcement measures may be required."[10]

This quote is a classic example of the benevolent yet threatening language that probation use to calmly control the individual under supervision and exert their authority, whilst trying to sound like they are avoiding taking disciplinary action. Yet again 'rehabilitation' is highlighted as a supportive veneer to an otherwise invasive attempt to modify an individual's behaviour. MSRP is the new name for what was the 'Thinking Skills Programme'. It is delivered 'in the community' and in prison.

### 'Developing Dialogues'

The 'good cop/bad cop' routine is a well-established dichotomy in mainstream culture, and anyone who has been nicked will be well aware that it is implemented a lot in the UK. My time on licence was no exception to this. As my offender supervisor was based quite some distance away (bad cop), my offender manager (good cop) over saw my weekly supervision, and they were responsible for trying to get me to engage with 'Developing Dialogues'.

Developing Dialogues is apparently concerned with "making you safe in the future"[11]. The ultimate goal is to get the individual to respond to 'high-risk' scenarios selected by the state (in my case riots and demonstrations, or the police killing someone) in a legal (or 'pro-social') way. Reaching this point is the rationale for ongoing attempts at psychological profiling and invasive procedures.

9 Kent, Surrey and Sussex Community Rehabilitation Company (KSS CRC) My Solution Rehabilitation Programme (MSRP), 2015
10 Kent, Surrey and Sussex Community Rehabilitation Company (KSS CRC) My Solution Rehabilitation Programme (MSRP), 2015
11 Probation officer 2016

I refused to participate in jail. Now it was on my licence. My strategy was to physically attend, whilst distracting probation as much as possible (you get good at deflecting attention away from yourself when you are locked into these institutional practices).

'Developing Dialogues' is a one-to-one project based on the old 'HI' model. It is a more intense version, and a programme for 'extremists'. Probation use it for "left wing, right wing and Islamic Fundamentalists"[12]. The programme uses the concept of 'identity' to interrogate an individual about their values and beliefs. The aim is to make them question them all. Prior to my case, the programme had used in on people they suspected to be involved in Daesh and right-wing individuals but not anarchists.

My advice on this programme is, as ever, be vague, deflect (ask probation what they think) and give information from childhood. For example, as part of the programme you are meant to describe a 'Relationship Web'; (at time of the 'offence', now, and at seven years old.) I talked for nearly a whole hour about how I played in the garden making perfume out of mud and flowers.

I'm not sure if it is part of a cunning plan, but the questions were fairly random. The usual targeted fishing exercises about my offence, were accompanied by queries like: "Do you think hospitality is important?", "What are your views on the elderly? Disabled? Women?"[13]

**Practical Suggestions**

A good friend gave me a few suggestions that helped me when I was feeling angry.

- Building your army: This is used in therapy, especially when fighting addiction. You try to think about all the resources and people who combined will create an exponentially stronger force against 'the enemy' (in my case, the state).

- Sensory grounding exercise: Try to think of different things you can touch, see, hear, feel, smell at any one time. I used to do this during my early morning laps of the wing in jail and it set me up for the day. Try to really focus in on something specific for each different sense, it takes you away from your head and roots you in your body.

---

12 Beth Weaver, and the Probation Journal, Control or Change? Developing Dialogues between Desistance Research and Public Protection Practices, 2014 Note: this article is not exactly related to the programme enforced by probation, but it does cover some of the key themes/issues.
13 Developing Dialogues, 2015

- Anchors: use a physical object to connect you to the moment. Touch this object when you can feel your head start to go. For me, it was a kettle-bell key ring my mate gave me, which I held when I need to be reminded of being in the 'here and now'.

# COMING HOME

"You are not meant to survive -not whole, not sane, not with a loving heart. Those who do survive find whatever means they can. To make it, you have to rebuild yourself: to rebuild the old you, whatever flaws and weaknesses you brought in, mortar in the gaps in the wall. It's a never ending job."[1]

So, you've made it through and you've come home. But the ride ain't over yet. Be prepared for a bit of a roller-coaster. You will most likely still feel the effects of your licence when you come home. I was so used to my curfew I felt slightly anxious when I stayed somewhere over night, or out late. And I still have a flight or fight response when someone knocks at the door, or I hear a lot of keys jangling.

The first few weeks I was back was the best high ever and I felt invincible (and to be honest, slightly manic). Then I started writing and became a total hermit. I don't regret it, but I wouldn't necessarily recommend it. In terms of settling in to being home and enjoying my freedom, it definitely didn't help!

One of the main things to remember when you return home is that throughout your sentence -inside and out- you have been in a highly controlled, artificial environment. Being released from this is *glorious* but not without its impacts. Using a computer was extremely draining the first few times I did it and I got frustrated with myself. When my new phone number got circulated I was overwhelmed by the number of people who wanted to say hi, but would then berate myself for feeling like this (what a privilege; to have so many friends!) If I knew people I cared about where having a hard time, I wanted to be able to support them (especially those

1 Imarisha, 2016

who had supported me inside), but after several attempts, I had to accept that I needed all my energy to support myself. Bumping into people in the street was way more challenging than it had been previously, and whilst I loved going out with my crew, I didn't like the unknown potential for random social interaction.

I have been aware since my arrest of the unasked questions that hang in the air, the inquisitive looks and attempts to find out what's been going on for me. I know that most of these have come from places of concern, but I have become highly suspicious of and resistant to them. I would warn anyone who is close to someone who has recently completed their sentence to be *patient* in dealing with them. You may want to spend time with them because you missed them. You may want to ask questions because you are concerned about them. Hopefully this text provides some insight, but you will never understand what they are going through unless you've been inside or on licence.

> "The most terrible thing about it is not that it breaks one's heart -hearts are made to be broken- but that it turns one's heart to stone."[2] *Wilde*

Prison changes everyone. I feel stronger in some ways than ever before, but I'm not going to lie, at times my rage has been ragged, fragile, and brittle. Like stains on a cell floor, prison has left a mark on me. I am sorry that I got caught, and I'm sorry that this has obvious security complications. I am sorry that I lost my anonymity. But I am not sorry that I have this stain, because it gives me strength, and it is a constant reminder of all that I despise. I do not think that I am special. I do not want sympathy. I attacked the state and it retaliated in the way that I knew it would.

> "Did you want to see me broken?
> Bowed head and lowered eyes?
> Shoulders falling down like tear drops,
> Weakened by my soulful cries?
>
> Does my haughtiness offend you?
> Don't you take it awful hard
> 'Cause I laugh like I've got gold mines
> Diggin' in my own backyard.

---

2 Wilde, 1904

You may shoot me with your words,
You may cut me with your eyes,
You may kill me with your hatefulness,
But still, like air, I'll rise."[3]

3 Maya Angelou, Still I Rise, 1978

# CONCLUSIONS

"Prison is power: control of the individual, community, people, nation. It is taking from our community and our spirits that which is not given. It is a threat to all of us."[1]

In the relentless power struggle between the state and those who refuse to conform to its violent logic and domination, there is no space for complacency or reform. Abolition is not enough. We are all part of a social war. As Faith has argued: "it is a mistake to generalize women as innocent victims of inevitable male violence. We are all innocent and we are all guilty. There are no 'good' or 'bad' people".[2]

"We desire to incriminate social neutrality and to constantly create a polarized condition which will force everyone to pick sides and lay out the dilemma: being an accomplice of authority or being with the law of rebellion. There are no middle ground solutions, no intermediate states. Neutrality must die because we have a war."[3]

The war that CCF have outlined can eat you up when you are on licence. The combination of isolation from your comrades, a narrowing of the forms of expression available to you, and the relentless interrogation of the state can suffocate. My advice to people on licence would be, get away with what you can, ask for as little as possible, and never, ever lose sight of who your enemy is. Being on licence can feel like a gross sell-out, a compliance, and a dilution of your political beliefs. But it is possible to use this time as a way to gather strength and access resources. They are

---

1 Imarisha, 2016
2 Faith, 2011
3 CCF, Chaotic Variables, 2016

*not* omnipotent and there are *always* cracks to be exploited in the system. Foucault outlined the totalitarian façade the prison estate presents:

> "Prison is the only place where power is manifested in its naked state, in its most excessive force, and where it is justified as moral force….For once, power doesn't hide or mask itself; it reveals itself as tyranny pursued into the tiniest details; it is cynical and at the same time pure and entirely 'justified', because its practice can be totally formulated within the framework of morality. Its brutal tyranny consequently appears as the serene domination of Good over Evil, or order over disorder."[4]

Even at its most "excessive" the force of the state can be attacked and there is always the capacity for rebellion, and rebellious thoughts. The aim of probation is to try to break down someone's 'offending behaviour' in order to remodel them as more acceptable individuals who will accept (and conform to) legal forms of action. If someone has refused to comply in jail, probation and licence conditions give the state a whole new tool kit of ways to try and break the individual and remodel them.

> "Do not go gentle into that good night,
> Old age should burn and rave at close of day;
> Rage, rage against the dying of the light."[5]

One of my probation officers used to say, "what resists persists"[6]. This is a commonly used approach by probation, a way to try to soften an individual's attitudes towards the system by giving them a slightly longer rope by which to hang themselves. Embrace, nurture, and strengthen resistance to this, especially when they are attempting to lure you in with promises of more relaxed conditions, or a slightly bigger cage. I never, ever want to lose the rage that I have against the system, and the contempt I feel for those who are part of it.

> "One thing prisons taught me is to be very strong, and that I am a worthwhile person. Nobody likes to have their freedom taken away from them, but all the abuse and everything they threw at me -it just made me stronger each time."[7]

---

4 Foucault, 1975
5 Dylan Thomas, Do Not Go Gentle Into That Good Night, 1952
6 Probation, 2016
7 Anonymous, Ex-prisoner

"We cannot win and winning is not our intention. We do what we have to do, all we can do, is keep at them until it becomes unbearable. To provoke them, and make them mad."[8]

Fire to the prisons! Solidarity, love and rage. x

---

8 Doyle, 1999

# Words I Never Want to Hear…..

Probation, rehabilitation, education, recommendation, adjudication, consideration, legislation, documentation, intervention, collaboration, protection, condition, application (your app is different from my app). Regime, pro-social, scenario, risk, management, community, dialogue, meaningful, development, safety, initiative, treatment, safeguarding, compliance, enabling, non-violent, minimising, duty of care, restraint, constructive, productive, offending behaviour, psychological profile, extremist, anti-terrorism, secure/security, approved/approval, justice, meaningful, opportunity, curfew.

# APPENDICES

Appendix One:

Childcare Resettlement Leave is *meant* to relate to the factors outlined below.

a) Article 8 of the European Convention on Human Rights on the right to a family life and Article 3 (1) of the UN Convention on the Rights of the Child;

b) The individual circumstances of the particular prisoner and her child. Make sure you reference these pieces of legislation if the prison doesn't act on your request, and, as with everything inside, keep a record of all staff spoken to, apps submitted, and dates.

If you feel that the prison service has not taken these issues into account in the decision-making process contact PAS.

Appendix Two:

Legislation for new mothers applying for a place on a Mother and Baby Unit:

- 'Children's Act' 1989 section 1 states that parental responsibility is to be retained by mother even if she is in prison.

- 'Children's Act' 2004 section 10 places a duty on local authorities to promote co-operation between authorities, including prisons.

- UN Convention on rights of the child 1989 Article 3, paragraph 1: "in any actions taken by authorities and public or private institutions, the best interests of the child *must* be of primary concern.

- European Convention on Human Rights 1950 Article 8: the right to respect for private and family life. "Everyone has the right to respect for *his* private and family life, *his* home and *his* correspondence". There should be no interference by public authorities in this process. (My italics; note the use of

the male pronoun again!)
- The publication 'All About MBUs' written by NOMS should be available at reception
Also see PSO 4800 'Women Prisoners'.

Appendix Three:
PSI 40/2011: 'The Categorisation of Female Prisoners'. For women, the official definitions of security categories are: "Category A - Prisoners whose escape would be highly dangerous to the public or the police or the security of the state and for whom the aim must be to make escape impossible. Restricted Status - Any female young person or adult prisoner convicted or on remand whose escape would present a serious risk to the public and who are required to be held in designated secure accommodation." -PAS

Appendix Four:
Birth Companions Birth Charter, 2016. Pregnant women in prison should:
1. Have access to the same standard of antenatal care as women in the community.
2. Be able to attend antenatal classes and prepare for their baby's birth.
3. Be housed, fed and moved in a way that ensures the well-being of mother and baby.
4. Be told whether they have a place on a Mother and Baby Unit as soon as possible after arriving in prison.
5. Have appropriate support if electing for termination of pregnancy.
During childbirth, women should:
6. Have access to a birth supporter of their choice.
7. Be accompanied by officers who have had appropriate training and clear guidance.
8. Be provided with essential items for labour and the early postnatal period.
9. Receive appropriate care during transfer between prison and hospital.
Women with babies in prison should:
10. Be encouraged and supported in their chosen method of infant feeding.
11. Be supported to express, store and transport their breast milk safely, if they are separated from their baby.
12. Be given the same opportunities and support to nurture and bond with their babies as women in the community.
13. Be entitled to additional family visits.
All pregnant women and new mothers should:

14. Be able to access counselling when needed.
15. Receive appropriate resettlement services after release from prison.

Appendix Five:
Legislation relating to trans prisoners' legal rights:
- Human Rights Act 1998 article 3: prohibits inhumane/degrading treatment, article 8 (right to privacy and family life -including gender identity) and article 24 prohibits discrimination.
- PSI 2016-017 (formerly PSI 7/2011) 'The Care and Treatment of Transsexual Prisoners'
- PSI 07/2016 'Searching of the Person' (see appendix 15)
- Equality Act 2010: those undergoing so-called 'gender reassignment' (an outdated and problematic term) should be protected. Individuals *do not* need a Gender Recognition Certificate in order for their rights to be recognised by the act. For what it's worth, the Equalities Act means it is unlawful to be discriminated (directly or indirectly), victimised or harassed as a trans person.

Appendix Six:
Justice Now! *Prison Abolition is a Queer Issue.*
1. Queers are over represented in the prison system.
2. Queers experience brutal human rights abuses in prisons, jails and detention centres.
3. Prisons magnify violence against queer people.
4. Prison expansion has continued to divert urgent resources away from queer communities.
5. Prisons enforce rigid, queer-phobic codes of gender and sexual expression and identity.
6. Prisons target communities of colour and low-income communities.
7. Prisons target women and families.
8. Prisons are highly lucrative for private corporations and public institutions.
9. The mainstream LGBT rights movement has consistently marginalised the participation, leadership and concerns of those who are most impacted by the prison system.
10. Queer liberation is only possible with the liberation of all oppressed and marginalised people.
Appendix Seven:
PAS overview on the main manifestations of racism in prison:
1) Direct racial abuse with or without physical violence, by staff or other

prisoners.
2) Ill treatment by staff because you have submitted, or are a witness to someone else's racist complaint.
3) Discriminatory provision of facilities and services between different racial groups.
4) Differential unfavourable treatment by staff.
5) Insufficient action by staff to address complaints of racism.

Appendix Eight:
Overview of Operation Nexus in relation to the use of police forces from outside the UK and prison infrastructure:
- Greater sharing of intelligence; to supposedly "support the removal of cases where previous charges have been dropped due to victims or witnesses refusing to cooperate with police because of intimidation or fear of retaliation".
- Unknown prints at police crime scenes and other forensic markers being run against UKBA biometric databases in a bid to solve previously unsolved crimes, both in the UK and abroad. This means that many people in detention who haven't even been *accused* of any criminal activity are having their forensics analysed by the police.
- Working with police officers from countries where high volumes of offenders are identified to help share information and further speed up removals.

Appendix Nine:
The Irish Council for Prisoners Overseas supports Irish prisoners and their families by:
- Identifying and responding to the needs of Irish prisoners and their families.
- Visiting prisoners and assisting families with travel and accommodation.
- Researching and providing relevant information to prisoners and their families including on issues such as deportation, repatriation and prison transfers.
- Representing prisoners' interests to the appropriate authorities (including embassies, welfare agencies, social welfare departments, probation, legal officers, etc.).
- Networking with prison-based agencies, as well as other groups and organisations concerned with the welfare of prisoners.
- Focusing public attention on issues affecting Irish prisoners.
- Engaging in practical work in aid of justice and human rights for Irish pris-

oners overseas.

Appendix Ten:
Prison Rule 051 'Offences Against Discipline' (OAD)
A prisoner is guilty of an offence against discipline if *he* – [my italics]
(1) commits any assault;
(1A) commits any racially aggravated assault;
(2) detains any person against his will;
(3) denies access to any part of the prison to any officer or any person (other than a prisoner) who is at the prison for the purpose of working there;
(4) fights with any person;
(5) intentionally endangers the health or personal safety of others or, by his conduct, is reckless whether such health or personal safety is endangered;
(6) intentionally obstructs an officer in the execution of his duty, or any person (other than a prisoner) who is at the prison for the purpose of working there, in the performance of his work;
(7) escapes or absconds from prison or from legal custody;
(8) fails to comply with any condition upon which he is temporarily released under Rule 9;
(9) administers a controlled drug to himself or fails to prevent the administration of a controlled drug to him by another person (but subject to Rule 52);
(10) is intoxicated as a consequence of knowingly consuming any alcoholic beverage;
(11) knowingly consumes any alcoholic beverage other than that provided to him pursuant to a written order under Rule 25(1);
(12) has in his possession –
(a) any unauthorised article, or
(b) a greater quantity of any article than he is authorised to have;
(13) sells or delivers to any person any unauthorised article;
(14) sells or, without permission, delivers to any person any article which he is allowed to have only for his own use;
(15) takes improperly any article belonging to another person or to a prison;
(16) intentionally or recklessly sets fire to any part of a prison or any other property, whether or not his own;
(17) destroys or damages any part of a prison or any other property, other than his own;
(17A) causes racially aggravated damage to, or destruction of, any part of a

prison or any other property, other than his own;

(18) absents himself from any place he is required to be or is present at any place where he is not authorised to be;

(19) is disrespectful to any officer, or any person (other than a prisoner) who is at the prison for the purpose of working there, or any person visiting a prison;

(20) uses threatening, abusive or insulting words or behaviour;

(20A) uses threatening, abusive or insulting racist words or behaviour;

(21) intentionally fails to work properly or, being required to work, refuses to do so;

(22) disobeys any lawful order;

(23) disobeys or fails to comply with any rule or regulation applying to him;

(24) receives any controlled drug, or, without the consent of an officer, any other article, during the course of a visit (not being an interview such as is mentioned in Rule 38);

(24A) displays, attaches or draws on any part of a prison, or on any other property, threatening, abusive or insulting racist words, drawings, symbols or other material;

(25) (a) attempts to commit,

(b) incites another prisoner to commit, or

(c) assists another prisoner to commit or to attempt to commit, any of the foregoing offences.


Appendix 11:

PSI 22/2012 'Secret Surveillance'

- Relates to the Regulation of Investigatory Powers Act (RIPA) 2000 and replaced the National Security Framework Function 4-4.6 (aka PSO1000).

- Expired 16/07/2016 but is still in use. It is reviewed by the 'Office of Surveillance Commissioners (OSC).'

- Specifically states at 3.12 "Information obtained by 'Secret' surveillance is shared securely with identified stakeholders". Unsurprisingly, prisoners are not informed who these 'stakeholders' are.

- Covers 'secret' surveillance by public authorities (directed surveillance) and 'secret' surveillance in a dwelling (including a cell) or private vehicle (intrusive surveillance).

> "All prisons will use 'secret' surveillance where it is necessary and proportionate to do so for the purposes of preventing or detecting crime/serious crime, preventing disorder, or on the

grounds of public safety. All prisons will have trained staff in the key roles to ensure that the 'secret' surveillance is undertaken in accordance with the law. Use of 'secret' surveillance will be an integral part of the intelligence gathering process within prisons. 'Secret' surveillance will assist with the maintenance of control in prisons and allow Managers to take informed decisions."

Appendix 12:
PSI 2010-029/ PSO 4700 *The Indeterminate Sentence Manual*
Chapters 3, 7, 8, 10, 11, 12 and 15'. This PSI replaces PSO 4700 Chapters 3, 10, 12 and 15 and means the immediate withdrawal of Chapters 7, 8 and 11. PSO 4700 set out policy and guidance for the management of prisoners serving an indeterminate sentence, both during custody and after release on licence. The previous version, issued in May 1999, replaced various 'Circular Instructions' and other guidance. The chapters now ready for issue are in this PSI.

Chapter 3 'Tariff', Chapter 10 'Young Male Offenders', Chapter 12 'Compassionate Release' and Chapter 15 'Mentally Disordered Indeterminate Sentenced Prisoners' have had minor amendments to ensure they apply equally to both Lifer and IPP prisoners and to ensure departments are correctly referenced. Chapter 7 'Risk Assessment' is being withdrawn as this policy is now covered by Chapter 9 of the *Public Protection Manual*. Chapter 8 'Life Sentence Plan' is being withdrawn as this policy is now covered by the *OM Implementation manual*. Chapter 11 'Temporary Release' is being withdrawn as it has been replaced by PSO 6300 'Release on Temporary Licence'.

Appendix 13:
PSI2015-015 'Adult Social Care':
"The prison estate was designed for young, fit men and not for its current ageing population. Often, small cells originally meant for one man now hold two. It is often not even possible to get a wheelchair into the cell and, in most prisons the majority of cells are not at ground floor level...Under the Care Act, where the prisoner meets the eligibility criteria for social care, local authorities are responsible for meeting those specific needs. Where prisoners do not meet the eligibility criteria for local authority care, the local authority should help with developing each support plan. This should set out

what needs to be done to meet a prisoner's current needs, and help to prevent or delay the prisoner developing additional needs. However, responsibility for delivering the plan rests with the prison."

Appendix 14:
PSI 49/2011 'Rule 39: Legal Correspondence':
"Prison Rule 39 requires that a prisoner's correspondence with the courts and their legal adviser may only be opened, stopped or read in specific circumstances. Rule 39 applies to both correspondence sent to the prisoner and sent out by the prisoner. Correspondence protected in this way is often referred to as a "Rule 39 letter...There must be strict compliance with the rules regarding privileged and confidential mail. Any breach, even if accidental, is likely to lead to legal challenge in both the domestic and international courts'. Governors should ensure 'that there are sufficient safeguards to avoid the possibility of such correspondence being opened inadvertently."
(PPO)

Appendix 15:
PSI 67/2011: 'Searching the person': updated August 2016
- There must be arrangements in place for keeping records of searches and finds and non-routine full-searches of prisoners must be recorded and records kept of any additional search procedure such as where a male prisoner is asked to squat as part of a full search.
- Emphasis that a prisoner must never be naked as part of a full search. Searching of anal/ genital area only applies to male prisoners.
- In open prisons, there is no mandate for searching women prisoners on return from ROTL or outside working party.
- Section 27 of the Offender Management Act (2007), a person who is not a direct employee of a prison can be authorised to conduct a rub-down search/ metal-detector scan of a prisoner.
- Religious issues and searches (for example the removal of underwear on Sikh prisoners, and protective clothing for Muslim prisoners and visitors; as well as washing facilities if they are touched by the dog).
- Pacemaker wearers to be allowed to walk through a metal detector portal and be searched with a hand-held metal detector.
- The routine searching of babies is not mandatory either on visiting a prison or on entry to a Mother and Baby Unit (MBU). Two trained officers of either sex can search a baby.

Annex B of PSI 67/2011 contains the full detailed instructions for different types of search and contains specific instructions relating to searches of young people (children and babies), female prisoners, and trans sexual prisoners. It also includes information on the use of technical aids for searching including X-Ray machines, metal detecting portals and hand held metal detectors, and the BOSS Chair. Annex F covers the searching of people using dogs. Annex H covers the searching guidance for transsexual prisoners and includes the legal obligations under the Gender Recognition Act (GRA) 2004. Annex H states; "Transsexual prisoners at all stages of the gender confirmation process must be encouraged to enter into a voluntary written agreement in respect of their searching arrangements on arrival to an establishment ... Prisoners who hold a GRC may insist on being searched by an officer of their acquired gender and if they do so then this must be adhered to."

Appendix 16:
Pre-Sentence Report overview:
The report will follow the structure below (note that I am using *their* language as this is how it will be presented to you):
- Sources of information (you can provide supplementary materials if you like, passed on to court via solicitor)
- Offence analysis (they will ask you repeatedly about the offence: brief details, why did the offence occur?)
- Offender accepts responsibility for the offence?
- Offender recognises the impact and consequences of offence(s) on the victim/community/wider society?
- Anti-social/discriminatory attitudes/behaviour associated with offending?
- Current offence(s) part of an established pattern of offending?
- Current offence(s) indicate escalation in seriousness from earlier offending?
- Offender assessment

Appendix 17:
PSIs (and PIs) for Foreign National Prisoners (FNPs)
PSI 18/2014 - Licences, Licence Conditions and Polygraph Examinations
PI 11/2014 - Licence Conditions, Polygraph Examinations and Temporary Travel Abroad
PI 10/2014- AI13/2014 -Managing Terrorist and Extremist Offenders in the

Community
PI 05/2014 / PSI 14/2014 - Case Allocation
PI06/2014 - Enforcement of Suspended Sentences
PI 07/2014 - Case Transfers
PI 08/2014 - Process For Community Rehabilitation Companies to refer cases in the Community to NPS for review/risk escalation review
PSI 52/2011 - Immigration, Repatriation and Removal Services
PSI 18/2012 -Tariff Expired Removal Scheme Target Operating Model Rehabilitation Programme v3

Appendix 18:
The 'Standard Six' Licence Conditions:
- To be of good behaviour behaved and not to commit any offence or do anything that undermines the purpose of supervision; (PI09/2015 the 'Good Behaviour Mechanism')
- To keep in contact with the supervising officer and in accordance with any instructions given;
- If required, to receive visits from the supervising officer at place of residence;
- Permanently reside at address approved by supervising officer and notify them in advance of any change or proposed stay;
- Undertake only such work (including voluntary) as approved by supervising officer and notify them in advance of any changes;
- Not travel outside the UK without permission (only given in exceptional circumstances).

Additional Licence Conditions:
PAS Overview of possible *additional* conditions; (correct as of April 2016): Psychiatric/Psychology contact; prohibitions on computer use; preventing activities and/or employment involving contact with children; a residency requirement; offending behaviour programmes; not to contact victims or family members; exclusion areas; non-association with named persons; drug or alcohol testing; polygraph testing. Also, you may be subject to conditions preventing you from contacting a certain person, engaging in a certain programme, disclosing an intimate relationship or having regular drug tests.

My additional licence conditions:
- Reside at AP
- Not to work with vulnerable adults

- Not use computer (directly or indirectly), data storage device or electronic device (including internet enabled mobile phone).
- Not delete usage history of devices and allow SO to access them
- Report to AP staff and sign at 11:00, 15:00 and 19:00.
- Curfew 21:00-07:00.
- Not go within 100 metres of "police establishments and training centres including Private Finance Initiatives (PFIs), equine establishments, and training centres." (if you have this condition you will also get issued with a whole heap of maps to prove this point).
- Comply with any specific requirements specified "for the purpose of ensuring that you address your thinking, attitudes and problem-solving skills."
- Provide details [such as make, model, colour, registration] of any vehicle you own, hire for more than a short journey, or have regular use of, prior to that journey taking place.
- Be escorted by police to AP upon release.
- Not to possess more than one mobile phone, and to give probation the IMEI number and telephone number of the mobile. (note that whilst you are at an AP hostel staff are particularly interested in hunting out illicit mobile phones during room searches)
- Comply with any problem solving/thinking attitudes work
As with the "good behaviour" clause the below conditions were also left vague to enable them to restrict me further...
- "Not to contact directly or indirectly any person who is a serving or remanded prisoner or detained in state custody without the prior approval of your supervising officer."
- "Not to groom any individual for the purposes of radicalisation or extremism (or discuss any ideas with them)"
- "Not to contact directly or indirectly any person whom you know or believe have been charged or convicted of any extremism related offence." (Note the use of the word *charged here*. It is common for the police to arrest people then drop charges with "no further action" or "no case to answer". This is an example of the police using the CJS to tie people up and restrict them when, even using their dubious system, they have done nothing "wrong").
- "Not to participate directly or indirectly in organising and/or contributing to any demonstration, meeting, gathering, or website"

Appendix 19:
MoJ rules of 'Approved Premises':

- No alcohol, non-prescribed drugs or solvents.
- Smoke outside building
- Must submit to drug or alcohol testing
- Hostel curfew plus licence conditions/curfews
- Staff to search bedrooms (and vehicle if parked in car park)
- No abusive/violent behaviour
- All meds kept in office
- 22:00 hostel curfew and 23:00 room curfew (till 07:00)
- Residents are not permitted in each other's bedrooms
- Engage in group work programme, every day from 10:00-13:15, unless excused by OS/PO.
- Morning meeting 09:15 and to do domestic duties
- Info on residents shared with police.
- Must comply with extra curfews etc.
- Keep myself and room clean
- No weapons, alcohol, drugs, drugs paraphernalia.
- No damage to AP, contractors, staff, visitors or residents
- No threatening or violent behaviour
- No non-residents allowed on premises
- No electronic or photographic items unless approved.
- Do not bring in any materials that may be considered offensive or "anti-social"
- No photograph, film anywhere on premises
- Not allow any residents in your room
- Hand in key when leaving premises
- Show all things to staff when returning to premises
- Use of internet to be approved by AP managers.
- No methadone, subutex, pethidine, morphine, co-codamol, codeine, ritalin, diazepam, temazepam
- Police may also take part in room searches
- AP not responsible for personal items
- Staff to open all post except "rule 39" (solicitor's correspondence) or post marked legal
- Rule 7 searching equipment applies

Note: Each hostel/AP will also have its own individual rules.

# RESOURCES/BIBLIOGRAPHY

Disclaimer: I don't like reformist organisations, but some of these might be useful if you are inside or supporting someone. Telephone numbers and postal addresses are included so that people in prison can try to add them to their PIN (though this is obviously highly likely to be refused by security).

**Letter Writing**
Anarchist Black Cross
Publish lists of anarchist prisoners to write to and information on practical solidarity and resistance to the prison regime.
Brighton brightonabc.org.uk ABC Brighton, PO Box 74, Brighton, BN1 4ZQ, UK brightonabc@riseup.net
Bristol bristolabc.wordpress.com bristol_abc@riseup.net ABC Bristol, Kebele, 14 Robertson Rd, Easton, Bristol, BS5 6JY
(also see Bristol ABC publications)
Cardiff cardiffabc.wordpress.com
Leeds leedsabc.org/leeds-abc-about-us/ (also see Leeds ABC publications).
London network23.org/londonabc/
Bent Bars bentbarsproject.org
Additional support to LGBT prisoners and publish newsletters.
P.O. Box 66754, London, WC1A 9BF bent.bars.project@gmail.com
Prisoners Penfriends prisonerspenfriends.org
Matches volunteers and prisoners.

**Anarchist /Contra-Info**
325 325.nostate.net/
Anarchist / anti-capitalist information clearing house and DIY media network for social war.

Contra-Info en-contrainfo.espiv.net/
Contra Info is an international multi-language counter-information
and translation node, maintained by anarchists, anti-authoritarians and
libertarians across the globe.
Act for Freedom Now actforfree.nostate.net/
News of insurrection and resistance from around the globe.
Anarchist News anarchistnews.org
Non-sectarian source for news about and of concern to anarchists.
Untorelli Press untorellipress.noblogs.org/
Anarchist publishing project
Elephant Editions
elephanteditions.net/
Collection of ideas, dreams and experiments
Anarchist Library
theanarchistlibrary.org
Site that collates many publications for reading/download.

**Prison specific**
Empty Cages Collective prisonabolition.org
People who have been imprisoned or engaged in prison-related struggle
and prisoner support over a number of years. Good resources section.
Community Action Against Prison Expansion (CAPE) cape-campaign.
org/
Grass-roots coalition of groups fighting prison expansion in our own
communities and in solidarity with others.
The Abolition Tool-kit criticalresistance.org/resources/the-abolitionist-
toolkit/
Practical ideas for prison abolition and community organising.
INCITE! incite-national.org/
Activist organization of radical feminists of colour advancing a
movement to end violence against women of colour and through direct
action, critical dialogue and organizing.
Instead of Prisons Handbook: A Toolkit for Abolitionists prisonpolicy.
org/scans/instead_of_prisons/
Everything you wanted to know about prison abolition.
Center for a Stateless Society c4ss.org/content/20326
Prison abolition as a political issue.
The Incarcerated Worker incarceratedworkers.org/
Publication and union of the Industrial Workers of the World (IWW) on
prison wage-slavery.
Critical Resistance criticalresistance.org
Building an international movement to end the PIC by challenging the

belief that caging and controlling people makes us safe.
Wild Fire wildfire.noblogs.org
Anarchist Prisoner Solidarity

**Advice/advocacy**
Prisoners Advice Service prisonersadvice.org.uk
Independent registered charity offering free legal advice and support to adult prisoners in England and Wales.
Prison Reform Trust prisonreformtrust.org.uk
Campaigning organisation for prisoners and their families and friends.
15 Northburgh Street, London EC1V 0JR, 0808 802 0060
Prison and Probation Ombudsman ppo.gov.uk
Allegedly independent ombudsman who investigate complaints of prisoners/probationers.
PO Box 70769, London, SE1P 4XY, Ashley House, 2 Monck Street, London, SW1P 2BQ
Howard League for Penal Reform howardleague.org
Works for young people in custody under the age of 21.
1 Ardleigh Road, London, N1 4HS, 0207 249 7373
Make Justice Work makejusticework.org.uk/
Campaign to boost public support for a change in how Britain deals with minor offenders.
Smash IPP smashipp.noflag.org.uk, smashipp.wordpress.com
Campaigning for the release of prisoners who are still in jail under the IPP laws.
Justice in Prisons justiceinprisons.org.uk/
Run by and for those with first-hand experience of the UK justice system.
National Preventive Mechanism nationalpreventivemechanism.org.uk/
To strengthen the protection of people in detention through independent monitoring.
Netpol netpol.org/resources/
Resources on Subject Access Requests.

**Women Specific**
Women's Breakout womensbreakout.org.uk
Voice for community based organisations offering gender specific alternatives to custody.
Birth Companions birthcompanions.org.uk
Charity for women experiencing severe disadvantage during pregnancy, birth and early parenting.
KeyChanges keychangesuwp.org.uk
Open Door women's centre offering particular support to those who have

experienced the criminal justice system.

Anawim anawim.co.uk
Supports women and their children, especially women vulnerable to exploitation.

Women and Prison womenandprison.org/
Stories and resources from incarcerated women in America.

HMP/Justice.Gov justice.gov.uk/offenders/types-of-offender/women
Information on the women's prison estate.

## Education

Prisoners Education Trust prisonerseducation.org.uk
Charity providing support for prisoners in England and Wales to access education.
The Foundry, 17-19 Oval Way, London, SE11 5RR

Books Unlocked literacytrust.org.uk/books_unlocked
Reading initiative targeting prison and young offender institution library reading groups.

National Prison Radio prisonradioassociation.org
The world's first national radio station made by prisoners, for prisoners.

Women in Prison womeninprison.org.uk
Provides education, training and practical support to women who are, or have been, in prison.

Koestler Trust koestlertrust.org.uk
Helps prisoners by encouraging them to make art and music.
168a Du Cane Road London W12 0TX

Shannon Trust shannontrust.org.uk/
Peer support charity promoting literacy in prison.
89 Albert Embankment, London, SE1 7TP

Haven Distribution havendistribution.org.uk
Practical support for prisoners, providing political and educational books.
27 Old Gloucester Street, London WC1N 3XX

## Health

Prison Phoenix Trust theppt.org.uk freedominside.org
Yoga and meditation for prisoners.

Vegan Prisoner Support Group vpsg.org/
Help, support, and information for vegans detained either in police custody or within the prison system in the United Kingdom.

Bent Bars bentbarsproject.org/resources
Health Section is an excellent reference on health issues facing prisoners.

Hep C Trust hepctrust.org.uk
National UK charity for hepatitis C.

Care Quality Commission cqc.org.uk
Independent regulator of all health and social care services in England.
03000616161.
Cruse Bereavement cruse.org.uk
National charity for bereaved people in England, Wales and Northern
Ireland.
Independent Advisory Panel on Deaths in Custody (IAP).
iapdeathsincustody.independent.gov.uk
Government watchdog on deaths in custody.
RAPT (Rehabilitation for Addicted Prisoners Trust) rapt.org.uk
Works with people with drug and alcohol dependency.
Diabetes UK Helpline 0345 123 2399 diabetes.org.uk
UK charity that cares for and campaigns on behalf of all people affected
by diabetes.
Alzheimers Society alzheimers.org.uk/
Dementia support and research charity, for anyone affected by any form
of dementia in England, Wales and Northern Ireland.
Rethink rethink.org/
Support group for people affected by mental illness.

**Counselling**
Counselling for Social Change counsellingforsocialchange.org.uk
Person-centred psychotherapists, experienced in issues surrounding
activism, care work and campaigning.
Self-care by CrimethInc crimethinc.com/2013/05/31/selfcare
Text outlining various aspects of PTSD and mental health for anarchists.
Free Psychotherapy Network freepsychotherapynetwork.com
Free psychotherapy for people on low incomes and benefits.

**Communications For Prisoners**
Jailmatecards.co.uk jailmatecards.co.uk/
Personalised greetings cards for prisoners and their loved ones.
Fonesavvy fonesavvy.co.uk/
Cheap way to bypass the extortionate prison phone tariffs.
Pics2prisons pics2prisons.com/
Personalised post card service for prisoners.
Emailaprisoner emailaprisoner.com
Helping people stay in touch with prisoners cheaply and quickly.
Prison Voice Mail prisonvoicemail.com
Voice-mail service for prisoners and their families. Leave messages at
any time.

**National Prison Newspapers** (Free from prison libraries, not great, but useful information. Published monthly)
Jailmail jailmail.co.uk/
Converse spyholepress.com/
Inside Time insidetime.org/ (IT is also a national charity that advocates for prisoners. It is increasingly reactionary, but it does publish some useful reports) PO BOX 251, SO30 4XJ, 08443 356483

**Foreign National Prisoners**
Hibiscus hibiscusinitiatives.org.uk/
Support for FNPs dealing with the CJS.
Language Line languageline.com
Translation services.
Institute of Race Relations irr.org.uk
Research and analysis for the struggle for racial justice in Britain, Europe and internationally.

**Miscarriages of Justice**
I am using the term 'miscarriage of justice' as it is a legally recognised term; and one used by Kev and Sam to describe their cases. These cases expose the violence and corruption at the heart of the CJS, and how it relies on arbitrary convictions.
justiceforkevan.org/
Website for long-term CSC prisoner Kevan Thakrar. Kev's case is a brutal example of the racism inherent in the 'justice' system in this country.
freedomforsam.org/
Sam Faulder is serving a minimum term of 24 years for the alleged murder of her best friend. She is over 10 years into her sentence.

**Traveller Support Organisations**
Irish Council for Prisoners Overseas (ICPO) icpo.ie
Charity supporting Irish prisoners anywhere in the world.
Columba Centre, Maynooth, Co. Kildare, Ireland+353 1 505 3156.
Traveller Movement travellermovement.org.uk
Advocacy group for Irish Travellers and Romany Gypsies.
The Traveller Movement, The Resource Centre, 356 Holloway Road, London, N7 6PA Tel 020 7607 2002.

**Families/Friends Outside**
Action for Prisoners Families familylives.org.uk
For prisoners' and offenders' families by supporting families affected by imprisonment. Action for Prisoners' and Offenders' Families 49-51 East

Road, London, N1 6AH
Prisoners Friends and Families prisonadvice.org.uk/
29 Peckham Road, London, SE5 8UA 0808 808 3444
Supports prisoners and their families to make a fresh start and to
minimise the harm that can be caused by imprisonment.
Affect (Action For Families Ending Criminal Trauma) affect.org.uk
A group of people who currently have, or have had, a family member in
prison.
Families Outside (Scotland) familiesoutside.org.uk
National charity in Scotland that works solely to support the families of
people affected by imprisonment.
Offenders Families Helpline offendersfamilieshelpline.org 0808 808 2003
Support for those with a family member who is interacting with with the
criminal justice system.
Partners of Prisoners partnersofprisoners.co.uk/
Information and support for offenders' families from the point of arrest
through to release and beyond.
1079 Rochdale Road, Manchester, M98AJ
Prison Widow UK prisonersfamiliesvoices.blogspot.co.uk
Blog written by the families of prisoners who are inside connected to
substance misuse.
PCUK prisonchatuk.com/
Online community for those with a loved one inside the British prison
system.
Assisted Prison Visits gov.uk/assisted-prison-visits Help with travel costs
if you're visiting a close friend or relative in prison 0300 063 2100.
National Association of (Official) Prison Visitors naopv.com/
Promotes and helps to maintain the work of Official Prison Visitors.
Lucy Faithfull lucyfaithfull.org.uk
Registered child protection charity which works across the UK to prevent
child sexual abuse.

## Support for Release
St Giles Trust peerassist.org.uk / stgilestrust.org.uk
Charity to help ex-prisoners and their families.
Shelter shelter.org.uk
Homeless charity.
Sanctuary Supported Living sanctuary-supported-living.co.uk
Support and housing services, to help residents to maintain independence,
in their own home or a supported environment.
National Careers Service nationalcareersservice.direct.gov.uk
Information, advice and guidance on learning, training and work.

Job Centre Plus gov.uk/contact-jobcentre-plus
UK Department for Work and Pensions.
Citizens Advice citizensadvice.org.uk/
Benefits advice, advocacy and support
Centrepoint centrepoint.org.uk/
Accommodation and support for homeless people 16-25.
St Mungo's mungos.org
Support for homeless people who are trying to "recover" from the issues
that create homelessness (note, be warned however, they also participate
in Operation Nexus).
NACRO nacro.org.uk/
Housing support, education provision and addiction support 020 7840
6464 / 020 7035.
Disclosure and Barring Service (DBS), disclosuresdbs.co.uk
Information about working with "vulnerable people" and recruitment
(formerly CRB).
The Policy Department, PO Box 165, Liverpool, L69 3JD.
Unlock unlock.org.uk
Information, advice, training and advocacy for those dealing with the
ongoing effects of criminal convictions 01634 247350.
Women in Prison womeninprison.org.uk/
Funding and resources (including Through the Gate services).
Direct Gov gov.uk
Everything about the government.
Working Chance workingchance.org
London-based charity that helps women with criminal convictions to find
work.
Working Links workinglinks.co.uk
Organisation dedicated to getting the long-term unemployed back to work
by matching people.
Turn2Us turn2us.org.uk
National charity helping people in financial hardship to gain access to
benefits, grants and support services.
Prisoner Funder Directory prisonerfunder.org.uk/
Funding for individual prisoners in The Hardman Directory.
Clinks clinks.org
Supporting voluntary organisations that work with prisoners and their
families.
The Clink theclinkcharity.org
Charity working with prisoners and ex-prisoners through horticulture.
Information Hub/Disclosure Calculator hub.unlock.org.uk/disclosure-
calculator/

Website managed by Unlock to help calculate information relating to your conviction.
Restore Support Network restoresupportnetwork.org.uk/
Provides support for older people in prison prior to their release, as well as older ex-offenders who are either over 50 years or with care, mental health or disability needs, or classified as a vulnerable adult.

**Helplines**
Alcoholics Anonymous alcoholics-anonymous.org.uk
0800 9177 650
Assistance in personal recovery and continued sobriety for alcoholics.
Narcotics Anonymous ukna.org 0300 999 1212
Official UK website of the international organisation, run by people in recovery.
Refuge (Domestic Violence) refuge.org.uk (aka National Domestic Violence Helpline) 0808 2000 247 For women and children. National charity, run in connection with Women's Aid.
Galop.org.uk galop.org.uk/domesticabuse/
National LGBT Domestic Abuse Helpline 0800 999 5428 help@galop.org.uk
Emotional and practical support for LGBT people experiencing domestic, psychological, emotional, financial and sexual abuse.
The Samaritans samaritans.org 116 123 (UK) 116 123 (ROI)
UK charity offering support to people who are suicidal or despairing, 24 hours a day, every day of the year.
B-eat b-eat.co.uk/ 0808 801 0677
Eating Disorder helpline.

**TEXTS RELATING TO PRISON**
Carl Cattermole, *HM Prison Service: A Survival Guide* 2011 prisonism.co.uk/
Joe Black and Bra Bros, *The Prison Works: Occasional Texts on the Roles of Prisons and Prison Labour* 2010 blackpigeons.noblogs.org/files/2016/01/the-prison-works.pdf
David Gilbert, *Our Commitment is to Our Communities* 2014 akpress.org/our-commitment-is-to-our-communities.html
Trans Prisoner Day of Action Zine 22nd January 2016 transprisoners.net/resources/
Rob Coronado, Jeff Luers, Jordan Halliday and Josh Harper, *After Prison: Words from Former Earth and Animal Liberation Prisoners* 2014 afterprisonzine.org/
Mark Barnsley, *If It Was Easy, They Wouldn't Call It 'Struggle'* 2005

katesharpleylibrary.net/pg4fwb
Albert Libertad, *We Go On*
theanarchistlibrary.org/library/albert-libertad-we-go-on
*Lockdown: Gender, Repression and Gender Nonconformity* 2008
bentbarsproject.org/sites/default/files/Lockdown_prison_gender_
nonconformity.pdf
Jean Weir, *A Passion for Freedom* 2010 leedsabc.org/publications-3/
publications-2/
*Tame Words from a Wild Heart* 2016 archive.elephanteditions.net/library/
jean-weir-tame-words-from-a-wild-heart
*Revolutionary Struggle trial: Statement to the terror court of Korydallos*
2012
theanarchistlibrary.org/library/jean-weir-revolutionary-struggle-trial
*A Primer for Understanding Prison Abolition* 2015 transprisoners.files.
wordpress.com/2015/11/primer-1pp.pdf transprisoners.net/resources/
 Inside Justice, *Miscarriages of Justice* 2014
insidejusticeuk.com/pdf/inside-justice-miscarriages-of-justice-guide.pdf
*The Struggle Against the Maxi-Prison in Brussels: A Chronology of
Attack and Antagonism* 2015
personsunknown.noblogs.org/post/2015/07/12/the-struggle-against-the-
maxi-prison-in-brussels-a-chronology-of-attack-antagonism/
Niall Harnett, *Jail! An Insight into Prison Life In Ireland, Namely
Castlerea Prison* 2013
dysophia.org.uk/wp-content/uploads/2013/08/jail_nh_web1.pdf
*Battle Tested: Solidarity with Anarchist Prisoner Eric King* 2015
supportericking.files.wordpress.com/2015/08/eric-king-writings-zine.pdf
Klaus Viehmann *Prison Round Trip* 2009 (English Edition, originally
published 2003)
secure.pmpress.org/index.php?l=product_detail&p=122
Conspiracy of Cells of Fire Imprisoned Members Cell *A Few Words Of
"Freedom": An interview with Alfredo Cospito* 2017
untorellipress.noblogs.org/post/2017/04/19/a-few-words-of-freedom-an-
interview-with-alfredo-cospito-by-conspiracy-of-cells-of-fire-imprisoned-
members-cell/
*The Sun Still Rises* 2012
darkmatter.noblogs.org/post/2012/03/25/the-sun-still-rises-by-the-
conspiracy-of-cells-of-fire-imprisoned-members-cell/
Bristol ABC *Close Supervision Centres -Torture Units in the UK (Parts
One and Two)* 2013
bristolabc.files.wordpress.com/2013/08/csc2-a-brief-follow-up.pdf
Bristol ABC and Empty Cages Collective *Never Alone* 2014
prisonabolition.org/wp-content/uploads/2014/10/Never-Alone-Final1.pdf

*Trans Prisoner Solidarity* transprisoners.net/
*Repression and Solidarity in Bristol* 2015
prisonabolition.org/new-zine-repression-solidarity-bristol-collection-writings-anarchist-prisoner-emma-sheppard-others/
John Bowden, *Tear Down the Walls*
leedsabc.org/wp-content/uploads/2011/12/Tear-Down-The-Walls-2010.pdf
Kevan Thakrar, selected writings
brightonabc.org.uk/kevantharar.html
Albert Libertad, We Go On
theanarchistlibrary.org/library/albert-libertad-we-go-on.html

## BOOKS (a small selection)

Baldwin, Lucy *Mothering Justice* 2015
Berger, Dan *The Struggle Within: Prisons, Political Prisoners, and Mass Movements in the United States* 2014
Carlen, Pat *Women and Punishment: The Struggle for Justice* 2002
Chigwada-Bailey, Ruth *Black Women's Experiences of Criminal Justice* 2002
CR10 Publishing Collective *Abolition Now! Ten Years of Strategy and Struggle Against the Prison Industrial Complex*; 2008.
Davis, Angela Y. *The Meaning of Freedom and Other Difficult Dialogues* 2012, *Are Prisons Obsolete?* 2003
Devlin, Angela *Invisible Women: What's Wrong with Women's Prisons?* 1998
Faith, Karlene *Unruly Women: The Politics of Confinement and Resistance* 2011
Flanders, L.J *Cell Workout Volume1* 2015
Foucault, Michel *Discipline and Punish: The Birth of the Modern Prison* 1975
Gilbert, David *No Surrender: Writings from an Anti-Imperialist Political Prisoner,* 2004
Gilmore, Ruth *Golden Gulag: Prisons, Surplus, Crisis and Opposition in Globalizing California (American Cross Roads)* 2007
Herivel, Tara and Wright, Paul *Prison Profiteers: Who Makes Money from Mass Incarceration* 2009
Imarisha, Walidah *Angels with Dirty Faces: Three Stories of Crime, Prison and Redemption,* 2016
Jackson, George *Soledad Brother: The Prison Letters of George Jackson* 1994
Kilgore, James *Understanding Mass Incarceration: A People's Guide to*

*the Key Civil Rights Struggle for our Time* 2015

Jackson, Lee *Dirty Old London: The Victorian Fight Against Filth,* 2014

Killjoy, Margaret *A Country of Ghosts* 2014

Kropotkin, Peter *Prisons and Their Moral Influence on Prisoners* 1887

Law, Victoria *Resistance Behind Bars: The Struggles of Incarcerated Women* 2012

Lorde, Audre *Zami: A New Spelling of My Name* 1983, *Sister Outsider: Essays and Speeches* 1984

Lloyd, Ann *Doubly deviant, Doubly Damned: Societies Treatment of Violent Women* 1993.

Lloyd, Jenna, Mitchelson, Matt and Burridge, Andrew (editors) *Beyond Walls and Cages: Prisons, Borders and Global Crisis* 2012

Malloch, Margaret *Women, Drugs and Custody* 2001

Mauer, Marc *Race to Incarcerate* 2006

Mayhew, Henry and Binny, John *The Criminal Prisons of London and Scenes of Prison Life,* 1863

Pflug-Back, Kelly-Rose *These Burning Streets* 2012

*Prisons Handbook* 2016

Rodriguez, Dylan *Forced Passages: Imprisoned Radical Intellectuals and the U.S. Prison Regime* 2006, *Suspended Apocalypse: White Supremacy, Genocide, and the Filipino Condition* 2009

Shakur, Assata *Assata: An Autobiography Second Edition* 2014

Stanley, Eric A and Smith, Nat *Captive Genders: Trans-Embodiment and the Prison Industrial Complex* 2015

Sudbury, Julia *Global Lockdown: Race, Gender and the Prison Industrial Complex* 2005

Wilde, Oscar *De Profundis* 1897, *The Ballad of Reading Gaol* 1904

# GLOSSARY

Prison is a minefield of jargon, slang, acronyms and legislation. Hopefully this glossary will help make sense of this.


Adjudication - Appearance before a governor when accused of some wrongdoing

App - General Application (form for requesting anything)

ASBO - Anti-Social Behaviour Order (legislation introduced by Tony Blair to target people who hadly allegedly behaved 'anti-socially' but not enough to be prosecuted.)

ASD - Autism Spectrum Disorder

Bang-up - Period of time when your door is locked

BME - Offensive term used by the system to describe so-called 'Black and Minority Ethnic' prisoners.

Bird - A prison sentence

Block - Solitary confinement

BOSS - Body Orifice Scanning Software

Burn - Ubiquitous jail term for tobacco

Canteen - Weekly shopping list

CA – Care Act

CCROTL - Child Care ROTL)

CJS - criminal justice system

CRC - Community Rehabilitation Company

CRD - Conditional Release Date

CSC - Close Supervision Centre

DBS - Disclosure and Barring Service (formerly the CRB – Criminal Records Board)

DIRF - Discrimination Incident Reporting Form

Dipping - Stealing
Dog ends - Cigarette butts
DPDU - Dangerous Personality Disorder Unit
EPP - Extended Public Protection Sentence
Escape - Don't even mention this word for a joke
EA - Equalities Act
EASS - Equality Advisory Support Service
ETE - Education and Employment (probation love this expression)
FNP - Foreign National Prisoner
Fresh Meat - New prisoners
Ghosted - To be moved from one prison to another unexpectedly
GTR - Gypsy Traveller Roma
Guv - A prison officer ('number one guv' is the head governor)
HDC - Home Detention Curfew
HMP - Her Majesty's Prison
HMIP - Her Majesty's Inspectorate of Prisons
HMPPS - Her Majesty's Prison and Probation Service (in the process of replacing NOMS at time of printing)
Hooch - Home brewed alcohol
HOOV - Hand Out On a Visit
IEP - Incentive Earned Privileges Scheme
IMB - Independent Monitor Board
IRC – Immigration Removal Centre
ISP - Indeterminate Sentence Prisoners
IPP – Imprisonment for Public Protection Sentence
IT – Inside Time
IWW - Industrial Workers of the World
JE - Joint Enterprise
JR - Judges Remand
JSA – Job Seekers Allowance
Judicial Review - Legal challenge of a decision made by a public body on the grounds that the decision was unlawful.
Kanga - Rhyming slang for a prison officer (screw – kangaroo – kanga)
MAPPA - Multi Agency Public Protection Arrangement
MBU - Mother and Baby Unit
MDT - Mandatory Drug Testing
Meds - Medicine, medication or the medical hatch
MRSP - My Solution Rehabilitation Programme (used by Kent CRC)
NACRO - National Association for the Care and Resettlement of

Offenders
NFI - Not For Issue
Nicking - Adjudication ("To be given a nicking" or "nicking sheet" - adjudication paperwork)
NPR - National Prison Radio
NPS - National Probation Service
NPS - New Psychoactive Substances
NOMS - National Offender Management System
OASys - Offender Assessment System
O/Ls - Letters the prison pays the postage. Each prisoner *should* get issued two second class letters per week, normally distributed by night staff on a Sunday. Foreign National Prisoners should get an overseas letter too.
OMU - Offender Management Unit
OM - Offender Manager
ORA - Offender Rehabilitation Act
OS - Offender Supervisor
Pad mate - Cell mate
Pelly, pad, peter (or yard) - Your cell
PO - Prison Officer
POCA - Proceeds of Crime Act
PPO - Prison and Probation Ombudsman
PSI - Prison Service Instruction (legal issues relating to all aspects of prison life)
PI - Probation Instruction
PIPES - Psychologically Planned Environments (residential programme in prison)
PSO - Prison Service Order
Prop - Your property (either in possession or 'stored prop')
PSR - Pre-Sentence Report
Remand - When you are awaiting sentencing or charge and have been denied bail
Restorative Justice - Process by which the alleged 'victims' and 'offenders' of a 'crime' mediate together to reach agreement on the issues surrounding the event which is satisfactory to the wider community.
ROTL - Release on Temporary Licence
RRA - Race Relations Act
SAR - Subject Access Request
Seg - Segregation unit

Shank - Homemade knife

Shipped out - To be moved from one prison to another

Shit 'n' a shave - A brief sentence

Screw - Prison Officer

SDO - Supervision Default Order

SO - Senior Officer

Spends - Money available in your account ('public' is what you can spend on canteen, 'private' is your total balance)

Spin - Cell search

Stretch - Sentence ("I got a ten stretch")

Sweatbox - Prison van

TC - Therapeutic Community (residential programme in prison)

Tear up - A fight

TERS - The Early Release Scheme

Thee Stripe - High ranking screw

Tick - To borrow drugs or tobacco

TOB - Tackling Offending Behaviour

Transformative Justice - Community approach to alleged "crimes" (similar to 'Restorative Justice', see definition earlier in glossary), but using a more systemic critique and analysis of factors involved in so-called "social exclusion". This process does not necessarily involve the alleged 'victim'.

VDT - Voluntary Drug Testing

VO - Visiting Order

Volumetric Control - Way for the prison to control the amount of belongings you have "in possession" (i.e. in your cell). Must have fit into two standard prison issue boxes at any one time.

ViSOR - Central store for information about MAPPA cases, accessed by the the police, prison service (both public and the contracted-out estate) and probation.

VPU - Vulnerable Prisoners Unit

WFI – Women for Independence (Scottish reform charity)

WIP - Women in Prison charity (UK wide reformist charity)

Window warrior - Someone who anonymously shouts insults out the windows after the cell doors are shut